Kinect for Windows SDK Programming Guide

Build motion-sensing applications with Microsoft's
Kinect for Windows SDK quickly and easily

Abhijit Jana

PUBLISHING

BIRMINGHAM - MUMBAI

Kinect for Windows SDK Programming Guide

First published: December 2012

Production Reference: 1191212

Published by Packt Publishing Ltd.
Livery Place
35 Livery Street
Birmingham B3 2PB, UK.

ISBN 978-1-84969-238-0

www.packtpub.com

Cover Image by Sandeep Babu (sandyjb@gmail.com)

Credits

Author

Abhijit Jana

Reviewers

Atul Gupta

Anoop Madhusudhanan

Atul Verma

Acquisition Editor

James Keane

Lead Technical Editor

Susmita Panda

Technical Editors

Prasanna Joglekar

Dipesh Panchal

Farhaan Shaikh

Nitee Shetty

Copy Editors

Brandt D'Mello

Insiya Morbiwala

Aditya Nair

Alfida Paiva

Project Coordinator

Yashodhan Dere

Proofreaders

Ting Baker

Matthew Humphries

Indexer

Rekha Nair

Graphics

Valentina D'silva

Aditi Gajjar

Production Coordinator

Nitesh Thakur

Cover Work

Nitesh Thakur

About the Author

Abhijit Jana works at Microsoft as a .NET Consultant, as part of Microsoft Services Global Delivery, India. As a consultant, his job is to help customers design, develop, and deploy enterprise-level secure solutions using Microsoft Technology. Apart from being a former Microsoft MVP, he is a speaker and author as well as an avid technology evangelist. He has delivered sessions at prestigious Microsoft events such as TechEd, Web Camps, Azure Camps, Community Tech Days, Virtual Tech Days, DevDays, and developer conferences. He loves to work with different .NET communities and help them with different opportunities. He is a well-known author and has published many articles on different .NET community sites.

He shares his thoughts on his personal blog at `http://abhijitjana.net`. You can follow him on Twitter at `@abhijitjana`. Abhijit lives in Hyderabad, India, with his wife, Ananya and a beautiful little angel Nilova.

Disclaimer
The opinions in this book are purely my personal opinions and do not reflect in any way the opinions of my employers.

Acknowledgement

Writing this book would not have been possible without the help of many people. I had a wonderful time while writing, which was mainly due to the skills, support, dedication, and motivation of the people around me.

First of all I am extremely thankful to Sachin Joshi, Pinal Dave, and Prasant Kraleti for the continuous support and motivation they gave me from the time I started writing this book. They have been awesome with their support at every stage of writing.

I am deeply thankful to the entire team at Packt Publishing, including Prasad, Susmita, Mayur, Prasanna, Dipesh, Farhaan, and Nitee. I would like to extend my thanks to the Project Coordinator, Yashodhan, for his support from the beginning. Thank you all for your effort and dedication.

A sincere thanks to Atul Gupta and Anoop Madhusudanan for their insightful and excellent technical review. They helped me to identify and fill the gaps and improve the overall quality of this book.

I would like to acknowledge the efforts of Atul Verma for his extended support for in-depth technical review, and also for his time in discussing, peer coding, and providing feedback on many topics.

I would like to thank Jebarson Jebamony for his excellent peer review for this book, and also for spending his time and effort in sharing his thoughts and feedback for improving the content. He also helped me to organize content and design many demo applications.

I would like to thank Arka Bhattacharya and Atul Sharma for their offline review of the book and for sharing their feedback. A big thank you to Rajesh R. Nair for helping me on designing sketches and icons, and also Rishabh Verma for capturing and sharing the dismantled sensor images with me.

My sincere thanks to Jag Dua and Sanjoyan Mitra, two true leaders I have worked with. I would like to extend my thanks to Jag for giving me his Kinect sensor when I was overseas and was urgently looking for a Kinect sensor for some experimentation.

I was fortunate enough to be present at many seminars and conferences over the past year, on Kinect. This helped me to interact with many developers and students who are really passionate about programming with Kinect. Thanks to each one of them for spending their time with me and discussing about their problems and questions.

A big thanks to the Kinect for Windows team, the Kinect for Windows Community, and my Community friends, and MSPs who helped me in writing this book. I would like to thank my friends Kunal Chowdhury, Abhishek Sur, Dhananjay Kumar, Suresh Bemagani, Sheo Narayan, and Sharavan Kasagoni for their continuous support and help while writing this book. I am also thankful to the bloggers on the various Kinect topics, and also the researchers who have been working and experimenting day in and day out with Kinect. On many occasions I have been reading their posts and referring to them.

I spent time in writing when I should have been sleeping, spending time with family, or playing with my newborn child. I'd never have been able to write this book without the support of my wife, Ananya. I cannot even express her love and support while I was writing this book. Thank you Ananya.

Being a Community lover and an active blogger, I have been writing blogs for the last couple of years; but this is the first time I am putting something in the form of a book. The credit goes to each one of you who has been connected with me and have been my blog reader and supporter.

I would really appreciate it if you would contact me at abhijitjana@outlook.com for any kind of clarification.

About the Reviewers

Atul Gupta is currently a Principal Technology Architect at Infosys' Microsoft Technology Center, Infosys Labs. With more than 16 years of experience working on Microsoft technologies, his expertise spans User Interface technologies, and he currently works on touch and gestural interfaces with technologies such as Windows 8 and Kinect. He has prior experience on Windows Presentation Foundation (WPF), Silverlight, Windows 7, Deepzoom, Pivot, PixelSense, and Windows Phone 7.

He has co-authored the book *ASP.NET 4 Social Networking, Packt Publishing*. Earlier in his career, he has also worked on technologies such as COM, DCOM, C, VC++, ADO.NET, ASP.NET, AJAX, and ASP.NET MVC. He is a regular reviewer for Packt Publishing and has reviewed books on topics such as Silverlight and Generics.

He has authored papers for industry publications and websites, some of which are available on Infosys' Technology Showcase (`http://www.infosys.com/microsoft/resource-center/pages/technology-showcase.aspx`). Along with his colleagues from Infosys, he is also an active blogger (`http://www.infosysblogs.com/microsoft`). Being actively involved in professional Microsoft online communities and developer forums, he has received Microsoft's Most Valuable Professional award for multiple years in a row.

Anoop Madhusudanan has been a Microsoft MVP in C# for the last 3 years and has more than 10 years of experience with Microsoft technologies. Presently, he is working as a Solution Architect with the Cloud & Mobile Center of Excellence, Marlabs Inc. He works across multiple Microsoft technologies and platforms including Windows 8, ASP.NET, Windows Azure, and so on, across domains including education, healthcare, and telecom.

He blogs at http://amazedsaint.com and is the developer of various open source frameworks such as BrainNet Neural Network Library, ElasticObject, SilverDraw, MetaCoder, and so on. He is also an active contributor to CodeProject. His Twitter handle is @amazedsaint.

Atul Verma is a Technical Consultant at Microsoft Services Global Delivery and is a graduate from NIT, Hamirpur. He has been developing enterprise-level secure and scalable solutions using agile software methodologies for the past seven years. His technical expertise includes WPF, ASP.NET, WCF, SharePoint, Dynamics CRM, and Kinect for Windows. Apart from this, he also contributes to technical communities, technical seminars, open source projects, and blogs. He is currently studying the essence of Indian culture and loves to spend quality time with his family.
You can follow him on Twitter at @verma_atul.

www.PacktPub.com

Support files, eBooks, discount offers and more

You might want to visit www.PacktPub.com for support files and downloads related to your book.

Did you know that Packt offers eBook versions of every book published, with PDF and ePub files available? You can upgrade to the eBook version at www.PacktPub.com and as a print book customer, you are entitled to a discount on the eBook copy. Get in touch with us at service@packtpub.com for more details.

At www.PacktPub.com, you can also read a collection of free technical articles, sign up for a range of free newsletters and receive exclusive discounts and offers on Packt books and eBooks.

http://PacktLib.PacktPub.com

Do you need instant solutions to your IT questions? PacktLib is Packt's online digital book library. Here, you can access, read and search across Packt's entire library of books.

Why Subscribe?

- Fully searchable across every book published by Packt
- Copy and paste, print and bookmark content
- On demand and accessible via web browser

Free Access for Packt account holders

If you have an account with Packt at www.PacktPub.com, you can use this to access PacktLib today and view nine entirely free books. Simply use your login credentials for immediate access.

Instant Updates on New Packt Books

Get notified! Find out when new books are published by following @PacktEnterprise on Twitter, or the *Packt Enterprise* Facebook page.

I dedicate this book to my parents, my lovely wife Ananya
and my little angel Nilova.

Table of Contents

Preface

Ever since its inception, Kinect has brought about a revolution in the field of NUI and hands-free gaming. There is no wonder that Kinect went on to shatter all records and become the fastest selling electronic device on earth. Although touted as a controller for Xbox console, Kinect applicability is beyond gaming domain and you can think of building applications for diverse domains such as health care, robotics, imaging, education, security, and so on. Thus we have the Kinect for Windows sensor, that enables applications to interacts with users via gestures and voice, and this opens up avenues that developers couldn't even have imagined before.

This book is mainly focussed on the Kinect for Windows SDK with which you can build applications that can leverage the power of the Kinect sensor. This book doesn't require any prior knowledge about the platform from the reader and its strength is the simplicity in which the concepts have been presented using code snippets, a step-by-step process, and detailed descriptions. This book covers:

- A practical step-by-step tutorial to make learning easy for a beginner
- A detailed discussion of all the APIs involved and the explanations of their usage in detail
- Procedures for developing motion-sensing applications and also methods used to enable speech recognition

What this book covers

Chapter 1, Understanding the Kinect Device, introduces Kinect as a hardware device. You will get an insight into the different components that make up Kinect and the technology behind this device, which makes the components work together. This chapter will also give an overview of the difference between Kinect for Xbox and Kinect for Windows sensor. You will also become familiar with different possibilities of domain specific applications that can be developed using the Kinect sensor.

Chapter 2, Getting Started, introduces the Kinect for Windows SDK, its features, and how to start working with the Kinect sensor. In this chapter, you will get to know about the requirements for preparing your development environment. This will also walk you through a step-by-step guide for downloading and installing the SDK. You will delve into the installed components to verify that everything is set up properly. This chapter will also provide you with a quick lap around the different features of the Kinect for Windows SDK as well as introduce the Kinect for Windows Developer Toolkit.

Chapter 3, Starting to Build Kinect Applications, explains the step-by-step process of building your first Kinect-based application. You will understand how applications interact with the Kinect sensor using the SDK libraries. This chapter will give you an in-depth guide on how to start building Kinect applications using the Kinect for Windows SDK and Visual Studio. You will also learn how to deal with applications when there is any change in the device status.

Chapter 4, Getting the Most Out of Kinect Camera, covers the in-depth discussion of the Kinect color camera and how to use it. In this chapter, you will learn about the different types of image streams and different approaches to retrieve them from the Kinect sensor. You will get an understanding of Color camera stream pipeline and its events. You will also explore the different features of the Kinect for Windows SDK that control the color camera and process the color data. This chapter will give you an understanding of processing color images and applying different effects to the captured images and how to save the image frames. You will also learn how you can use the Kinect camera to capture images in low light.

Chapter 5, The Depth Data – Making Things Happen, explores the fundamentals of the Kinect depth sensors and how they produce depth information. This chapter describes how to work with object distances and player indices from the captured depth data. You will also learn about the capturing of data using the near mode and also get a quick view of generating 3D depth data.

Chapter 6, Human Skeleton Tracking, describes how a Kinect sensor tracks the human skeleton and how you can leverage the features of the Kinect for Windows SDK to play around with tracked skeletons and joints. You will also learn how to change the sensor elevation angle based on the player position. This chapter also explores how skeletons can be tracked in a seated mode. You also learn about details of the skeleton joints and bone hierarchy. The sample application in this chapter will help you to understand the APIs for skeleton tracking in better ways such as using Kinect as an intrusion detector. At the end of this chapter, you will be familiar with a few debugging tips and tricks to boost your development speed.

Chapter 7, Using Kinect's Microphone Array, introduces the microphone array that captures and processes the audio signal. You will learn why Kinect uses an array of microphones rather than a single microphone. In this chapter you will get an insight into the Kinect audio processing pipeline that helps Kinect to capture good-quality audio signals and makes Kinect a highly directional audio device. This chapter provides you with information on how to capture and record audio signals using the Kinect microphone array and process the audio data for better quality. You will also learn about different concepts such as Noise Suppression, Automatic Gain Control, Echo Cancellation, and Beam forming.

Chapter 8, Speech Recognition, introduces the building of speech-enabled applications using Kinect. You will explore how speech recognition works and how Kinect's microphone array helps Kinect to recognize human speech. This chapter also shows how you can use Kinect as the default speech recognition device for your PC. You will also learn about the Microsoft Speech API and how it is integrated with Kinect for Windows SDK, which helps us to build speech-enabled applications.

Chapter 9, Building Gesture-controlled Applications, describes how to build applications that can be controlled by human gestures. You will learn different approaches for recognizing gestures and how to apply these approaches in the form of programs to build motion-sensing applications using the Kinect sensor. This chapter will also help you understand how to build some gestured-enabled controls.

Chapter 10, Developing Applications Using Multiple Kinects, explains how multiple Kinect sensors can be placed together and used to build applications. This chapter describes how to set up environments for developing applications using multiple Kinects and walks you through building applications by reading data from multiple devices. You also learn how multiple Kinects work together and different scenarios where multiple Kinects can be used, along with the challenges while developing applications using multiple devices.

Chapter 11, Putting Things Together, introduces us to more advanced developments using Kinect by integrating it with other devices such as Windows Phone, microcontrollers, and so on. This chapter addresses how we can take things up from Kinect to Windows Azure and control the Kinect sensor using Windows Phone via Windows Azure. You will also learn how Kinect can be integrated with the Netduino microcontroller and how you can use a Kinect device for face tracking.

What you need for this book

The basic requirements for this book are as follows:

- Microsoft Visual Studio 2010 Express or higher editions of Visual Studio
- Microsoft .NET Framework 4.0 or higher
- Kinect for Windows Sensor or Kinect for Xbox Sensor
- Kinect for Windows SDK

Please refer *Chapter 02*, *Getting Started* , for detailed information on installation of SDK and the development environment setup.

Who this book is for

The purpose of this book is to explain how to develop applications using the Kinect for Windows SDK. If you are a beginner and looking to start developing applications using the Kinect for Windows SDK, and if you want to build motion-sensing, speech-recognizing applications with Kinect, this book is for you.

This book uses C# and WPF (Windows Presentation Foundation) in the examples, so you need to know the basics of C# and WPF. You should be familiar with the Visual Studio IDE as well. You don't have to know anything about the Kinect for Windows SDK.

Conventions

In this book, you will find a number of styles of text that distinguish between different kinds of information. Here are some examples of these styles, and an explanation of their meaning.

Code words in text are shown as follows: "Each Kinect device represents an instance of the `Microsoft.Kinect.KinectSensor` class."

A block of code is set as follows:

```
public sealed class KinectSensorCollection : ReadOnlyCollection<Kinec
tSensor>
{
    public KinectSensor this[string instanceId] { get; }

    public event EventHandler<StatusChangedEventArgs> StatusChanged;
}
```

When we wish to draw your attention to a particular part of a code block, the relevant lines or items are set in bold:

```
public partial class MainWindow : Window
{

    KinectSensor sensor;
    // remaining code goes here
}
```

New terms and important words are shown in bold. Words that you see on the screen, in menus or dialog boxes for example, appear in the text like this: "Move to the Listen tab and select the Listen to this device checkbox and click on Apply".

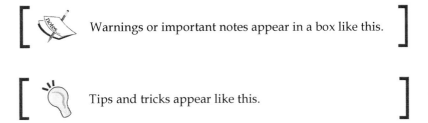

Warnings or important notes appear in a box like this.

Tips and tricks appear like this.

Reader feedback

Feedback from our readers is always welcome. Let us know what you think about this book—what you liked or may have disliked. Reader feedback is important for us to develop titles that you really get the most out of.

To send us general feedback, simply send an e-mail to feedback@packtpub.com, and mention the book title via the subject of your message.

If there is a topic that you have expertise in and you are interested in either writing or contributing to a book, see our author guide on www.packtpub.com/authors.

Customer support

Now that you are the proud owner of a Packt book, we have a number of things to help you to get the most from your purchase.

Downloading the example code

You can download the example code files for all Packt books you have purchased from your account at `http://www.PacktPub.com`. If you purchased this book elsewhere, you can visit `http://www.PacktPub.com/support` and register to have the files e-mailed directly to you.

Errata

Although we have taken every care to ensure the accuracy of our content, mistakes do happen. If you find a mistake in one of our books—maybe a mistake in the text or the code—we would be grateful if you would report this to us. By doing so, you can save other readers from frustration and help us improve subsequent versions of this book. If you find any errata, please report them by visiting `http://www.packtpub.com/support`, selecting your book, clicking on the **errata submission form** link, and entering the details of your errata. Once your errata are verified, your submission will be accepted and the errata will be uploaded on our website, or added to any list of existing errata, under the Errata section of that title. Any existing errata can be viewed by selecting your title from `http://www.packtpub.com/support`.

Piracy

Piracy of copyright material on the Internet is an ongoing problem across all media. At Packt, we take the protection of our copyright and licenses very seriously. If you come across any illegal copies of our works, in any form, on the Internet, please provide us with the location address or website name immediately so that we can pursue a remedy.

Please contact us at `copyright@packtpub.com` with a link to the suspected pirated material.

We appreciate your help in protecting our authors, and our ability to bring you valuable content.

Questions

You can contact us at `questions@packtpub.com` if you are having a problem with any aspect of the book, and we will do our best to address it.

1
Understanding the Kinect Device

Welcome to the world of motion computing with Kinect. Kinect was originally known by the code name "Project Natal". It is a motion-sensing device which was originally developed for the Xbox 360 gaming console. One of the distinguishing factors that makes this device stand out among others in this genre is that it is not a hand-controlled device, but rather detects your body position, motion, and voice. Kinect provides a **Natural User Interface** (**NUI**) for interaction using body motion and gesture as well as spoken commands. Although this concept seems straight out of a fairytale, it is very much a reality now. The controller that was once the heart of a gaming device finds itself redundant in this Kinect age. You must be wondering where its replacement is. The answer, my friend, is YOU. It's you who is the replacement for the controller, and from now on, you are the controller for your Xbox. Kinect has ushered a new revolution in the gaming world, and it has completely changed the perception of a gaming device. Since its inception it has gone on to shatter several records in the gaming hardware domain. No wonder Kinect holds the Guinness World Record for being the "fastest selling consumer electronics device". One of the key selling points of the Kinect was the idea of "hands-free control", which caught the attention of gamers and tech enthusiasts alike and catapulted the device into instant stardom. This tremendous success has caused the Kinect to shatter all boundaries and venture out as an independent and standalone, gesture-controlled device.

It has now outgrown its Xbox roots and the Kinect sensor is no longer limited to only gaming. Kinect for Windows is a specially designed PC-centric sensor that helps developers to write their own code and develop real-life applications with human gestures and body motions. With the launch of the PC-centric Kinect for Windows devices, interest in motion-sensing software development has scaled a new peak.

As Kinect blazed through the market in such a short span of time, it has also created a necessity of resources that help people learn the technology in an appropriate way. As Kinect is still a relatively new entry into the market, the resources for learning how to develop applications for this device are scant. So how does a developer understand the basics of Kinect right from scratch? Here comes the utility of this book.

This book assumes that you have basic knowledge of C# and a great enthusiasm to program for Kinect devices. This book can be enjoyed by anybody interested in knowing more about the device and learning how to interact with devices using Kinect for Windows **Software Development Kit (SDK)**. This book will also help you explore how to process video depth and audio stream, and build applications that interact with human body motion. The book has deliberately been kept simple and concise, which will aid in the quick grasping of the concepts.

Before delving into the development process, we need a good understanding of the device and, moreover, what the different types of applications are, which we can develop using these devices. In order to develop standard applications using the Kinect for Windows SDK, it is really important for us to understand the components it interacts with.

In this chapter we will cover the following topics:

- Identifying the critical components that make up Kinect
- Looking into the functionalities of each of the components
- Learning how they interact with each other
- Choosing between Kinect for Windows and Kinect for Xbox
- Exploring different application areas where we can use Kinect

Components of Kinect for Windows

Kinect is a horizontal device with depth sensors, color camera, and a set of microphones with everything secured inside a small, flat box. The flat box is attached to a small motor working as the base that enables the device to be tilted in a horizontal direction. The Kinect sensor includes the following key components:

- Color camera
- Infrared (IR) emitter
- IR depth sensor
- Tilt motor
- Microphone array
- LED

Apart from the previously mentioned components, the Kinect device also has a power adapter for external power supply and a USB adapter to connect with a computer. The following figure shows the different components of a Kinect sensor:

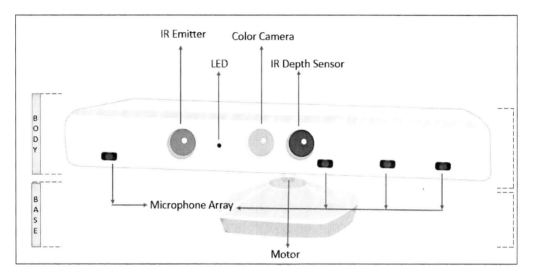

Inside the Kinect sensor

From the outside, the Kinect sensor appears to be a plastic case with three cameras visible, but it has very sophisticated components, circuits, and algorithms embedded. If you remove the black plastic cover from the Kinect device, what will you see? The hardware components that make the Kinect sensor work.

The following image shows a front view of a Kinect sensor that's been unwrapped from its black case. Take a look (from left to right) at its IR emitter, color camera, and IR depth sensor:

Let's move further and discuss about component.

The color camera

This color camera is responsible for capturing and streaming the color video data. Its function is to detect the red, blue, and green colors from the source. The stream of data returned by the camera is a succession of still image frames. The Kinect color stream supports a speed of 30 **frames per second (FPS)** at a resolution of 640 x 480 pixels, and a maximum resolution of 1280 x 960 pixels at up to 12 FPS. The value of frames per second can vary depending on the resolution used for the image frame.

The viewable range for the Kinect cameras is 43 degrees vertical by 57 degrees horizontal. The following figure shows an illustration of the viewable range of the Kinect camera:

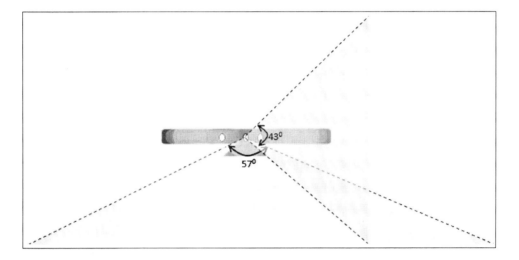

The following image shows a color image that was captured using Kinect color sensors with a resolution of 640 x 480 pixels:

IR emitter and IR depth sensor

Kinect depth sensors consist of an IR emitter and an IR depth sensor. Both of them work together to make things happen. The IR emitter may look like a camera from the outside, but it's an IR projector that constantly emits infrared light in a "pseudo-random dot" pattern over everything in front of it. These dots are normally invisible to us, but it is possible to capture their depth information using an IR depth sensor. The dotted light reflects off different objects, and the IR depth sensor reads them from the objects and converts them into depth information by measuring the distance between the sensor and the object from where the IR dot was read. The following figure shows how the overall depth sensing looks:

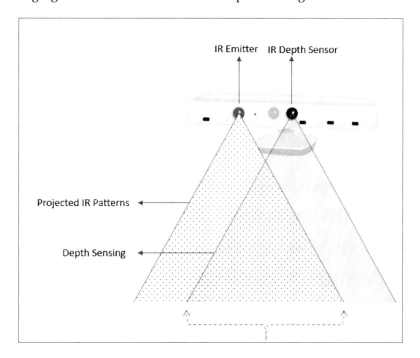

 It is quite fun and entertaining to know that these infrared dots can be seen by you. All we need is a night vision camera or goggles.

The depth data stream supports a resolution of 640 x 480 pixels, 320 x 240 pixels, and 80 x 60 pixels, and the sensor viewable range remains the same as the color camera.

The following image shows depth images that are captured from the depth image stream:

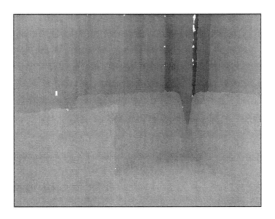

How depth data processing works

The Kinect sensor has the ability to capture a raw, 3D view of the objects in front of it, regardless of the lighting conditions of the room. It uses an **infrared (IR)** emitter and an IR depth sensor that is a monochrome **CMOS (Complimentary Metal-Oxide-Semiconductor)** sensor. The backbone behind this technology is from PrimeSense, and the following diagram shows how this works:

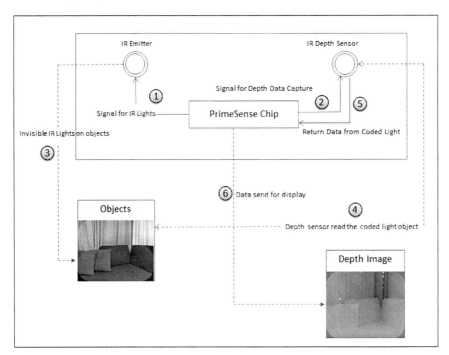

The sequence explained in the diagram is as follows:

When there is a need to capture depth data, the PrimeSense chip sends a signal to the infrared emitter to turn on the infrared light (1), and sends another signal to the IR depth sensor to initiate depth data capture from the current viewable range of the sensor (2). The IR emitter meanwhile starts sending an infrared light invisible to human eyes (3) to the objects in front of the device. The IR depth sensor starts reading the inferred data from the object based on the distance of the individual light points of reflection (4) and passes it to the PrimeSense chip (5). The PrimeSense chip then analyzes the captured data, and creates a per-frame depth image and passes it to the output depth stream as a depth image (6).

The IR emitter emits an electromagnetic radiation. The wavelengths of the radiations are longer than the wavelength of the visible light, which makes the sensor's IR lights invisible. The wavelengths need to be consistent to minimize the noise within the captured data. Heat generated by the laser diode when the Kinect sensor is running can impact the wavelength. The Kinect sensor has a small, inbuilt fan to normalize the temperature and ensure that the wavelengths are consistent.

Tilt motor

The base and body part of the sensor are connected by a tiny motor. It is used to change the camera and sensor's angles, to get the correct position of the human skeleton within the room. The following image shows the motor along with three gears that enable the sensor to tilt at a specified range of angles:

The motor can be tilted vertically up to 27 degrees, which means that the Kinect sensor's angles can be shifted upwards or downwards by 27 degrees. The following figure shows an illustration of the angle being changed when the motor is tilted:

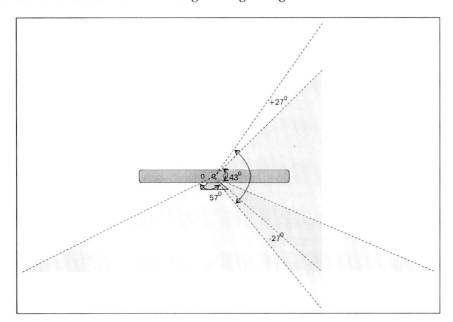

 Do not physically force the device into a specific angle. The Kinect for Windows SDK has a few specific APIs that can help us control the sensor's motor tilting. Do not tilt the Kinect motor frequently; use this as few times as possible and only when it's required.

Microphone array

The Kinect device exhibits great support for audio with the help of a microphone array. The microphone array consists of four different microphones that are placed in a linear order (three of them are spread on the right side and the other one is placed on the left side, as shown in the following image) at the bottom of the Kinect sensor:

The purpose of the microphone array is not just to let the Kinect device capture the sound but to also locate the direction of the audio wave. The main advantages of having an array of microphones over a single microphone are that capturing and recognizing the voice is done more effectively with enhanced noise suppression, echo cancellation, and beam-forming technology. This enables Kinect to be a highly bidirectional microphone that can identify the source of the sound and recognize the voice irrespective of the noise and echo present in the environment:

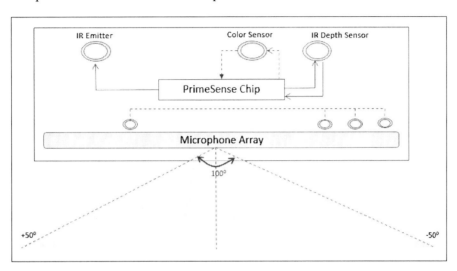

LED

An LED is placed in between the camera and the IR projector. It is used for indicating the status of the Kinect device. The green color of the LED indicates that the Kinect device drivers have loaded properly. If you are plugging Kinect into a computer, the LED will start with a green light once your system detects the device; however for full functionality of your device, you need to plug the device into an external power source.

Kinect for Windows versus Kinect for Xbox

Although "Kinect for Windows" and "Kinect for Xbox" are similar in many respects, there are several subtle differences from a developer's point of view. We have to keep in mind that the main purpose of Kinect for Xbox was to enhance the gaming experience of the players. Developing applications was not its primary purpose. In contrast, Kinect for Windows is primarily a developing device and not for gaming purposes.

You can develop applications that use either the Kinect for Windows sensor or the Kinect for Xbox sensor. The Kinect for Xbox sensor was built to track players that are up to 12 feet (4.0 meters) away from the sensor. But it fails to track objects that are very close (80 cm), and we might need to track objects at a very close range for different applications. The Kinect for Windows sensor has new firmware, which enables **Near Mode** tracking. Using Near Mode, Kinect for Windows supports the tracking of objects as close as 40 cm in front of the device without losing accuracy or precision. In terms of range, both the sensors behave the same.

 Kinect for Windows SDK exposes APIs that can control the mode of the sensors (Near Mode or Default Mode) using our application, however the core changes for this feature are built within the firmware of the Kinect for Windows sensor.

Both the Kinect for Windows and Kinect for Xbox sensors need additional power for the sensors to work with your PC. This might not be required when connected to the Xbox device as the Xbox port has enough power to operate the device. There is no difference between Xbox Kinect and Kinect for Windows in this respect. However in Kinect for Windows, the USB cable is small and improved to enable more reliability and portability across a wide range of computers.

And finally, the Kinect for Windows sensor is for commercial applications, which means that if you are developing a commercial application, you must use the Kinect for Windows device for production, whereas you can use Kinect for Xbox for general development, learning, and research purposes.

Where can you use Kinect

By now it has already struck you that this is something more than just gaming. The Kinect sensor for Windows and the Kinect for Windows SDK unwrap a new opportunity for the developer to build a wide range of applications. These can include:

- Capturing real-time video using the color sensor
- Tracking a human body and then responding to its movements and gestures as a natural user interface
- Measuring the distances of objects and responding

- Analyzing 3D data and making a 3D model and measurement
- Generating a depth map of the objects tracked
- Recognizing a human voice and developing hands-free applications that can be controlled by voice

With this you can build a number of real-world applications that fall under a different domain. The following are a few examples, which will help you understand the applicability of Kinect sensors:

- **Healthcare**: Using the Kinect sensor, you can build different applications for healthcare, such as exercise measurement, monitoring patients, their body movements, and so on
- **Robotics**: Kinect can be used as a navigation system for robots either by tracking human gestures, voice commands, or by human body movements
- **Education**: You can build various applications for students and kids to educate and help them to learn subjects either by their gesture and voice commands
- **Security system**: Kinect can be used for developing security systems where you can track human body movement or face and send the notifications
- **Virtual Reality**: With the help of Kinect 3D technology and human gesture tracking, several virtual reality applications can be build using the Kinect sensor
- **Trainer**: Kinect can potentially be used as a trainer by measuring the movements of human body joints, providing live feedback to users if the joints are moving in an appropriate manner by comparing the movements with previously stored data
- **Military**: Kinect can be used to build intelligent drones to spy on enemy lines

Well these were just a few specific examples of domains where you can use Kinect, but at the end of the day it's up to your imagination; where and how you want this device to work.

Summary

This chapter gave you an inside look at the different components of the Kinect sensor. You saw that the major components of a Kinect device are its color sensor, IR depth sensors, IR emitter, microphone arrays, and a stepper motor that can be tilted to change the Kinect camera angles. While the color sensor and depth sensors ensure video and depth data input, which is of prime importance for the functioning of the device, the microphone arrays on the other hand ensure that the audio quality is also at par. Also worthwhile is mentioning about how kinect processes the depth data, and the array of microphones, which is a design novelty that helps in clear voice recognition with the use of the noise suppression and echo cancelation mechanisms. Kinect for Windows is also capable of tracking humans at a close range of approximately 40 centimeters using Near Mode. It wouldn't be wrong to say that it is this combination of technological innovations that make Kinect the awe-inspiring device that it is. You have also gone through the different possibilities of applications that can be developed using Kinect. In the next chapter, we will walk you through the step-by-step installation and configuration of the development environment setup along with different troubleshooting tips and tricks that will help you to be sure about everything before beginning with development.

2
Getting Started

The Kinect for Windows SDK is a toolkit for developing applications for Kinect devices. Developing applications using Kinect SDK is fairly easy and straightforward. The SDK provides an interface to interact with Kinect via system drivers. The SDK includes drivers for the Kinect sensor, which interact with the device, and the OS and APIs interact with the device through program. Overall, the SDK provides an opportunity to the developers to build an application using either managed code (C# and VB.NET) or unmanaged code (C++) using Visual Studio 2010 or higher versions, running on Windows 7 or Windows 8.

Kinect for Windows Developer Toolkit is an additional installer that comes with a set of extended components, such as Face Tracking SDK, which helps to track human faces, and Kinect Studio to record and playback the depth and color stream data. The Developer Toolkit also contains samples and documentation to give you a quick hands-on reference.

While the application development with Kinect SDK is fascinating and straightforward, there are certain things that need to be taken care of during the SDK installation, configuration, and setting up of your development environment. The following is a quick overview of various aspects we'll be discussing in this chapter:

- Understanding the system requirements
- The evolutionary journey of Kinect for Windows SDK
- Installing and verifying the installed components
- Troubleshooting tips and tricks
- Exploring the installed components of SDK
- A quick lap around different features of Kinect for Windows SDK
- The Coding4fun toolkit

By the end of this chapter, you will have everything set up to start development with the Kinect sensor.

System requirements for the Kinect for Windows SDK

While developing applications for any device using an SDK, compatibility plays a pivotal role. It is really important that your development environment must fulfill the following set of requirements before starting to work with the Kinect for Windows SDK.

Downloading the example code

You can download the example code files for all Packt books you have purchased from your account at http://www.PacktPub.com. If you purchased this book elsewhere, you can visit http://www.PacktPub.com/support and register to have the files e-mailed directly to you.

Supported operating systems

The Kinect for Windows SDK, as its name suggests, runs only on the Windows operating system. The following are the supported operating systems for development:

- Windows 7
- Windows Embedded 7
- Windows 8

The Kinect for Windows sensor will also work on Windows operating systems running in a virtual machine such as Microsoft HyperV, VMWare, and Parallels.

System configuration

The hardware requirements are not as stringent as the software requirements. It can be run on most of the hardware available in the market. The following are the minimum configurations required for development with Kinect for Windows:

- A 32- (x86) or 64-bit (x64) processor
- Dual core 2.66 GHz or faster processor
- Dedicated USB 2.0 bus
- 2 GB RAM

The Kinect sensor

It goes without saying, you need a Kinect sensor for your development. You can use the Kinect for Windows or the Kinect for Xbox sensor for your development.

 Before choosing a sensor for your development, make sure you are clear about the limitations of the Kinect for Xbox sensor over the Kinect for Windows sensor, in terms of features, API supports, and licensing mechanisms. We have already discussed this in the *Kinect for Windows versus Kinect for Xbox* section in *Chapter 1, Understanding the Kinect Device*.

The Kinect for Windows sensor

By now, you are already familiar with the Kinect for Windows sensor and its different components. The Kinect for Windows sensor comes with an external power supply, which supplies the additional power, and a USB adapter to connect with the system. For the latest updates and availability of the Kinect for Windows sensor, you can refer to `http://www.microsoft.com/en-us/kinectforwindows/site`.

The Kinect for Xbox sensor

If you already have a Kinect sensor with your Xbox gaming console, you may use it for development. Similar to the Kinect for Windows sensor, you will require a separate power supply for the device so that it can power up the motor, camera, IR sensor, and so on.

 If you have bought a Kinect sensor with an Xbox as a bundle, you will need to buy the adapter / power supply separately. You can check out the external power supply adapter at `http://www.microsoftstore.com`. If you have bought only the Kinect for Xbox sensor, you will have everything that is required for a connection with a PC and external power cable.

Development tools and software

The following are the software that are required for development with Kinect SDK:

- Microsoft Visual Studio 2010 Express or higher editions of Visual Studio
- Microsoft .NET Framework 4.0 or higher
- Kinect for Windows SDK

Kinect for Windows SDK uses the underlying speech capability of a Windows operating system to interact with the Kinect audio system. This will require Microsoft Speech Platform – Server Runtime, the Microsoft Speech Platform SDK, and a language pack to be installed in the system, and these will be installed along with the Kinect for Windows SDK. The system requirements for SDK may change with upcoming releases. Refer to http://www.microsoft.com/en-us/ kinectforwindows/ for the latest system requirements.

Evaluation of the Kinect for Windows SDK

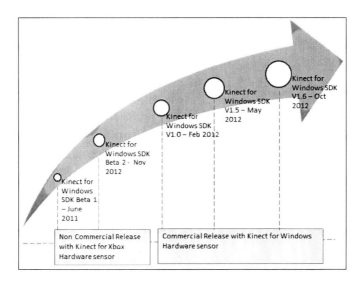

Though the Kinect for Xbox sensor has been in the market for quite some time, Kinect for Windows SDK is still fairly new in the developer paradigm, and it's evolving. The book is written on **Kinect for Windows SDK v1.6**. The Kinect for Windows SDK was first launched as a Beta 1 version in June 2011, and after a thunderous response from the developer community, the updated version of Kinect for Windows SDK Beta 2 version was launched in November 2011. Initially, both the SDK versions were a non-commercial release and were meant only for hobbyists. The first commercial version of Kinect for Windows SDK (v1.0) was launched in February 2012 along with a separate commercial hardware device. SDK v1.5 was released on May 2012 with bunches of new features, and the current version of Kinect for Windows SDK (v1.6) was launched in October 2012. The hardware hasn't changed since its first release. It was initially limited to only 12 countries across the globe. Now the new Kinect for Windows sensor is available in more than 40 countries. The current version of SDK also has the support of speech recognition for multiple languages.

Downloading the SDK and the Developer Toolkit

The Kinect SDK and the Developer Toolkit are available for free and can be downloaded from `http://www.microsoft.com/en-us/kinectforwindows/`.

The installer will automatically install the 64- or 32-bit version of SDK depending on your operating system. The Kinect for Windows Developer Toolkit is an additional installer that includes samples, tools, and other development extensions. The following diagram shows these components:

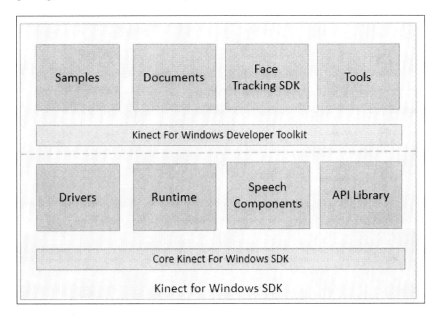

 The main reason behind keeping SDK and Developer Toolkit in two different installers is to update the Developer Toolkit independently from the SDK. This will help to keep the toolkit and samples updated and distributed to the community without changing or updating the actual SDK version. The version of Kinect for Windows SDK and that for the Kinect for Windows Developer Toolkit might not be the same.

Installing Kinect for Windows SDK

Before running the installation, make sure of the following:

- You have uninstalled all the previous versions of Kinect for Windows SDK
- The Kinect sensor is not plugged into the USB port on the computer
- There are no Visual Studio instances currently running

Start the installer, which will display the start screen as **End User License Agreement**. You need to read and accept this agreement to proceed with the installation. The following screenshot shows the license agreement:

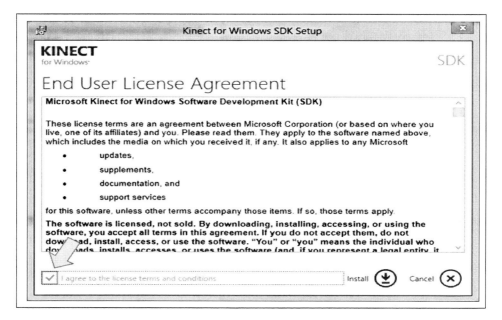

Accept the agreement by selecting the checkbox and clicking on the **Install** option, which will do the rest of the job automatically.

Before the installation, your computer may pop out the **User Access Control (UAC)** dialog, to get a confirmation from you that you are authorizing the installer to make changes in your computer.

Once the installation is over, you will be notified along with an option for installing the Developer Toolkit, as shown in the next screenshot:

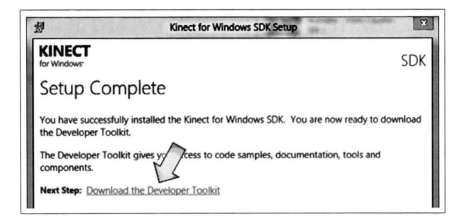

Is it mandatory to uninstall the previous version of SDK before we install the new one?

The upgrade will happen without any hassles if your current version is a non-Beta version. As a standard procedure, it is always recommended to uninstall the older SDK prior to installing the newer one, if your current version is a Beta version.

Installing the Developer Toolkit

If you didn't downloaded the Developer Toolkit installer earlier, you can click on the **Download the Developer Toolkit** option of the SDK setup wizard (refer to the previous screenshot); this will first download and then install the Developer Toolkit setup. If you have already downloaded the setup, you can close the current window and execute the standalone Toolkit installer. The installation process for Developer Toolkit is similar to the process for the SDK installer.

Components installed by the SDK and the Developer Toolkit

The Kinect for Windows SDK and Kinect for Windows Developer Toolkit install the drivers, assemblies, samples, and the documentation. To check which components are installed, you can navigate to the **Install and Uninstall Programs** section of **Control Panel** and search for Kinect. The following screenshot shows the list of components that are installed with the SDK and Toolkit installer:

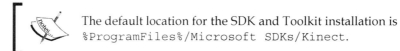

> The default location for the SDK and Toolkit installation is %ProgramFiles%/Microsoft SDKs/Kinect.

Kinect management service

The Kinect for Windows SDK also installs **Kinect Management**, which is a Windows service that runs in the background while your PC communicates with the device. This service is responsible for the following tasks:

- Listening to the Kinect device for any status changes
- Interacting with the COM Server for any native support
- Managing the Kinect audio components by interacting with Windows audio drivers

You can view this service by launching **Services** by navigating to **Control Panel | Administrative Tools**, or by typing Services.msc in the **Run** command.

Is it necessary to install the Kinect SDK to end users' systems?

The answer is *No*. When you install the Kinect for Windows SDK, it creates a `Redist` directory containing an installer that is designed to be deployed with Kinect applications, which install the runtime and drivers. This is the path where you can find the setup file after the SDK is installed:

`%ProgramFiles%/\Microsoft SDKs\Kinect\v1.6\Redist\`
`KinectRuntime-v1.6-Setup.exe`

This can be used with your application deployment package, which will install only the runtime and necessary drivers.

Connecting the sensor with the system

Now that we have installed the SDK, we can plug the Kinect device into your PC. The very first time you plug the device into your system, you will notice the LED indicator of the Kinect sensor turning solid red and the system will start installing the drivers automatically.

The default location of the driver is `%Program Files%\Microsoft Kinect Drivers\Drivers`.

The drivers will be loaded only after the installation of SDK is complete and it's a one-time job. This process also checks for the latest Windows updates on USB Drivers, so it is good to be connected to the Internet if you don't have the latest updates of Windows.

The check marks in the dialog box shown in the next screenshot indicate successful driver software installation:

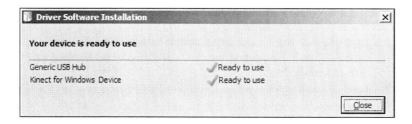

When the drivers have finished loading and are loaded properly, the LED light on your Kinect sensor will turn solid green. This indicates that the device is functioning properly and can communicate with the PC as well.

Verifying the installed drivers

This is typically a troubleshooting procedure in case you encounter any problems. Also, the verification procedure will help you to understand how the device drivers are installed within your system. In order to verify that the drivers are installed correctly, open **Control Panel** and select **Device Manager**; then look for the **Kinect for Windows** node. You will find the **Kinect for Windows Device** option listed as shown in the next screenshot:

Not able to view all the device components

At some point of time, it may happen that you are able to view only the **Kinect for Windows Device** node (refer to the following screenshot). At this point of time, it looks as if the device is ready. However, a careful examination reveals a small hitch. Let's see whether you can figure it out or not! The Kinect device LED is on and **Device Manager** has also detected the device, which is absolutely fine, but we are still missing something here. The device is connected to the PC using the USB port, and the system prompt shows the device installed successfully — then where is the problem?

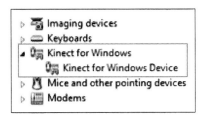

The default USB port that is plugged into the system doesn't have the power capabilities required by the camera, sensor, and motor. At this point, if you plug it into an external power supplier and turn the power on, you will find all the driver nodes in **Device Manager** loaded automatically.

 This is one of the most common mistakes made by the developers. While working with Kinect SDK, make sure your Kinect device is connected with the computer using the USB port, and the external power adapter is plugged in and turned on.

The next picture shows the Kinect sensor with USB connector and power adapter, and how they have been used:

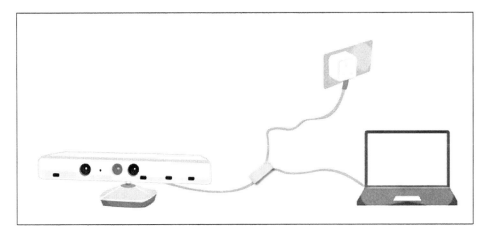

With the aid of the external power supply, the system will start searching for Windows updates for the USB components. Once everything is installed properly, the system will prompt you as shown in the next screenshot:

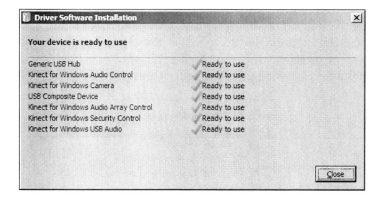

All the check marks in the screenshot indicate that the corresponding components are ready to be used and the same components are also reflected in **Device Manager**.

 The messages prompting for the loading of drivers, and the prompts for the installation displaying during the loading of drivers, may vary depending upon the operating system you are using. You might also not receive any of them if the drivers are being loaded in the background.

Detecting the loaded drivers in Device Manager

Navigate to **Control Panel | Device Manager**, look for the **Kinect for Windows** node, and you will find the list of components detected. Refer to the next screenshot:

The **Kinect for Windows Audio Array Control** option indicates the driver for the Kinect audio system whereas the **Kinect for Windows Camera** option controls the camera sensor. The **Kinect for Windows Security Control** option is used to check whether the device being used is a genuine Microsoft Kinect for Windows or not. In addition to appearing under the **Kinect for Windows** node, the **Kinect for Windows USB Audio** option should also appear under the **Sound, Video and Game Controllers** node, as shown in the next screenshot:

Once the Kinect sensor is connected, you can identify the Kinect microphone like any other microphone connected to your PC in the **Audio Device Manager** section. Look at the next screenshot:

Testing your device

Once the SDK installation is complete, you are ready to start the development. But let's start with a few bits of testing.

Testing Kinect sensors

The Developer Toolkit has a set of sample applications; you can choose any of them to test the device. To quickly check it out, you can run the Kinect Explorer application from the Developer Toolkit. The Kinect Explorer demonstrates the basic features of the Kinect for Windows SDK, which retrieves color, depth, and skeleton data and displays them on the UI. The next screenshot shows the UI reference of the application:

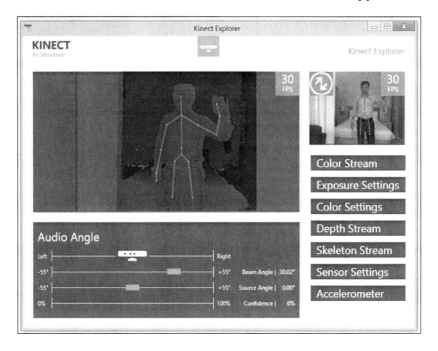

If you are also able to view a similar-looking output, where you can see the Kinect sensor returning the depth, color, and skeleton data, you can be sure that your device has been installed properly.

Testing the Kinect microphone array

You can use Kinect as a microphone. Navigate to the **Sound** section in **Control Panel** and select the **Recording** tab to see Kinect's **Microphone Array**. This is shown in the following screenshot. You can also see the bar along with the microphone array, which indicates the level of sound. You can do everything that a PC's audio tool is capable of doing.

To ensure that the Kinect microphone array is capturing the sound clearly and passing it to your system, you can use the **Listen To this device** option. To enable this, right-click on **Microphone Array** and select **Properties**. This is shown in the next screenshot:

This will launch the **Microphone Array Property** window. Move to the **Listen** tab, select the **Listen to this device** checkbox, and click on **Apply**. This is shown in the next screenshot:

Now, if your system's speaker is turned on and you speak in front of the Kinect device, you should get to hear the same voice via your system's speaker. This ensures that your Kinect audio device is also configured properly.

If you want to use multiple Kinect sensors for your application, you can see the detailed procedure given in *Chapter 10, Developing Application Using Multiple Kinects*.

Looking inside the Kinect SDK

The Kinect SDK provides both managed and unmanaged libraries. If you are developing an application using either C# or VB.NET, you can directly invoke the .NET Kinect Runtime APIs; and for C++ applications, you have to interact with the Native Kinect Runtime APIs. Both the types of APIs can talk to the Kinect drivers that are installed as a part of SDK installation.

> The unmanaged and managed libraries provide access to the same set of Kinect sensor features.

For managed code, the Kinect for Windows SDK provides **Dynamic Link Library (DLL)** as an assembly (**Microsoft.Kinect.dll**), which can be added to any application that wants to use the Kinect device. You can find this assembly in the SDK installation directory, as shown in the next screenshot:

The Kinect driver can control the camera, depth sensor, audio microphone array, and the motor. Data passes between the sensor and the application in the form of data streams of the following types:

- Color data stream
- Depth data stream
- Audio data stream

> The Kinect for Windows SDK is capable of capturing Infrared data stream as a part of color data stream channel as well as can read the sensor accelerometer data.

The next diagram illustrates the overall layered components for the Kinect SDK, and it shows how an application interacts with different layers of components:

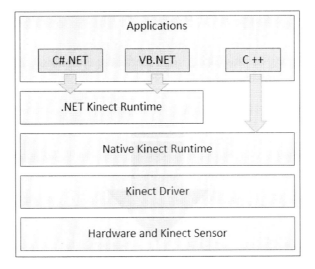

Features of the Kinect for Windows SDK

Well, as of now we have discussed the components of the Kinect SDK, system requirements, installation of SDK, and setting up of devices. Now it's time to have a quick look at the top-level features of Kinect for Windows SDK.

The Kinect SDK provides a library to directly interact with the camera sensors, the microphone array, and the motor. We can even extend an application for gesture recognition using our body motion, and also enable an application with the capability of speech recognition. The following is the list of operations that you can perform with Kinect SDK. We will be discussing each of them in subsequent chapters.

- Capturing and processing the color image data stream
- Processing the depth image data stream
- Capturing the infrared stream
- Tracking human skeleton and joint movements
- Human gesture recognition
- Capturing the audio stream
- Enabling speech recognition
- Adjusting the Kinect sensor angle
- Getting data from the accelerometer
- Controlling the infrared emitter

Capturing the color image data stream

The color camera returns 32-bit RGB images at a resolution ranging from 640 x 480 pixels to 1280 x 960 pixels. The Kinect for Windows sensor supports up to 30 FPS in the case of a 640 x 480 resolution, and 10 FPS for a 1280 x 960 resolution. The SDK also supports retrieving of YUV images with a resolution of 640 x 480 at 15 FPS.

Using the SDK, you can capture the live image data stream at different resolutions. While we are referring to color data as an image stream, technically it's like a succession of color image frames sent by the sensor. The SDK is also capable of sending an image frame on demand from the sensor.

Chapter 4, Getting the Most Out of Kinect Camera, talks in depth about capturing color streams.

Processing the depth image data stream

The Kinect sensor returns 16-bit raw depth data. Each of the pixels within the data represents the distance between the object and the sensor. Kinect SDK APIs support depth data streams at resolutions of 640 x 480, 320 x 240, and 80 x 60 pixels.

Near Mode

The **Near Mode** feature helps us track a human body within a very close range (of approximately 40 centimeters). We can control the mode of sensors using our application; however, the core part of this feature is built in the firmware of the Kinect sensor.

 This feature is limited to the Kinect for Windows sensor only. If you are using the Xbox sensor, you won't be able to work with Near Mode.

We will talk about depth data processing and Near Mode in *Chapter 5, The Depth Data – Making Things Happen*.

Capturing the infrared stream

You can also capture images in low light conditions, by reading the infrared stream from the Kinect sensor. The Kinect sensor returns 16 bits per pixel infrared data with a resolution of 640 x 480 as an image format, and it supports up to 30 FPS. The following is an image captured from an infrared stream:

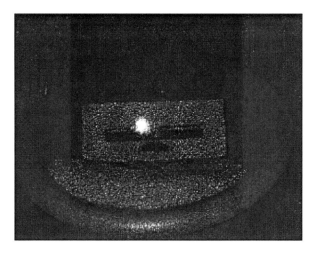

 You cannot read color and infrared streams simultaneously, but you can read depth and infrared data simultaneously. The reason behind this is that an infrared stream is captured as a part of a color image format.

Tracking human skeleton and joint movements

One of the most interesting parts of the Kinect SDK is its support for tracking the human skeleton. You can detect the movement of the human skeleton standing in front of a Kinect device. Kinect for Windows can track up to 20 joints in a single skeleton. It can track up to six skeletons, which means it can detect up to six people standing in front of a sensor, but it can return the details of the full skeleton (joint positions) for only two of the tracked skeletons.

The SDK also supports tracking the skeleton of a human body that is seated. The Kinect device can track your joints even if you are seated, but up to 10 joint points only (upper body part).

The next image shows the tracked skeleton of a standing person, which is based on depth data:

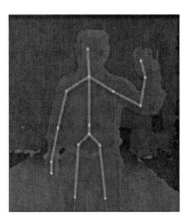

The details on tracking the skeletons of standing and seated humans, its uses, and the development of an application using skeletal tracking, is covered in *Chapter 6, Human Skeleton Tracking.*

Capturing the audio stream

Kinect has four microphones in a linear configuration. The SDK provides high-quality audio processing capabilities by using its own internal audio processing pipeline. The SDK allows you not only to capture raw audio data, but also high-quality audio processing by enabling the noise suppression and echo cancellation features. You can also control the direction of the beam of the microphone array with the help of the SDK.

We have covered the details of audio APIs of Kinect SDK in *Chapter 7, Using Kinect's Microphone Array.*

Speech recognition

You can take advantage of the Kinect microphone array and Windows Speech Recognition APIs to recognize your voice and develop relevant applications. You can build your own vocabulary and pass it to the speech engine, and design your own set of voice commands to control the application. If a user says something with some gestures, say while moving a hand as shown in the following picture, an application can be developed to perform some work to be done depending on the user's gestures and speech.

In *Chapter 8, Speech Recognition*, we will discuss the APIs and build some sample applications by leveraging the speech recognition capability of the Kinect for Windows SDK.

Human gesture recognition

A **gesture** is nothing but an action intended to communicate feelings or intentions to the device. Gesture recognition has been a prime research area for a long time. However, in the last decade, a phenomenal amount of time, effort, and resources have been devoted to this field in the wake of the development of devices. Gesture recognition allows people to interface with a device and interact naturally with body motion, as with the person in the following picture, without any device attached to the human body.

In the Kinect for Windows SDK, there is no direct support for an API to recognize and deal with human gestures; however, by using skeleton tracking and depth data processing, you can build your own gesture API, which can interact with your application.

Chapter 9, Building Gesture-controlled Applications, has a detailed discussion about building gesture-controlled applications using the Kinect for Windows SDK.

Tilting the Kinect sensor

The SDK provides direct access to controlling the motor of the sensor. By changing the elevation angles of the sensors, you can set the viewing angle for the Kinect sensor as per your needs. The maximum and minimum value of elevation angle is limited to +27 degrees and -27 degrees, in SDK. If you try to change the sensor angle more or less than these specified ranges, your application will throw an invalid operation exception.

 The tilting is allowed only for the vertical direction. There is no horizontal tilting with Kinect sensors.

We will cover the details of tilting motors and the required APIs in *Chapter 4, Getting the Most Out of Kinect Camera.*

Getting data from the accelerometer of the sensor

Kinect treats the elevation angle as being relative to the gravity and not its base, as it uses its accelerometers to control the rotation. The Kinect SDK exposes the APIs to read the accelerometer data directly from the sensor. You can detect the sensor orientation by reading the data from accelerometer of the sensor.

Controlling the infrared emitter

Controlling the infrared emitter is a very small but very useful feature of the Kinect SDK, where you can forcefully turn the infrared emitter off. This is required while dealing with the data from multiple sensors, and when you want to capture data from specific sensors by turning off the IR emitters of other sensors.

 This feature is limited only to the Kinect for Windows sensor. If you are using the Xbox sensor, you will get `InvalidOperationException` with the **The feature is not supported by this version of the hardware** message.

The Kinect for Windows Developer Toolkit

Kinect for Windows Developer Toolkit is an additional set of components that helps you to build sophisticated applications easily by providing access to more tools and APIs. This toolkit has a number of samples, documentation for SDK API libraries, the **Kinect Studio** tool (a tool that can help you record and play Kinect and data during debugging), as well as the **Face Tracking SDK**.

After the installation of Developer Toolkit, you will get a standalone executable within the toolkit that is installed in the directory. Run the application; it will display the screen as shown in the following screenshot. You can navigate through it for resources and samples.

The Face Tracking SDK

The **Face Tracking SDK** is a part of the Kinect for Windows Developer Toolkit. It contains a few sets of APIs that you can use to track a human face, by taking advantages of Kinect SDK APIs. The SDK detects and tracks the positions and orientations of faces, and it can also animate eye brow positions and the shape of mouth in real time. The Face Tracking SDK can be used in several places, such as recognizing facial expressions, NUI interaction with the face, and tasks that are related to the face.

The next image shows a basic face tracking instance using the Kinect for Windows and Face Tracking SDKs.

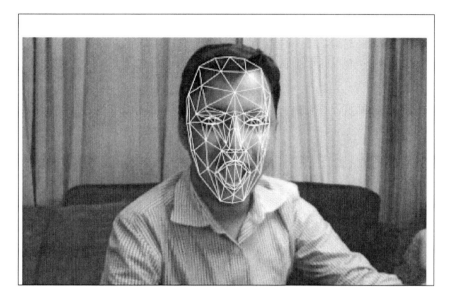

Kinect Studio

Kinect Studio can record and playback the sensor's data stream. It's a very handy and useful tool for developers during testing and while dealing with debugging of Kinect applications. The Kinect data stream can be recorded and saved in a `.xed` file format for future use. What does that mean? How does that help? Well, let's say you are developing an application based on gestures, and you need to perform that gesture every time to test or debug your application; in this case, using the Kinect Studio you can record your action once and just play the recording again and again.

 The permission level for both Kinect Studio and the application that is used by Kinect Studio, has to be the same.

The next screenshot shows a quick view of Kinect Studio, which is displaying the color view, depth view, and 3D view of the data captured by Kinect:

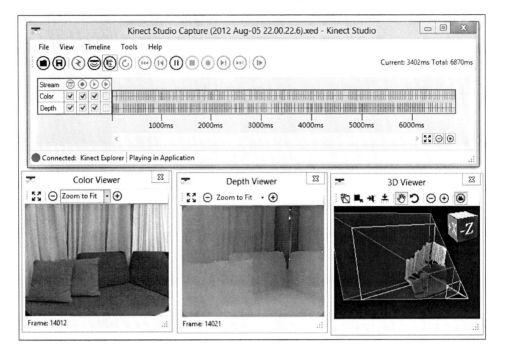

I have covered more on the Face Tracking SDK and Kinect Studio in the latter part of this book.

Making your development setup ready

While the device and driver setup look good, you need to ensure your development environment is ready as well.

The basic software you require for setting up the development environment are Visual Studio 2010 Express Edition or any higher edition along with .NET 4.0 Framework, which we have already discussed as a part of system requirement.

If you are already familiar with development using Visual Studio, the basic steps for implementing an application using a Kinect device should be straightforward. You simply have to perform the following operations:

1. Launch a new instance of Visual Studio.
2. Create a new project.
3. Refer to the `Microsoft.Kinect.dll` file.
4. Declare the appropriate namespaces for the added assembly.
5. Start using the Kinect SDK API library.

We will be discussing the details about development in the next chapter.

The Coding4Fun Kinect Toolkit

The **Coding4Fun Kinect Toolkit** provides several necessary extension methods to make developing of application using the Kinect for Windows SDK faster and easier. You can download the Coding4Fun Kinect Toolkit from `http://c4fkinect.codeplex.com/`.

 The Coding4Fun Kinect Toolkit is also available as a NuGet package. You can install it using the NuGet Package Manager console within Visual Studio.

We will explore some of the extension methods and the installation procedure of Coding4Fun Kinect Toolkit in the upcoming chapters.

Summary

In this chapter we have covered the prerequisites of an SDK installation, that is, the hardware and software requirements for the installation. A brief step-by-step guide for the installation, loading of drivers, and for setting up the development environment is also discussed. We have seen a quick overview of the Kinect SDK features and also the new Kinect SDK Developer Toolkit. We have also seen how the SDK provides an opportunity to developers to build applications using different languages such as C#, VB.NET, or C++. The knowledge gained from this chapter will help you fully grasp the subjects discussed in the subsequent chapters.

In the next chapter you will get started with development with the Kinect for Windows SDK.

3
Starting to Build Kinect Applications

Let's begin our journey towards developing our first application with Kinect. For the development of every Kinect application, there are certain common operations we need to perform, listed as follows:

- The application must detect the connected Kinect device and needs to start it.
- Once the sensor is started, the application has to initialize and subscribe the type of data required from the sensor.
- During the overall execution cycle of an application, a sensor can change its state. The application must monitor the changes in the state for the connected device and handle them appropriately.
- When the application quits/ends, it should shut down the device properly.

This chapter will cover the basic understanding of the Kinect SDK APIs and the development of applications with the Kinect SDK. We will discuss in a step-by-step manner the development of the applications in this chapter so that it helps you in upcoming chapters. The following is an overview of various aspects we'll be covering in this chapter:

- Getting familiar with the application's interaction with the Kinect device
- Understanding the classification of APIs based on the Kinect SDK libraries used
- Building a Kinect Info Box application by reading sensor information
- Using Kinect libraries in your application
- Exploring SDK libraries that read device information

- Different ways to examine whether Kinect devices are correctly connected and installed and are in working condition
- Building a KinectStatusNotifier application to notify the sensor state change in the system tray

How applications interact with the Kinect sensor

The Kinect for Windows SDK works as an interface between the Kinect device and your application. When you need to access the sensor, the application sends an API call to the driver. The Kinect driver controls access to sensor data. To take a granular look inside the application interfacing with the sensor, refer to the following diagram:

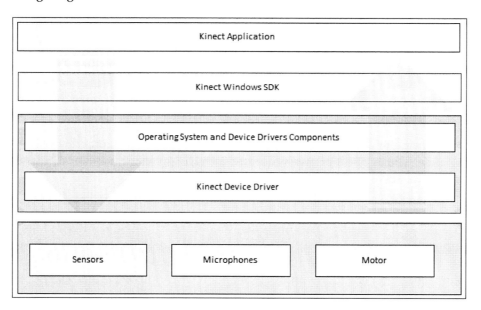

The installed drivers for the sensors sit with the components of system device drivers and can talk to each other. The drivers help to stream the video and audio data from the sensors and return it to the application. These drivers help to detect the Kinect microphone array as a default audio device and also help the array to interact with the Windows default speech recognition engine. Another part of the Kinect device driver controls the USB hubs on the connected sensor as well.

Understanding the classification of SDK APIs

To understand the functionality of different APIs and to know their use, it is always good to have a clear view of the way they work. We can classify the SDK libraries into the two following categories:

- Those controlling and accessing Kinect sensors
- Those accessing microphones and controlling audio

The first category deals with the sensors by capturing the color stream, infrared data stream, and depth stream, by tracking human skeletons and taking control of sensor initialization. A set of APIs in this category directly talks to the sensor hardware, whereas a few APIs on processing apply the data that is captured from the sensor.

On the other hand, the audio APIs control the Kinect microphone array and help to capture the audio stream from the sensors, controlling the sound source and enabling speech recognition, and so on. The following diagram shows a top-level API classification based on the type of work the API performs:

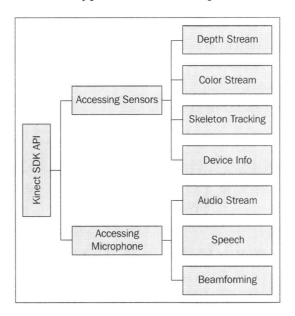

We can also define the SDK API as a **Natural User Interfaces** (**NUI**) API, which retrieves the data from the depth sensor and color camera and captures the audio data stream. There are several APIs that are written on top of the NUI APIs, such as those for retrieving sensor information just by reading sensor details and for tracking human skeletons based on the depth data stream returned from the sensor.

Kinect Info Box – your first Kinect application

Let's start developing our first application. We will call this application **Kinect Info Box**. To start development, the first thing we are going to build is an application that reads the device information from a Kinect sensor. The Info Box application is self-explanatory. The following screenshot shows a running state of the application, which shows the basic device information such as **Connection ID**, **Device ID**, and **Status**. The Info Box also shows the currently active stream channel and the sensor angle. You can also start or stop the sensor using the buttons at the bottom of the window.

We will build this application in a step-by-step manner and explore the different APIs used along with the basic error-handling mechanisms that need to be taken care of while building a Kinect application.

Creating a new Visual Studio project

1. Start a new instance of Visual Studio.

2. Create a new project by navigating to **File | New Project**. This will open the **New Project** window.

3. Choose **Visual C#** from the installed templates and select the **WPF Application**, as shown in the following screenshot:

 You can select the **Windows Forms Application** template instead of **WPF Application template**. In this book, all the sample applications will be developed using WPF. The underlying Kinect SDK API is the same for both **Windows Forms Application** and **WPF Application**.

4. Give it the name `KinectInfoBox`, and then click on **OK** to create a new Visual studio project.

Adding the Kinect libraries

The next thing you need to do is add the Kinect libraries to the Visual Studio project using the following steps:

1. From the **Solution Explorer** window, right-click on the **References** folder and select **Add Reference...**, as shown in the following screenshot:

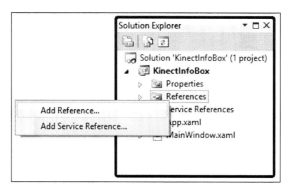

2. This will launch the **Add Reference** window. Then, search for the `Microsoft.Kinect.dll` file within the Kinect SDK folder. Select `Microsoft.Kinect.dll` and click on **OK**, as shown in the following screenshot:

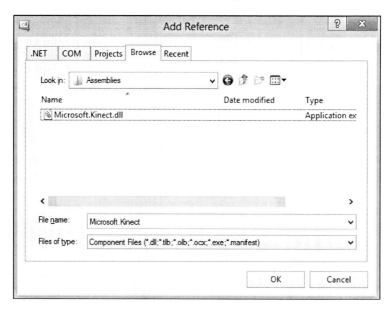

3. This will add `Microsoft.Kinect.dll` as a reference assembly into your project, which you can see within the **References** folder, as shown in the following screenshot:

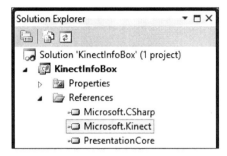

We now have a default project ready with the Kinect library added. The next thing to do is to access the library APIs for our application.

Getting the Kinect sensor

The `KinectSensor` class is provided as part of the SDK libraries, which are responsible for most of the operation with the Kinect sensor. You need to create an instance of the `KinectSensor` class and then use this to control the Kinect sensor and read the sensor information.

While writing code, the first thing you need to do is to add the `using` directives, which will enable the program to use the Kinect SDK reference. Open the `MainWindow.xaml.cs` file from **Solution Explorer**, and then add the following line of code at the top of your program with the other `using` statement:

```
using Microsoft.Kinect;
```

The Kinect sensor

In a Kinect application, each Kinect device represents an instance of the `Microsoft.Kinect.KinectSensor` class. This represents the complete runtime pipeline for the sensor during the life span of the application.

The following diagram illustrates the usage of Kinect sensors over a life span of an application:

Defining the Kinect sensor

Defining the sensor objects is as simple as defining other class objects. The defined object will come into action only when you initialize for a specific Kinect operation, such as color image streaming and depth image streaming. We can define a Kinect sensor object using the following code snippet:

```
public partial class MainWindow : Window
{
    KinectSensor sensor;
    // remaining code goes here
}
```

The `sensor` objects need a reference to the Kinect device that is connected with the system and can be used by your application. You can't instantiate the `KinectSensor` object as it does not have a `public` constructor. Instead, the SDK creates `KinectSensor` objects when it detects a Kinect device attached to your system.

The collection of sensors

The `KinectSensor` class has a static property of the `KinectSensorCollection` type, named `KinectSensors`, which consists of the collection of sensors that are connected with your system. The `KinectSensor.KinectSensors` collection returns the collection of Kinect devices connected with your system. `KinectSensorCollection` is a read-only collection of the `KinectSensor` type. Each `KinectSensorCollection` class consists of an indexer of the `KinectSensor` object and an event named `StatusChanged`. The following code block shows the definition of the `KinectSensorCollection` class:

```
public sealed class KinectSensorCollection : ReadOnlyCollection<Kinect
Sensor>, IDisposable
    {
        public KinectSensor this[string instanceId] { get; }
        public event EventHandler<StatusChangedEventArgs>
        StatusChanged;
        public void Dispose();
    }
```

As this returns a collection of Kinect devices, you can use any index of that collection to get the reference of a particular sensor. As an example, if you have two devices connected with your system, `KinectSensor.KinectSensors[0]` will represent the first Kinect device and `KinectSensor.KinectSensors[1]` will represent the second Kinect device.

Consider that you have connected a device, so you will get a reference of this connected sensor as shown in this code:

```
this.sensor = KinectSensor.KinectSensors[0];
```

Once you have the sensor object for the Kinect device, invoke the `KinectSensor.Start()` method to start the sensor.

Check whether any device is connected before you start the sensor

It is always good practice to first check whether there is any sensor connected with the system before carrying out any operation with the `KinectSensor` objects. `KinectSensors` holds the reference to all connected sensors, and as this is a collection, it has a `Count` property. You can use `KinectSensors.Count` to check the number of devices.

```
int deviceCount = KinectSensor.KinectSensors.Count;
if (deviceCount > 0)
{
    this.sensor = KinectSensor.KinectSensors[0];
    // Rest operation here
}
else
{
    // No sensor connected. Take appropriate action
}
```

Starting up Kinect

Starting up Kinect means initializing the Kinect sensors with different data streams. The sensor has to first start before reading from itself. You can write a method, such as the following one, that handles the sensor start:

```
private void StartSensor()
{
    if (this.sensor != null && !this.sensor.IsRunning)
    {
        this.sensor.Start();
    }
}
```

The KinectSensor class has a property named IsRunning, which returns true if the sensor is running. You can take advantage of this property to check whether the sensor is running or not. When you call the sensor.Start() method, the SDK checks the current sensor status internally before it actually starts the sensor. So, if you forgot to check sensor.IsRunning, the SDK will take care of this automatically; however, checking it well in advance will save an unnecessary call. Similarly, calling the Start() method multiple times won't cause any problems as the SDK will start the sensor only if it is not running.

In this application, we are instantiating the sensor in the Window_Loaded event, as shown in the following code snippet. This will start the sensor when the application starts; however, you can take the connected sensor as a reference and can start it anywhere in your application, based on your requirements.

```
protected void MainWindow_Loaded(object sender, RoutedEventArgs e)
{
    if (KinectSensor.KinectSensors.Count > 0)
    {
        this.sensor = KinectSensor.KinectSensors[0];
        this.StartSensor();
    }
    else
    {
        MessageBox.Show("No device is connected with system!");
        this.Close();
    }
}
```

In the preceding code block, you can see that, first of all, we check the count of the connected sensors and proceed if the number of the connected devices is greater than 0, otherwise we prompt a message to the user and close the application. This is always a good practice. Once we have connected the sensor, we take the sensor as a reference and start the sensor by calling the StartSensor method that we defined earlier.

Inside the sensor.Start() method

Before taking any further action, the `sensor.Start()` method first checks for the status of the sensor(with the `Status` term). The initialization of the sensor happens only if the sensor is connected. If the sensor is not connected and you are trying to start the sensor, it will throw an `InvalidOperationException` object with the `KinectNotReady` message.

If the sensor is connected, the `Start()` method initializes the sensor and then tries to open the `color`, `depth`, and `skeleton` data stream channels with the default values if they are set to `Enable`.

> Initialization of different stream channels does not mean to start sending data from the sensor. You have to explicitly enable the channel and register an appropriate event to feed data from the sensor.

The initialization of the sensor happens with a set of enumeration flags, which provides the type of channel that needs to be initialized. The following table lists the types of initialization options and their descriptions:

Initialization option	Description
None	This is the default option, so the sensor will just initialize the channels but it won't open any of them unless we explicitly mention the type of initialization we need.
UseDepthAndPlayerIndex	This option is used to capture depth stream data as well as the player index from the skeleton tracking engine.
UseColor	This option enables the color image stream.
UseSkeletonTracking	This option opens the channel for reading the positions of the skeleton joints from the sensor.
UseDepth	This option is used to enable the depth data stream.
UseAudio	To start the audio source, the sensor uses the `UseAudio` initialization option.

The initialization of the stream channel is achieved by setting the options internally. From a developer's perspective, you just need to call the `Start()` method, and the rest will be taken care of by the SDK.

Enabling the data streams

The KinectSensor class provides specific events that help to enable and to subscribe image stream, depth stream, and skeleton stream data. We will be dealing with details of each and every data stream in subsequent chapters. As of now, we will learn how to enable stream data in our application.

Within the Kinect for Windows SDK, the color, depth, and skeleton data streams are represented by the types of ColorImageStream, DepthImageStream, and SkeletonStream methods respectively. Each of them has an Enable method that opens up the stream pipeline. For example, to enable the ColorStream type, you need to write the following line of code:

```
this.sensor.ColorStream.Enable();
```

You can explicitly enable the stream only after the StartSensor() method, as shown in the following code snippet. In our Info Box application, we did the same by enabling the color, depth, and skeleton data streams after starting the sensor.

```
if (KinectSensor.KinectSensors.Count > 0)
{
    this.sensor = KinectSensor.KinectSensors[0];
    this.StartSensor();
    this.sensor.ColorStream.Enable();
    this.sensor.DepthStream.Enable();
    this.sensor.SkeletonStream.Enable();
}
```

Identifying the Kinect sensor

Each Kinect sensor can be identified by the DeviceConnectionId property of the KinectSensor object. The connection ID of this device returns the Device Instance Path of the USB port on which it is connected.

To have a look at it, open **Control Panel** and navigate to **Device Manager**. Then, change the view of Device Manager to **Device by Connection**. Select **Generic USB Hub** for the **Kinect for Windows Device** node and open the **Properties** menu. There you will find the same device ID as you have seen previously. See the following screenshot:

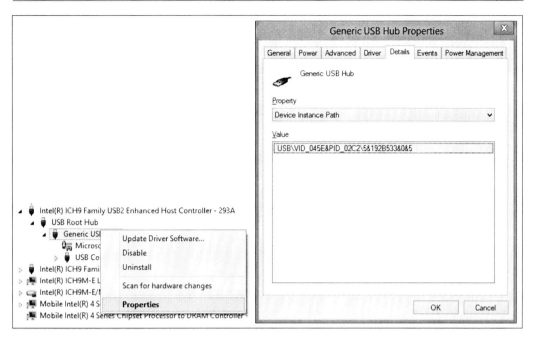

Initializing the sensor using device connection ID

If you know the device connection ID for your Kinect sensor, you can use the same for instantiating the senor instead of using an index. This will make sure that you are initializing the correct device if there are multiple devices and if you are not sure about the device index. In the following code snippet we have used the previously received unique instance ID:

```
KinectSensor  sensor = KinectSensor.KinectSensors [@" USB\VID_045E&PID
_02C2\5&192B533&0&5"];
This.sensor.Start()
```

As this Connection ID returns the USB hub device instance path ID, it will be changed once you plug the device into a different USB hub.

If you are aware of your device ID, you can always refer to the device using the ID as stated in the following code block:

```
KinectSensor sensor = KinectSensor.KinectSensors[@"USB\
VID_045E&PID_02AE\A00362A01385118A"];
int position = 0;
var collection = KinectSensor.KinectSensors.Where(item => item.
DeviceConnectionId == sensor.DeviceConnectionId);
var indexCollection = from item in collection
let row = position++
select new { SensorObject = item, SensorIndex = row };
```

If it's a single sensor, the index should be 0, but this code block will return the actual position from the list of sensors as well. Currently, we have tested the code with one sensor, so we have the sensor index value 0 as shown in the following screenshot:

```
IMMEDIATE WINDOW                                                      ▾ ☐ ✕
indexCollection.ToList();
Count = 1
    [0]: { SensorObject = {Microsoft.Kinect.KinectSensor}, SensorIndex = 0 }
```

 The KinectSensor object has another property, named UniqueKinectId, that returns a unique ID for the Kinect sensor. You can use this ID to identify the sensor uniquely. Also you can use the same to map the index of the sensor.

Stopping the Kinect sensor

You should call the sensor.Stop() method of the KinectSensor class when the sensor finishes its work. This will shut down the instance of the Kinect sensor. You can write a method such as the following that deals with stopping the sensor.

```
private void StopSensor()
{
    if (this.sensor != null && this.sensor.IsRunning)
    {
        this.sensor.Stop();
    }
}
```

 Like sensor.Start(), the Stop() method also internally checks for the sensor's running state. The call goes to stop the sensor only if it is running.

The Stop() method does the clean-up operation

It's good practice to call Stop() once you are done with the Kinect sensor. This is because the Stop() method does some clean-up work internally before it actually shuts down the device. It completes the following tasks:

- It stops the depth, color, and skeleton data streams individually by calling the Close method if they are open
- It checks for the open Kinect audio source and stops it if it's running

- It kills all the threads that were spawned by events generated by the Kinect device
- It shuts down the device and sets the sensor initialization option to `None`

The following diagram shows the actual flow of the `Stop()` method of a Kinect device:

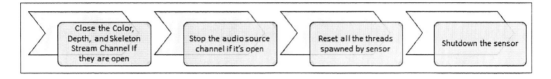

The Kinect sensor internally uses unmanaged resources to manage the sensor data streams. It sends the stream to the managed application and the `KinectSensor` class uses it. When we close the application, it cannot dispose of the unmanaged stream automatically if we don't forcefully send a termination request by calling the `Stop()` method. The managed `Dispose` method does this as well. So to turn off the device, the application programmer needs to call the `Stop()` method to clear unmanaged resources before the managed application gets closed.

For instance, if you are running the application while debugging, your application will be directly hosted in your `vshost` file and the Visual Studio debugger allows you to run your code line by line. If you close the application directly from Visual Studio, it will ensure that the process gets stopped without any code getting executed. To experience this situation, you can stop the application directly from Visual Studio without calling the `Stop()` method, and you will see the IR light of the device is still on.

Turning off the IR light forcefully

You can turn off the IR emitter using the `KinectSensor. ForceInfraredEmitterOff` property. By default, this property is set to `false`. To turn the IR light off, set the property to `true`.

You can test this functionality easily by performing the following steps:

- Once the sensor is started, you will find a red light is turned on in the IR emitter.
- Set `ForceInfraredEmitterOff` to `true`, which will stop the IR emitter; you will find that the IR light is also stopped.

Again, set the `ForceInfraredEmitterOff` property to `false` to turn on the emitter.

Displaying information in the Kinect Info Box

So far, you have seen how you can use Kinect libraries in your application and how to identify, stop, and start it. In short, you are almost done with the major part of the application. Now, it's time to look at how to display information in the UI.

Designing the Info Box UI

This application displays information using the `System.Windows.Controls.TextBlock` class inside a `System.Windows.Controls.Grid` class. That is, each cell on the grid contains a `Textblock` component. The following excerpt from the `MainWindow.xaml` file shows how this is accomplished in XAML:

```
<TextBlock Text="Connection ID" Grid.Row="1" Grid.Column="0"
Style="{StaticResource BasicTextStyle}"  />
<TextBlock Text="{Binding ConnectionID}" Grid.Row="1" Grid.Column="1"
Style="{StaticResource BasicContentStyle}" />
```

As we are going to display the information in text format, we will be splitting the window into a number of columns and rows, where each of the individual rows is responsible for showing information for one single sensor. As you can see in the preceding code, we have two `TextBlock` controls. One of them shows the label and another is bound to a property that shows the actual data.

Similar to this, we have several `TextBlock` controls that display the data for different information types. Apart from the text controls, we have button controls to start and stop the sensor.

Binding the data

Data binding in WPF can be done very easily using the property notification API built into WPF applications. `INotifyPropertyChanged` is a powerful interface in the `System.Component` namespace and provides a standard way to notify binding to UI on a property change.

Implementing the `INotifyPropertyChanged` interface is not mandatory for data binding. You can use direct binding of data by just assigning data into control. Implementing `INotifyPropertyChanged` will allow changes to property values to be reflected in the UI and will help keep your code clean and get the most out of the complex work done by implementing data binding in the UI. As the standard process of data binding, in this section we will give you a step-by-step look into the application as we will be following the same approach across the book for all demo applications.

A quick look at INotifyPropertyChanged

The INotifyPropertyChanged interface itself is a simple. It has no properties and no methods. It has just one event called PropertyChanged with two parameters. Refer to the following code snippet; the first parameter is the sender, and the second parameter is PropertyChangedEventArgs, which has a property named PropertyName:

```
this.PropertyChanged.Invoke(this, new PropertyChangedEventArgs(proper
tyName));
```

Using INotifyPropertyChanged for data binding

Within our Kinect Info Box project, add a new class named MainWindowViewModel. cs and implement the INotifyPropertyChanged interface.

The very first thing we are going to do here is wrap the PropertyChanged event within a generic method so that we can call the same method for every property that needs to send the notifications.

As shown in the following code block, we have a method named OnNotifyPropertyChange, which accepts the propertyName variable as a parameter and passes it within PropertyChangedEventArgs:

```
public void OnNotifyPropertyChange(string propertyName)
{
    if (this.PropertyChanged != null)
    {
        this.PropertyChanged.Invoke(this, new PropertyChangedEventArgs
        (propertyName));
    }
}
```

The class also contains the list of properties with PropertyChanged in the setter block to see if a value is changing. Any changes in the values will automatically notify the UI. This is all very simple and useful. Implementation of any property that needs a notification looks like the following code snippet:

```
private string connectionIDValue;
public string ConnectionID
{
    get
    {
        return this.connectionIDValue;
    }
    set
    {
```

```
            if (this.connectionIDValue != value)
            {
                this.connectionIDValue = value;
                this.OnNotifyPropertyChange("ConnectionID");
            }
        }
    }
```

We need all the properties to be defined in the same way for our `MainWindowViewModel` class. The following diagram is the class diagram for the **MainWindowViewModel** class:

Setting the DataContext

Binding of the data occurs when the **PropertyChanged** event of the `MainWindowViewModel` class is raised. The `DataContext` property of the `MainWindow` class is set when the class is first initialized in the constructor of the `MainWindow` class:

```
private MainWindowViewModel viewModel;
public MainWindow()
{
    this.InitializeComponent();
    this.Loaded += this.MainWindow_Loaded;
    this.viewModel = new MainWindowViewModel();
    this.DataContext = this.viewModel;
}
```

Setting up the information

The last thing we need to do is to fill up the `MainWindowViewModel` class instance with the values from the sensor object. The `SetKinectInfo` method does the same job in our Kinect Info Box application. Refer to the following code snippet; we have assigned the `DeviceConnectionId` value of the sensor object, which is nothing but the currently running sensor, to the `connectionID` property of the `ViewModel` object.

```
private void SetKinectInfo()
{
    if (this.sensor != null)
    {
        this.viewModel.ConnectionID = this.sensor.DeviceConnectionId;
        // Set other property values
    }
}
```

Whenever the `SetKinectInfo` method is called, the value of `DeviceConnectionId` is assigned to `ViewModel.connectionID`, and it immediately raises the `OnNotifyPropertyChange` notification, which notifies the UI about the changes and updates the value accordingly.

That's all!

You are done! You have just finished building your first application. Run the application to see the information about the attached Kinect sensor. While starting the application it will automatically start the sensor; however, you can start and stop the sensor by clicking on the **Start** and **Stop** buttons. In the code behind these two buttons that were just mentioned, are the `SensorStart()` and `SensorStop()` methods, respectively.

Dealing with the Kinect status

The Kinect sensor needs an external power supply to get the camera, IR sensor, and motor to work properly. Even after following all the standard practices and measures, your system might not detect any of the components of Kinect if there is any problem with your device. Other scenarios that may occur, and that are indeterministic in nature, could be the power suddenly going off while your application is running, , some error occurring in the device, or the device getting unplugged. All the earlier cases can cause your application to crash or throw an unknown exception.

It is of paramount importance to track the device status while your sensor is used by the application. The `KinectSensor` object has a property named `Status`, which indicates the current state of the devices. The property type is of the `KinectStatus` enumeration.

The following table has listed the different status values with their descriptions:

Status	Description
Connected	This indicates that the device is connected properly with the system and that it can be used for receiving data using an application.
Error	The SDK will return this status if the system fails to detect the device properly or there is some internal error.
Disconnected	This is the status if the device gets disconnected at any point in time while the application is running, which could happen in different scenarios such as a power cut, unplugging the external power source, or even unplugging the USB device from system.
NotReady	This is the status returned when the device is detected but not loaded properly. Generally, the Kinect SDK detects the device once you have plugged it into the system, but the system loads actual drivers once external power is supplied. This is the intermediate status when the device is not ready to be used.
NotPowered	This is the status if the device is connected to the system using a USB port, but the external power supplier is not plugged in or is turned off.
Initializing	This is the status when the device is getting connected or initialized. Generally, this occurs during reconnecting after disconnection or shutdown.
DeviceNotSupported	This is the status if the device is not supported by the SDK. This is not applicable to the Kinect for Xbox device.
DeviceNotGenuine	This status can be used to make your application check that you are using only Kinect for Windows devices. This is not applicable to the Kinect for Xbox device.
InsufficicentBandwith	This is the status when the USB hub is not able to process the complete data sent by the sensor.
Undefined	This is the status raised for any kind of unhandled issues that can cause the sensor to be undefined or erroneous.

To understand the flow of the Kinect status and the scenarios in which it can occur can be explained in a simpler way refer to the following diagram. Once the device is connected and the power is turned off, it will show the Not Powered status. Similarly, unplugging the device from USB port will return the Disconnected status. If you plug it back in or turn the power on, it will first show the Initializing status before changing to the Connected status.

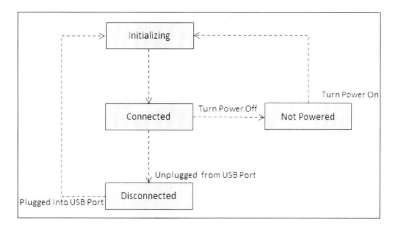

Monitoring the change in sensor status

The KinectSensorCollection object has only an event named StatusChanged, which can be registered as follows:

```
KinectSensor.KinectSensors.StatusChanged += KinectSensors_
StatusChanged;
```

Once the event is registered, it will fire automatically if there are any changes in the device status, internally or externally.

 The StatusChanged event is registered at the start of your application during the initialization of the sensor.

The StatusChanged event fires up with a StatusChangedEventArgs class, which holds the KinectStatus property and the instance of the sensor by which this event has been raised.

Properties of the StatusChangedEventArgs class

The following table shows the properties of the `StatusChangedEventArgs` class:

Name	Description
Sensor	This property refers to the Kinect sensor that raised this event. This information is useful if you are handling any operation on any status change. If there are multiple Kinect devices, you will get the reference of individual sensors using the property itself.
Status	This property provides the current status of the Kinect device that raised the events. `KinectStatus` is a flag enumeration defined in Microsoft. Kinect namespaces.

In the `StatusChanged` event handler, you can check for the status that is returned by the `KinectStatus` enumeration and display the proper message to end users. The uses of different statuses with the `StatusChanged` event handler are shown in the following code snippet:

```
void Kinects_StatusChanged(object sender, StatusChangedEventArgs e)
{
    switch (e.Status)
    {
        case KinectStatus.Connected:
            // Device Connected;
            break;
        case KinectStatus.DisConnected:
            // Device DisConnected;
            break;
    }
}
```

So, you must have noticed that the Kinect SDK is flexible enough to detect the device status this well. This will really help avoid unnecessary exceptions and application crashes.

The `StausChanged` events are attached to all the elements of `KinectSensorCollection`. So, you can track the status change of each and every Kinect device if there is more than one device connected. When the `StatusChanged` event is fired, it invokes the event handler with `StatusChangedEventArgs`, which has associated with the sensor. The following image shows the sensor property of the Kinect `StatusChangedEventArgs` class within the event handler that is raised by the `StatusChanged` event:

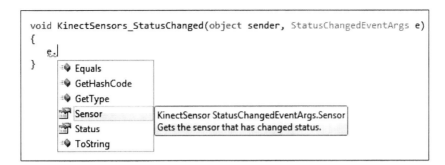

Resuming your application automatically

You have also seen that, during the lifespan of a Kinect application the status of the sensor can change. You can start the sensor only when it's in the connected state and you need to call the `Start()` method explicitly to start it. We can take advantage of the `StatusChanged` event to start the sensor and resume our application automatically when it is connected. You can save the state of your application when the status is `Disconnected` or `NotPowered` and can resume it automatically once it is connected by starting the sensor and reloading your application state. This is shown in the following diagram:

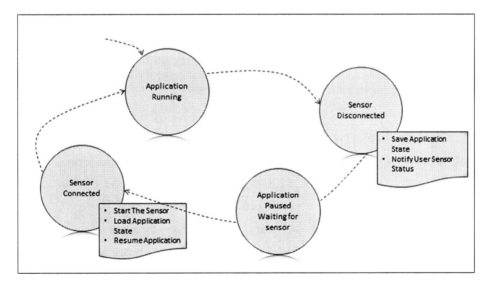

Building KinectStatusNotifier

In this section, we are going to learn how to build a notification application named KinectStatusNotifier that uses the Kinect sensor and shows the sensor status in the system tray. KinectStatusNotifier will pop up a notification icon in the system tray whenever there is a change in the sensor status (refer to the following screenshot).

If you want to show some custom messages with the status change, you can also explicitly call KinectStatusNotifier to notify of a status change in the system tray, as shown in the following screenshot:

 The KinectStatusNotifier application can be useful for any Kinect application, so we will implement it as a general class library so that we can inject it into any Kinect application.

Setting up an application

We will start this application from scratch with a new `ClassLibrary` project, as follows:

1. Start a new instance of Visual Studio.

2. Create a new project by navigating to **File** | **New Project**.

3. Select the **Visual C#** template and pick the **Class Library** option from the template options.

4. Name the library `KinectStatusNotifier`, as shown in the following image. Click on **OK** to create the project.

NotifyIcon is a class in the System.Windows.Forms namespace and can be used to invoke the default notification from the system tray. By default, the WPF application does not have NotifyIcon, so we are going to create a wrapper around System.Windows.Forms.NotifyIcon so that we can easily invoke it from any application.

Perform the following steps to set up our projects:

5. Remove the exiting classes from the **KinectStatusNotifier** project and add a new class by right-clicking on **Project | Add New Item | Class**. Give it the name StatusNotifier and click on **OK**.

6. Add a reference to System.Windows.Forms and System.Drawing to the KinectStatusNotifier project.

How it works

Once we have the project set up, the first thing we need to do is to create an instance of NotifyIcon, as follows:

```
private NotifyIcon kinectNotifier = new NotifyIcon();.
```

KinectNotifier now holds the reference to NotifyIcon and can be invoked by a status change of the sensor. Hence, we need the reference to KinectSensorCollection in the KinectStatusNotifier project.

Add a property of type KinectSensorCollection, as follows:

```
private KinectSensorCollection sensorsValue;
public KinectSensorCollection Sensors
{
    get
    {
        return this.sensorsValue;
    }
    set
    {
        this.sensorsValue = value;
        this.AutoNotification = true;
    }
}
```

Sensors is a public property of the StatusNotifier class that holds the reference to KinectSensorCollection that is passed from the calling application. If you have noticed, we have an additional AutoNotification property, which is by default set to true; however, if you look inside the definition of this property, you will find this:

```
private bool autoNotificationValue;
public bool AutoNotification
{
    get
    {
        return this.autoNotificationValue;
    }
    set
    {
        this.autoNotificationValue = value;
        if (value)
        {
            this.Sensors.StatusChanged += this.Sensors_StatusChanged;
        }
        else
        {
```

```
        this.sensors.StatusChanged -= this.Sensors_StatusChanged;
    }
  }
}
```

We are subscribing to the `StatusChanged` event handler only when `AutoNotification` is set to `true`. This will give you a choice between using the automatic notification with status change and not using it, as shown in the following screenshot:

The `StatusNotifer` class has a few more properties for the notification title, message, and sensor status, as shown in the preceding class diagram. The `StatusNotifer` class has a defined enumeration called `StatusType`, which is either the information or a warning. The `NotifierMessage` and `NotifierTitle` properties are set in the `Sensor_StatusChanged` event handler, which was registered from the `AutoNotification` property as follows:

```
protected void Sensors_StatusChanged(object sender,
StatusChangedEventArgs e)
{
    this.SensorStatus = e.Status;
    this.NotifierTitle = System.Reflection.Assembly.
    GetExecutingAssembly().GetName().Name;
    this.NotifierMessage = string.Format("{0}\n{1}", this.
    SensorStatus.ToString(), e.Sensor.DeviceConnectionId);
    this.StatusType = StatusType.Information;
    this.NotifyStatus();
}
```

As you can see in the preceding code, the NotifierTitle property is set to the name of the application, and the NotifierMessage property is set to SensorStatus and DeviceConnectionId. Finally, the call to the NotifyStatus() method sets the StatusNotifier property to the kinectNotifier instance of the NotifyIcon class and invokes the ShowBallonTip() method to notify an icon on the system tray. The NotifyStatus class is shown in the following code snippet:

```
public void NotifyStatus()
{
    this.kinectNotifier.Icon = new Icon(this.GetIcon());
    this.kinectNotifier.Text = string.Format("Device Status : {0}",
    this.SensorStatus.ToString());
    this.kinectNotifier.Visible = true;
    this.kinectNotifier.ShowBalloonTip(3000, this.NotifierTitle,
    this.NotifierMessage, this.StatusType == StatusType.Information ?
    ToolTipIcon.Info : ToolTipIcon.Warning);
}
```

Using KinectStatusNotifier

KinectStatusNotifier is not a self-executable; it generates a KinectStatusNotifier.dll assembly that can be used with a Kinect application. Let's integrate this to our previously built Kinect Info Box application and see how it works. This can be done simply by performing the following steps:

1. Add the KinectStatusNotifier.dll assembly as a reference assembly to the Kinect Info Box application from the **Add References** window.

2. Add the following namespace in the application:

    ```
    using KinectStatusNotifier;
    ```

3. Instantiate a new object for the StatusNotifier class, as follows:

    ```
    private StatusNotifier notifier = new StatusNotifier();
    ```

4. Assign the KinectSensor.KinectSensors collection as a reference to notifer.Sensors, as follows:

    ```
    this.notifier.Sensors = KinectSensor.KinectSensors;
    ```

That's all! The StatusNotifer class will take care of the rest. Whenever there is a change in the status of the sensor, you can see a notification with the current status in the System Tray icon.

You can set the value of `AutoNotification` to `false`, which will stop the automatic notification in the system tray at the `StatusNotifer` class level and invoke the `NotifyIcon` class explicitly when there is a status change. It will do this by handling the `StatusChanged` event handler in your application itself. You can also handle it from both places, while you can change the status in the tray icon from a single place.

Test it out

To test the application out and see how the application and the sensor work together, first run the Kinect Info Box application and then switch off the power to the sensor and switch it back on. As shown in the following screenshot, you will able to see exactly three different changes in sensor status in the system tray notification:

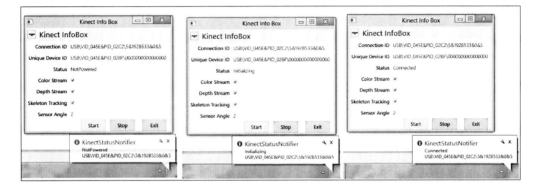

Summary

In this chapter we discussed the fundamentals of building Kinect applications. As the sensor is prevalent in many other platforms and devices, the Kinect applications also make substantial use of it in device identification, initialization, and disposing. Thus we have learned a comprehensive view of these approaches in this chapter. We have explored several APIs that help to start and stop the sensor, as well as identifying them and enabling different types of streams by building a small utility. Tracking the Kinect status will safeguard the application from failures and crashes, and we have also discussed a way to do so by notifying the state change in the system tray. With the knowledge gained from this chapter, we will be building a few more complex applications by directly consuming Kinect camera information in the next chapter.

4
Getting the Most out of Kinect Camera

You are all set to take your development experience to the next level. This time you will leverage your learning towards the Kinect SDK API by accessing the Kinect camera and playing around with the data captured by the camera. The Kinect device has a video camera that delivers the three basic color components, namely *red*, *green*, and *blue*. As part of the Kinect sensor, the camera helps in capturing the color stream, enabling face tracking and more. This color stream is the least complex process in terms of the way it returns the data and how the SDK processes it. Working with a Kinect image stream majorly involves the following steps:

1. Enabling the stream.
2. Capturing the stream frame by frame in the application.
3. Processing the image frames.

In this chapter, you will learn how to enable and retrieve the color stream, extract frames, play around with the color pixels, control the device motor, and apply effects on camera images. We will start with building a camera application that uses the Kinect color camera, and then we will be extending the camera with various features, such as extracting frames, saving frames, changing pixels formats and others. You will also learn how to change the camera's color brightness, contrasts, hue, and other different settings to fine-tune color images, along with applying backlight compensation. The following is an overview of the various aspects that we'll be covering in this chapter:

- Understanding the Kinect image stream
- Understanding different ways of retrieving stream data
- Building a KinectCam application that uses the Kinect camera

- Studying Kinect APIs in depth for color image streams
- Manipulating individual color pixels
- Changing the sensor elevation angle
- Applying effects on the Kinect camera
- Making your camera see in low light conditions
- Improving the performance of your application

Understanding the Kinect image stream

An image stream is nothing but a succession of still image frames. Kinect can deliver the still image frame within a range of 12 to 30 frames per second (fps). The frame rate can change as per the requested type and resolution. The SDK supports two types of image stream formats:

- Color image stream
- Depth image stream

Different streams are transferred in different pipelines, which you must enable along with the type of data that you want from the sensor. The type of image frames depend on input parameters such as the frame resolution, image type, and frame rate. Based on your inputs, the sensor will initialize the stream channel for data transfer. If you are not specifying anything, the SDK will pick up the default image type and resolution defined in the SDK for that particular channel.

The image frames are stored into a buffer before they are used by the application. If there is any delay in reading the buffer data and rendering it as images, the buffer will fill with a new image frame by discarding the old frame data. The unprocessed frames will be dropped, which means you are losing the image frames, and the frame rate will be decreased. One of the reasons can be a lack of hardware resources due to which Kinect may go out of sync with the application.

The Kinect SDK provides a top-level base class ImageStream, which is an abstract class; this is implemented by both the color and depth stream classes.

Having said that Kinect supports the image stream in the format of color and depth; in this chapter we will be focusing only on the details of the color image stream.

Types of color images

The Kinect sensor supports the following types of color image formats:

- RGB
- YUV
- Bayer

The first one, as the name suggests, is the Red-Green-Blue color space known as RGB color. Each RGB pixel of the Kinect color image frame is an array of size four and arranged in the following way, where the first three values are for red, green, and blue. Alpha, the fourth value in the array, gives the transparency:

Blue	Green	Red	Alpha	Blue	Green	Red	Alpha
Blue	Green	Red	Alpha	Blue	Green	Red	Alpha
Blue	Green	Red	Alpha	Blue	Green	Red	Alpha
Blue	Green	Red	Alpha	Blue	Green	Red	Alpha

And the second one is Luminance YUV, where Y is the luminance channel, U is the blue channel, and V is the red channel. Both YUV data and RGB data represent the same image frame as they are captured using the same camera; the only difference is in the representation of the color space. You can choose the image format that is most convenient for your application.

The Kinect video camera can return a 32 bits per pixel RGB image stream in two different resolutions:

- 640 x 480 (at 30 frames per second)
- 1280 x 960 (at 12 frames per second)

On the other side, YUV provides 16 bits per pixel and is used as part of the color image pipeline. The Kinect color camera supports YUV data only at the following resolution:

- 640 × 480 (at 15 frames per second)

The YUV image stream uses less memory than the RGB image stream to hold bitmap data and allocates less buffer memory. You can choose this stream channel if you compromise on the image quality and use the same memory buffer for other purposes in your application.

The Kinect camera also returns a raw Bayer color image format with a combination of red, green, and blue color; but the color filter pattern uses 50 percent green, 25 percent red, and 25 percent blue. The pattern is called a **Bayer color filter array** or a **Bayer filter**. This color filter is used in this way because the human eye is more sensitive to green and can see more changes in green lights. The pattern for the Bayer color format is shown in the following figure, where half of the total number of pixels are green while the other half are of the total number of red and blue:

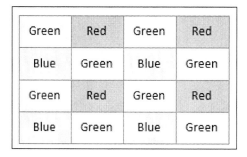

The resolutions supported by the Bayer color format are the following formats:

- 640 x 480 (at 30 frames per second)
- 1280 x 960 (at 12 frames per second)

The sensor returns 16 bits per pixel infrared data with the following resolution as a part of the color image stream:

- 640 × 480 (at 30 frames per second)

 The Kinect SDK also exposes the IR emitter lights as *infrared stream* data in a format of the color image stream.

Different ways of retrieving the color stream from Kinect

The image frames are a type of the `ColorImageFrame` class. Depending on the type of images you are using, the sensor will return the image frame. To get any color frame from the sensor, you need to either subscribe to the event handler or explicitly send the request to the sensor to send a frame:

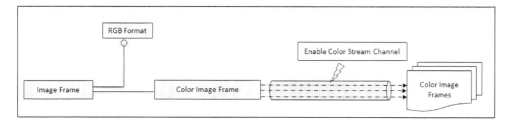

There are two ways of capturing the same in your application:

- Event model
- Polling model

Event model

Using the event model, the Kinect sensor sends the frame to the application whenever a new frame is captured by the sensor. For that you need to subscribe to the specific event handler using your code, where you need to process the incoming frames. Before subscribing to the event, you must tell the SDK the color type and resolution of image streams you are looking for. Once it's subscribed to, the sensor will send the data continuously unless you disable and unsubscribe the channel, or stop the sensor.

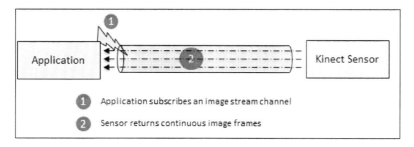

Polling model

The polling model is an on-demand model where you need to send a request to the sensor whenever there is a necessity to get an image frame. For the polling model, you have to pass the time interval after which the sensor will return the image frame.

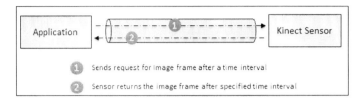

If there is any open color channel and there is no subscriber event on that channel, the SDK will automatically pick up the existing channel to get an image frame. If there is no channel open, the SDK will create a new channel to get the frame from the sensor. You can't send a request for images to a channel that is already subscribed by an event handler.

KinectCam – a Kinect camera application

The first thing that developers with Kinect programming often do is read the color stream data from the sensor. This also verifies that the camera is working properly and that you can successfully create and run a simple application.

In this section you are going to learn how to consume the color data stream from the sensor and use other Kinect SDK APIs to play around with the color data. And you will learn everything by building a complete application called **KinectCam**. Refer to the following screenshot, which shows how the end application will look:

And this is how the application will work:

1. On starting the application, the Kinect camera will start capturing the color stream, and you can view the live stream in your application.
2. You can click on the **Save** button to save the current frame as an image.
3. The **Start** and **Stop** buttons will do the job of starting and stopping the sensor, whereas the **Exit** button will close the camera.

Is this what you are going to build? Of course not! There is another button, which we missed out. Yes, the **Settings** button. On clicking the **Settings** button, the application will show you the **KinectCam Settings** dialog window, which is shown in the following screenshot:

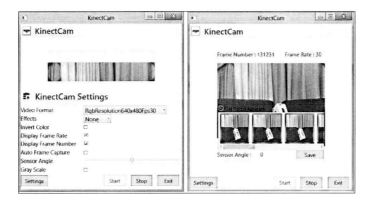

The setting options will allow you to:

1. Change the video format and camera elevation angle.
2. Enable and disable the frame rates and frame number.
3. Perform an automatic image capture.
4. Apply effects such as the RGB filter, grayscale, and inverted color on the stream.

So let's go ahead and build the KinectCam application now.

Setting up the project

The very first thing that you need to do is create and set up the project by adding the assemblies that are required for accessing the sensor. Follow these steps to set up a blank project for your KinectCam application:

1. Start a new instance of Visual Studio.
2. Create a new project by navigating to **File** | **New Project**.

3. You will see the **New Project** dialog box. Choose **Visual C#** as our development language, select **WPF Application Template**, and type the name as KinectCam.

4. From **Solution Explorer**, right-click on the **References** folder and select **Add References**.

5. Include a reference of the **Microsoft.Kinect** assembly.

Designing the application – XAML and data binding

The application design is very simple and straightforward. This application displays the information using the TextBlock and Image controls inside various types of panel controls such as Grid and Stackpanel. There are several buttons that perform different actions. The following is a part of the document outline view from MainWindow.xaml, which shows how this UI is accomplished in XAML:

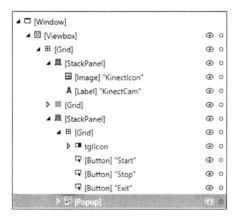

We will be following the same approach for data binding as we did for the KinectInfoBox application in the previous chapter; however this data-binding approach is not an area of concern as we will mostly be focusing on Kinect APIs.

Add a new class named MainWindowViewModel.cs that implements the INotifyPropertyChanged interface and has the following listed property that calls OnNotifyPropertyChange() if there is any value change:

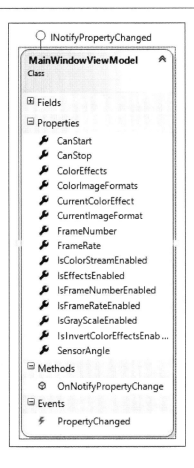

The XAML markup will be using these properties to bind the data. For example, for displaying the frame number, you have to use the following XAML snippet:

```
<TextBlock Name="FrameNumberText" Text="{Binding FrameNumber}" />
```

The `MainWindow` constructor of the KinectCam application instantiates `MainWinodowViewModel` and sets `DataContext` for the application:

```
MainWindowViewModel viewModel;
public MainWindow()
{
  InitializeComponent();
  viewModel = new MainWindowViewModel();
  this.DataContext = this.viewModel;
}
```

Now if your application updates the values `this.viewModel.FrameNumber`, it will reflect in the UI. The same approach holds for all the properties of the `MainWindowViewModel` class.

Capturing color image from the Kinect camera

Capturing the color image stream from the sensor and displaying it to the UI can be done by following these steps:

1. Enable the color stream channel with an image format.
2. Attach the event handler with the stream channel.
3. Process the incoming image frames.
4. Render the image frames on the UI.
5. Starting the sensor before the sensor starts producing image frames and stopping and monitoring the sensor status will be the common job for all of your applications, which you are already familiar with.

Let's have a look inside the individual steps for capturing a color image.

Enabling the color stream channel

The `KinectSensor` class has a property `ColorStream` of type `ColorImageStream`, which actually handles everything that is required for capturing the color image. The first thing it must do is get the reference of the connected sensor and start it.

```
this.sensor = KinectSensor.KinectSensors.FirstOrDefault( sensorItem =>
sensorItem.Status == KinectStatus.Connected);
this.StartSensor();
```

Here `sensor` is an object of the type `KinectSensor` class. Once you have the `sensor` object and reference of the Kinect sensor, you can enable the stream by calling the `Enable()` method of the `ColorImageStream` class, as follows:

```
this.sensor.ColorStream.Enable();
```

When the sensor is running and the color stream is enabled, it will initialize the Kinect sensor to generate a stream of color images.

The next thing you must do is to tell the sensor what to do when it has captured a new image frame. To achieve this, you need an event handler that has to be attached to the sensor stream channel.

Enabling a channel with the image format

By default `Enable` does not accept any argument and enables the color stream with a `RgbResolution640x480Fps30` color image format, which is an enumeration of the type `ColorImageFormat`.

The `ImageStream` class has an overloaded method for `Enable()`. If you want to initialize the color stream with a different image format, use the overloaded method that accepts `ColorImageFormat` as an argument, as shown in the following snippet:

```
this.sensor.ColorStream.Enable(ColorImageFormat.
RgbResolution640x480Fps30);
```

How to check if the color stream is already enabled or not

The `ColorStreamImage` class also includes an `IsEnabled` property, which is read only. `IsEnabled` returns the current status of the color stream channel. You can use the `IsEnabled` property just before enabling the stream channel at any point in time, to check if the channel is open for the color stream before you access the stream data. Here's the code snippet that uses the `IsEnabled` property before enabling the color stream.

```
if (!this.sensor.ColorStream.IsEnabled)
{
  this.sensor.ColorStream.Enable();
}
```

Choosing the image format

`ColorImageFormat` is a public enumeration defined in the `Microsoft.Kinect` assembly. You can specify the color image format along with the resolution within the single specified value. The following is a list of color image formats available of the type `ColorImageFormat` enumeration that you can specify for your application:

- `RgbResolution640x480Fps30`
- `RgbResolution1280x960Fps12`
- `YuvResolution640x480Fps15`
- `RawYuvResolution640x480Fps15`
- `InfraredResolution640x480Fps30`
- `RawBayerResolution640x480Fps30`
- `RawBayerResolution1280x960Fps12`
- `Undefined`

For example, by specifying `ColorImageFormat.RgbResolution640x480Fps30` with the `Enable()` method you are informing the sensor to send an image frame of the RGB type with a resolution of 640 x 480. If you specify Undefined, the SDK will throw an `ArgumentException` with the `ImageFormatNotSupported` message.

 You can enable only one *type* of color stream at a time.

The following are a couple of things you must consider while enabling the stream channel:

- If you are trying to enable the stream multiple times with different color image formats, the *last one* will take precedence
- If you are trying to reenable the stream with the same image format, the SDK does not perform anything and your application continues with the existing stream channel

The call goes to the open stream channel only if it is a new request or the requested `ColorImageFormat` is new.

Disabling the color stream channel

You can disable or close the stream channel by just calling the `Disable()` method of the `ImageStream` class, as shown in the following line of code:

```
this.sensor.ColorStream.Disable();
```

The `Disable()` method just closes the connection channel for the current open stream irrespective of `ColorImageFormat` that you have specified.

`IsEnabled` is automatically set to `false` internally when you stop the sensor or disable the color stream by calling the `Disable()` method.

Till now what you have seen is how to enable the color stream and how you can apply a color image format while enabling the stream. With that let's have a look at how to attach the event handler.

Attaching the event handler

The KinectSensor class has an event ColorFrameReady, which is invoked whenever there is new frame sent by the sensor. You can subscribe to the event just by using the following line:

```
this.sensor.ColorFrameReady += sensor_ColorFrameReady;
```

The event handler has two arguments; the first one is sender and the second one is the ColorImageFrameReadyEventArgs.

The default method stub for the sensor_ColorFrameReady event handler will look like the following code snippet:

```
void sensor_ColorFrameReady(object sender,
ColorImageFrameReadyEventArgs e)
{
}
```

> **How to generate the event handler automatically in Visual Studio**
>
> Visual Studio provides you with a nice feature; you can automatically create the event handler by just pressing *Tab* twice after associating the event name, as follows:

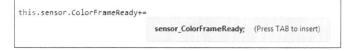

So if you put together whatever you have done so far in a method called StartKinectCam(), the method should look like:

```
private void StartKinectCam()
{
  if (KinectSensor.KinectSensors.Count > 0)
  {
    this.sensor = KinectSensor.KinectSensors.FirstOrDefault
(sensorItem =>sensorItem.Status == KinectStatus.Connected);
    this.StartSensor();
    this.sensor.ColorStream.Enable();
```

```
      this.sensor.ColorFrameReady += sensor_ColorFrameReady;
    }
    else
    {
      MessageBox.Show("No device is connected with system!");
      this.Close();
    }
}
```

With this, the control of your application moves to the `sensor_ColorFrameReady` event handler where image frame processing has to be done.

Processing the incoming image frames

Once the event handler is called, it means there is a new frame that has been sent by the sensor and it's time to process it. The event arguments for this event handler expose a method `OpenColorImageFrame()` that returns an image frame of the type `ColorImageFrame`. You can now use this exact same code to work image frames.

```
void sensor_ColorFrameReady(object sender,
ColorImageFrameReadyEventArgs e)
{
  using (ColorImageFrame imageFrame = e.OpenColorImageFrame())
  {
    // Check if the incoming frame is not null
    if (imageFrame == null)
    {
      return;
    }
      else
      {
      // Get the pixel data in byte array
      this.pixelData = new byte[imageFrame.PixelDataLength];

      // Copy the pixel data
      imageFrame.CopyPixelDataTo(this.pixelData);

      // Calculate the stride
      int stride = imageFrame.Width * imageFrame.BytesPerPixel;

      // assign the bitmap image source into image control
      this.VideoControl.Source = BitmapSource.Create(
      imageFrame.Width,
      imageFrame.Height,
```

```
      96,
      96,
      PixelFormats.Bgr32,
      null,
      pixelData,
      stride);
    }
  }
}
```

The number of lines in the previous code snippet can be overwhelming at first sight. However, on a more meticulous and step-by-step inspection, we can decipher the meaning of the individual lines quite easily. In reality the steps are quite simple; whenever there is a new frame sent by the sensor, this event handler invokes the `ColorFrameReady` handler, and in the first step, it reads `ColorImageFrame`, which returns the image frame of the type returned by the `OpenColorImageFrame()` method.

```
using (ColorImageFrame imageFrame = e.OpenColorImageFrame())
{
}
```

 We have used the `using` block, which defines the scope of an object, outside of which an object will be disposed. The `imageFrame` object is declared in a `using` block. This means that when the execution completes the block of code that follows the `using` statement, the `imageFrame` object is no longer required and can be destroyed. It is important to do this because the frame will take up a lot of memory as there are about 30 frames in each second.

In the next step, we perform a null detection on the incoming image frame.

```
if (imageFrame == null)
{
  Return;
}
```

This is just to make sure that if there is any dropped frame in between frames, your application should be smart enough to take care of it.

After that, we calculate the size of the incoming frame in the `byte[]` array. `PixeDataLength` is a read-only property that returns the length of the pixel data. Internally, this is an abstract property of the `ImageFrame` class and has been overridden in the `ColorImageFrame` class. The pixel data length provides the integer length of the image frame.

```
this.pixelData = new byte[imageFrame.PixelDataLength];
```

Copy the `byte[]` array of the pixel data into the color image frame by calling the `CopyPixelDataTo()` method.

```
imageFrame.CopyPixelDataTo(this.pixelData);
```

Finally, create a bitmap image source with the incoming image frame and assign the same in the image control:

```
this.VideoControl.Source = BitmapSource.Create(
    imageFrame.Width,
    imageFrame.Height,
    96,
    96,
    PixelFormats.Bgr32,
    null,
    pixelData,
    stride);
```

The `BitmapSource.Create()` method creates a `BitmapSource` from an array of pixels. We have the pixel information stored in the `imageframe` and `pixelData` variables. The only one parameter that you might need to know more about is the last parameter that passes the `stride` value, which we have created as follows:

```
int stride = imageFrame.Width * imageFrame.BytesPerPixel;
```

 Stride is the width in bytes of a single row of pixel data including padding.

As shown in the following figure, the total image row width is the stride where the pixel data is the actual image width (`ImageFrame.width`) and an extra pixel is calculated for padding.

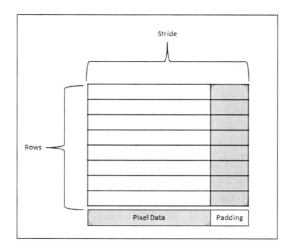

What you have seen till now was for a single image frame; a similar succession of similar image frame operations produces the video stream.

How to change the pixel format of a color image stream

You can display the image stream in a different pixel format. This pixel format has to be defined while you are creating the object of writeable bitmap. As shown in the following code snippet, we have changed the pixel format to Cmyk32:

```
this.colorimageControl.Source = BitmapSource.Create(
imageFrame.Width,
imageFrame.Height,
96,
96,
PixelFormats.Cmyk32,
null,
pixelData,
stride);
```

The only thing you need to keep in mind while working with different types of pixel formats is the buffer size for the pixel data, which should be equal to or more than the required image frame buffer. Otherwise, it won't be able to write, and will throw an exception because different pixel format images use different sizes of buffer.

Rendering image frames on the UI

The final part is about displaying the frames in the UI. And you were already done with most of the rendering part within the event handler while creating BitmapSource from the image frame.

```
this.VideoControl.Source = BitmapSource.Create(
...
```

The BitmapSource was assigned to the source property of an image control. The image control is defined in the MainWindow.Xaml file, which is shown as follows:

```
<Image Name="VideoControl" Stretch="Fill" />
```

Running the KinectCam

With this, you are done with the development of your first interactive application that not only controls your sensor but also reads the color image stream from the Kinect sensor.

Run your application (from Visual Studio press *F5*), and here is the result. You will be able to view the video streaming on your application that was captured by your sensor.

Our next job is to extend it to an advanced version where we can control the image frames, capture images, calculate the frame rates, and so on. To do so, we need to have a clear understanding of what else the Kinect SDK provides us.

Looking inside color image stream helpers

You just developed the application by reading the image stream directly from the Kinect sensor. When we walked through the code implementation, you must have noticed that we were talking about two classes, and they are `ColorImageStream` and `ColorImageFrame`. Truly, they are the core of image streaming from the sensor. Both of these classes are derived from the `ImageStream` and `ImageFrame` base classes respectively. Let's focus on the individual class members.

The ColorImageStream class

The `ColorImageStream` class represents the succession of color image frames coming from Kinect devices. `ColorImageStream` is nothing but a stream of `ColorImageFrame` objects. The `ColorImageStream` class is derived from an `ImageStream` base class. The `ColorImageStream` class is a sealed class, so you can't inherit it in the next level. This class defines the properties and method for working with the color image stream.

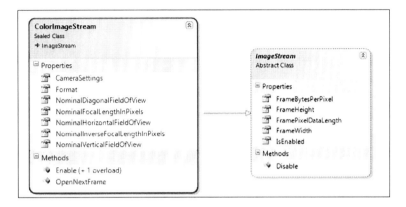

The ColorImageFrame class

The `ColorImageFrame` class is also a sealed class and is derived from an `ImageFrame` class. This class defines the properties and method for working with the color image frame.

The following class diagram shows the properties and methods available within the `ColorImageFrame` class:

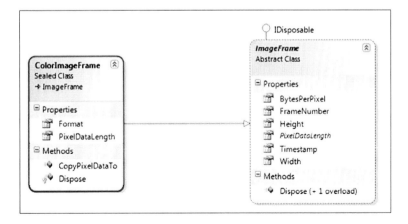

The following diagram is just for quickly recalling what we have discussed till now about the color image frame. `ColorImageFrame` is derived from the `ImageFrame` base class. Whenever there is a frame from the sensor, `ColorFrameReady` events fire up with `ColorImageFrameReadyEventArgs`, which has the `OpenColorImageFrame()` method exposed. `OpenColorImageFrame()` returns the type of `ColorImageFrame` with the `ColorImageFormat` type that was specified during stream channel initialization:

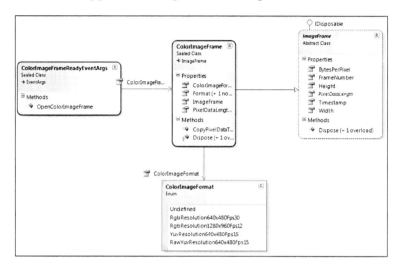

How to retrieve the image format from current image frame

You can retrieve the color image format for the current image frame using the `ImageFrame.Format` property. `ColorImageFrameReadyEventArgs` exposes the `OpenColorImageFrame ()` method that returns the currently received image frame from the sensors.

```
using (ColorImageFrame imageFrame =
e.OpenColorImageFrame())
{
  // Check if the incoming frame isnot null
  if (imageFrame != null)
  {
    this.ImageFormat = imageFrame.Format;
  }
}
```

Here `ImageFormat` is a user defined property and is defined as:

```
public ColorImageFormat ImageFormat {get;set;}
```

Once you have the `ImageFormat` assigned with this property, you can use it anywhere in your application.

ImageFrame.Format is a read-only property. You cannot set the value directly to change the color image format. You have to enable the stream with proper ColorImageFormat to change the value of the image format.

Capturing frames on demand

The ColorImageStream class has a public method named OpenNextFrame(). Using the OpenNextFrame() method, you can request an image frame from the sensor. This is how the polling model works for retrieving image frames.

In the polling model, the application opens a channel for the stream, and whenever the application needs a frame, it sends a request to get the frame. OpenNextFrame () accepts one parameter called millisecondsWait, which specifies how long the sensor should wait before it sends the image frame. If there is no frame ready within the provided time, the method will return null. The following is the general syntax of using OpenNextFrame(); in our case we have used a waiting time of 10 milliseconds:

```
int millisecondsWait = 10;
if (this.sensor.ColorStream.IsEnabled)
{
    ColorImageFrame colorImageFrame = this.sensor.ColorStream.
    OpenNextFrame(millisecondsWait);
}
```

The colorImageFrame class will return an image frame after the provided waiting time. This frame will be the same as the frame captured using the ColorFrameReady event. (Refer to the following screenshot that shows an image frame that was captured using the polling model.) The only difference is that you have to send an explicit request to the sensor to get the image frame:

Name	Value
⊟ ◉ colorImageFrame	{Microsoft.Kinect.ColorImageFrame}
⊟ ◉ base	{Microsoft.Kinect.ColorImageFrame}
⚙ BytesPerPixel	4
⚙ FrameNumber	70
⚙ Height	480
⚙ PixelDataLength	1228800
⚙ Timestamp	2296
⚙ Width	640

You can't call `OpenNextFrame()` after the `ColorFrameReady` is already attached to the color stream. By attaching an event handler, you are notifying the sensor to send the image continuously. If you are doing so, you will receive an `InvalidOperationException`.

Extending the KinectCam

So far we have built the basic KinectCam application, which can feed and display the color stream from the sensor. Our next job is to extend it by leveraging the features of Kinect for Windows SDK.

In this section, you will start with displaying frame numbers, displaying and calculating the frame rates, followed by changing image formats, and finally you will learn how to apply color effects by manipulating the color pixels.

Getting the frame number

The Kinect sensor sends the data as an individual frame, and every frame has a number just to identify the frame. This number is incremented with every single frame when you are using the event model to retrieve the image. Whereas for the polling model, with the `OpenNextFrame()` method it returns the frame numbers of that particular image frame. `FrameNumber` is a read-only property of the `ImageFrame` class and can be accessed as follows:

```
int frameNumber=imageFrame.FrameNumber;
```

The `FrameNumber` property is a unique number that identifies the frame. It increases with each frame, but it doesn't necessarily increase by 1 or the same value each time. It might increase by 1 or more.

To make it generic, in our KinectCam application we will write a method called `GetCurrentFrameNumber()`, which accepts the image frame and returns the frame number:

```
private int GetCurrentFrameNumber(ColorImageFrame imageFrame)
{
  return imageFrame.FrameNumber;
}
```

Now the frame number has to be updated from each and every frame, and we process single frames inside the `ColorFrameReady` event handler. Hence the final task you need to do would be to call the `GetCurrentFrameNumber()` method from the `ColorFrameReady` event handler and assign the value to the `FrameNumber` property of the view, which will update the UI automatically:

```
this.viewModel.FrameNumber = this.GetCurrentFrameNumber(imageFrame);
```

 The `ImageFrame` class has a `Timestamp` property that gives you a time value in milliseconds, representing when the frame was captured by the sensor. The difference values from frame-to-frame will tell you how much time elapsed between the frames.

Changing image format on the fly

You have seen that while enabling the color stream we provide the specific color format using the `ColorImageFormat` enumeration. The `ImageStream` class has an overloaded method for `Enable()`. If you want to initialize the color stream with a different image format, use the overloaded method that accepts `ColorImageFormat`.

Let's have a look at how we can use this in our KinectCam application and change the format.

Bind available image formats

The very first things we need to do are that we need to bind the available image formats in a dropdown using binding. The dropdown will contain the list of image formats whereas the label control is just used for showing a message. The following is the XAML snippet for the combobox:

```
<ComboBox  Name="ColorImageFormatSelection" ItemsSource="{Binding
ColorImageFormats}" SelectionChanged="ComboBox_SelectionChanged"  />
```

In the next step, you need to bind the available color image formats. You can bind them as a string value with the list controls and then use them as a value converter when enabling the stream, but here we have done so using the property `ColorImageFormats` which returns `ObservableCollection` of `ColorImageFormat` as assigned, similar to `ItemsSource` of `ComboBox`.

```
private ObservableCollection<ColorImageFormat> colorImageFormatvalue;

public ObservableCollection<ColorImageFormat> ColorImageFormats
```

```
{
  get
  {
    colorImageFormatvalue = new ObservableCollection<ColorImageForm
    at>();
    foreach (ColorImageFormat colorImageFormat in Enum.GetValues
    (typeof(ColorImageFormat)))
    {
      colorImageFormatvalue.Add(colorImageFormat);
    }
    return colorImageFormatvalue;
  }
}
```

At this point, if you run the application and select the **Video Format** dropdown, you should able to see all the image formats populated in the dropdown:

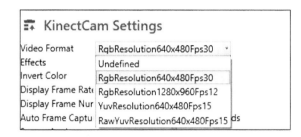

Changing the color image format

Now you have the list of color image formats, and you want to see them in action when you are changing the selections from the combobox. ChangeColorImageFormat looks like the following, which you can call when the ColorImageFormatSelection selection is changed.

```
private void ChangeColorImageFormat()
{
  if (this.sensor.IsRunning)
  {
    this.viewModel.CurrentImageFormat = (ColorImageFormat)this.
    ColorImageFormatSelection.SelectedItem;
    this.sensor.ColorStream.Enable(this.viewModel.
    CurrentImageFormat == ColorImageFormat.Undefined ?
    ColorImageFormat.RgbResolution640x480Fps30 : this.viewModel.
    CurrentImageFormat);
  }
}
```

Yes, this is very straightforward; just enable the color stream with the selected value from the list control. In the case of an undefined image format we have used `RgbResolution640x480Fps30`.

 For the Bayer image format, you have to write your own conversion logic that will convert Raw Bayer color to RGB color. To convert an image from a Bayer filter format to an RGB format, we need to interpolate the two missing color values in each pixel. The interpolation algorithm for deriving the two missing color channels at each pixel is called **demosaicing**. There are several standard interpolation algorithms, such as nearest neighbor, bilinear interpolation, bicubic, spline, and lanczos that can be used for this conversion. The KinectCam application does not handle this conversion.

To know more about the Bayer color filter and the different conversion algorithms for converting Bayer color to RGB, you can refer to the URLs `http://en.wikipedia.org/wiki/Demosaicing` and `http://en.wikipedia.org/wiki/Bayer_filter`.

Calculating frame rate

Frame rate is the number of frames produced per second and is denoted as fps. In terms of the Kinect sensor image stream, the frame rate is the number of image frames coming from the sensor per second. Frame rates depend on the resolution and type of the color format you are using.

How to calculate frame rate

There is no direct API to read the frame rate of the current image stream. But you must have noticed that the `ColorImageFormat` value has the frame rate mentioned within it. For example, when you are providing the color image frame format as `ColorImageFormat.RgbResolution640x480Fps30`, the color stream will have a frame rate of 30 fps at maximum. But the frame number may vary due to the compression and decompression on the image stream channel. The following code snippet shows how you can keep track of the frame rate every time:

```
private int TotalFrames { get; set; }
private DateTime lastTime = DateTime.MaxValue;
private int LastFrames { get; set; }
int currentFrameRate = 0;

private int GetCurrentFrameRate()
{

    ++this.TotalFrames;
```

```
  DateTime currentTime = DateTime.Now;
  var timeSpan = currentTime.Subtract(this.lastTime);
  if (this.lastTime == DateTime.MaxValue || timeSpan >= TimeSpan.
FromSeconds(1))
  {
    currentFrameRate = (int)Math.Round((this.TotalFrames - this.
LastFrames) / timeSpan.TotalSeconds);
    this.LastFrames = this.TotalFrames;
    this.lastTime = currentTime;
  }
  return currentFrameRate;
}
```

Just as with the frame number, we have to invoke this method during frame processing itself so that our counts keep updated with every frame if there is any change. Call the `GetCurrentFrameRate()` method from the `ColorFrameReady` event handler and assign the value to the `FrameRate` property:

```
this.viewModel.FrameRate = this.GetCurrentFrameRate();
```

To test the frame rate follow these steps:

1. Run the KinectCam application; at this point of time you can't view the frame rates as this is not possible from **Settings**.
2. Check the **Display Frame Rate** checkbox from **Settings**. This will start to display the frame rate in the application.
3. Change **Video Format** from the drop-down box to see the changed frame rates.

Capturing and saving images

KinectCam not only allows you to display captured video, but also captures a particular image frame and saves it as an image in your hard drive. Images can be saved on a drive as follows:

```
private void SaveImage()
{
  using (FileStream fileStream = new FileStream(string.Format("{0}.
Jpg", Guid.NewGuid().ToString()), System.IO.FileMode.Create))
  {
    BitmapSource imageSource = (BitmapSource)VideoControl.Source;
    JpegBitmapEncoder jpegEncoder = new JpegBitmapEncoder();
    jpegEncoder.Frames.Add(BitmapFrame.Create(imageSource));
    jpegEncoder.Save(fileStream);
    fileStream.Close();
  }
}
```

In the previous code block, we are first taking the reference of `imageSource` from the source of our UI image control, named `VideoControl`, and then saving the image by converting the image source to a `.jpeg` image using `JpegBitmapEncoder`:

 Here we have used `JpegBitmapEncoder` to encode the images in the `.jpeg` format; you can use other encoders such as `PngBitmapEncoder` and `PngBitmapEncoder` as well.

The following highlighted code block calls the `SaveImage()` method. You can call this method with some specific events, such as on the KinectCam application where we have called it by clicking on the **Save** button.

```
if (this.sensor.IsRunning && this.sensor.ColorStream.IsEnabled)
{
   this.SaveImage()
}
```

Run the application, and capture a few images by clicking on the **Save** button. Then click on the **Captured Images** expander to see the images that have been captured by the application:

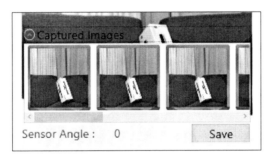

Saving images periodically

You can enable the automatic image save from the KinectCam settings. Saving images periodically is also an easy task. You just need to call the `SaveImage ()` method on a `Tick` event of `DispatcherTimer`. You can achieve the automatic image save by performing the following steps:

1. Define the `DispatcherTimer` object, which you can find under the `System.Windows.Threading` namespace:

   ```
   private DispatcherTimer timer = new DispatcherTimer();
   ```

2. Write the start method, as shown in the following snippet, with an interval of 10 seconds and attach the `Tick` event handler:

```
public void StartTimer()
{
  this.timer.Interval = new TimeSpan(0, 0, 10);
  this.timer.Start();
  this.timer.Tick += this.Timer_Tick;
}
```

3. On the `Tick` event handler, call the `SaveImage()` method. That's it.

```
public void Timer_Tick(object sender, object e)
{
  if (this.sensor.IsRunning && this.sensor.ColorStream.IsEnabled)
  {
    this.SaveImage();
  }
}
```

The timespan defined for the timer is 10 seconds. So `Timer_Tick` will be invoked every 10 seconds and capture the image frame.

4. The only thing you need do next is call the `StartTimer()` method on the checked event of the Auto Frame Capture checkbox.

Trying to save image frames directly

In the previous section, we saved the images by taking the reference of the image source from the source property of an image control where the image frames are already processed. Consider a situation where you want to save the images directly from the image frame. The call to the `SaveImage()` method would look like:

```
using (ColorImageFrame imageFrame = e.OpenColorImageFrame())
{
  if (imageFrame != null)
  {
    ...
    this.SaveImage(imageFrame);
    ...
}
```

Here the image frame is the current image frame captured by the sensor. Though it looks quite simple and similar to how we performed saving earlier, the problem will start when you try to access the image frame from the `SaveImage()` method. It will throw an `ObjectDisposedException` exception, because the frame you are trying to access on the `imageFrame` object has already been disposed of or might have changed.

To handle this type of situation with the image frames, you can write a wrapper class that implements the `IDisposable` interface, as follows:

```
internal class ColorImageWrapper :IDisposable
{
  public ColorImageWrapper(ColorImageFrame frame)
  {
    this.ImageFrame = frame;
    this.NeedDispose = true;
  }

  internal ColorImageFrame ImageFrame { get; set; }

  internal bool NeedDispose { get; set; }

  public void Dispose()
  {
    if (this.ImageFrame != null && this.NeedDispose)
    this.ImageFrame.Dispose();
    this.NeedDispose = false;
  }
}
```

Once you have the `ColorImageWrapper` class, you can define an `ImageFrame` property of the type `ColorImageWrapper` within your application:

```
private ColorImageWrapper imageFramevalue;
ColorImageWrapper ImageFrame
{
  get
  {
    return this.imageFramevalue;
  }
```

```
   set
   {
     if (this.imageFramevalue != null &&
 this.imageFramevalue.NeedDispose)
       this.imageFramevalue.Dispose();
       this.imageFramevalue = value;
   }
 }
```

Now within the `ColorFrameReady` handler, take the reference of the current image frame within the `ImageFrame` property:

```
ColorImageFrame imageFrame = e.OpenColorImageFrame();
{
  if (imageFrame != null)
  {
    ...
    this.ImageFrame = new ColorImageWrapper(imageFrame);
    ...
  }
}
```

Finally, click on the **Save** button and pass `imageFrame` to the `SaveImage()` method, as follows:

```
using (this.ImageFrame)
{
  ColorImageFrame imageFrame = this.ImageFrame.ImageFrame;
  this.SaveImage(imageFrame);
}
```

With this approach, you can save the current image frame directly to an image. This is very useful when you are not displaying the captured stream in the UI and want to save the frames directly or from the event handler.

Changing the sensor elevation angle

The Kinect sensor has a motor in the basement. This is used to change the camera and the sensor's angles to get the correct position of players within the room. The sensor motor can be tilted vertically up to 27 degrees, which means that the Kinect sensor's angles can be shifted upwards or downwards by 27 degrees:

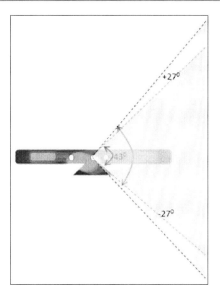

The default elevation angle is 0 degrees, which indicates that the sensor is pointing to a perpendicular gravity. So when the Kinect sensor is on the default angle, it considers a perpendicular gravity as the base. Changing the sensor angle involves just changing the base of the gravity with respect to the previous base, because the base depends on the gravity and not on the sensor base.

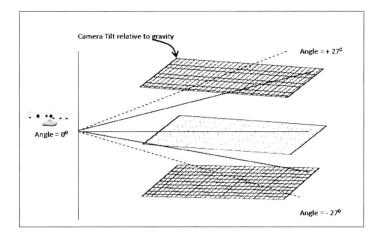

 Do not physically force the device into a specific angle; allow the position to be set by your application automatically, as few times as possible.

Maximum and minimum elevation angles

The Kinect sensor can be tilted upwards or downwards by up to 27 degrees in a vertical position; these values are fixed. The Kinect SDK has two read-only properties MaxElevationAngle and MinElevationAngle, which return the maximum and minimum elevation angle for the Kinect sensor. The values of these two properties are simply defined with +27 and -27 in the class library.

> The MaxElevationAngle and MinElevationAngle properties defined the boundary values of the Kinect sensor elevation angle. You can't move the angle beyond those two values. If you try to do so, it will throw an ArgumentOutOfRangeException exception.

Adjusting the Kinect sensor angle

The sensor angle can be adjusted using the ElevationAngle property. You can change the angle of the Kinect camera within the range of the ElevationAngle property. The specified value is in degrees and must be between the MaxElevationAngle and MinElevationAngle properties. The following code snippet shows how you can change the sensor elevation angle:

```
//Sets the sensor angle.
private void SetSensorAngle(int angleValue)
{
   if(angleValue > sensor.MinElevationAngle || angleValue < sensor.
MaxElevationAngle)
   {
     this.sensor.ElevationAngle = angleValue;
   }
}
```

In the KinectCam application, we are controlling the sensor angle by a slider control, where the slider max and min values are defined as +27 and -27; we are changing a value of five on every tick of the slider.

```
<Slider TickPlacement="BottomRight" IsSnapToTickEnabled="True"
Minimum="-27" Maximum="27" SmallChange="5" LargeChange="5"
ValueChanged="Slider_ValueChanged"  />
```

Call the SetSensorAngle() method on the Slider_ValueChanged event handler:

```
this.SetSensorAngle(Int32.Parse(e.NewValue.ToString()));
```

One of the most important things to keep in mind while doing any implementation with the elevation angle is to use the Kinect motor tilt operation only when it's absolutely required. Changing the sensor angle frequently will result in an error code.

> You can handle the changes in the sensor elevation angle in an asynchronous mode such that it does not freeze the actual UI to deliver the updates as to which sensor movement is happening. You are free to use the `BeginInvoke` pattern in the `Dispatcher` thread to make sure the UI thread affinity is maintained, yet calling the code asynchronously.

Playing around the color pixels

Each RGB pixel of the Kinect color image frame is an array of size four. The first three values represent the values of blue, green, and red, whereas the fourth value is the alpha value for that pixel:

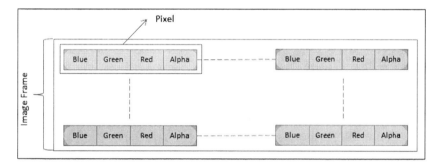

The previous diagram is the representation of each pixel within an image frame. The maximum value of each color is 255 and the minimum is 0. The following screenshot shows the color values for blue, green, and red along with the alpha values from an image frame:

pixelData	{byte[1228800]}
[0]	151
[1]	171
[2]	207
[3]	0

We could use values from the array to set or change the color value. Pixel manipulation has to be done while we are processing the images inside the `ColorFrameReady` event handler, as this has to be taken care of for all the pixels.

Applying RGB effects

While processing color pixels, applying red, green, and blue effects is the easiest. You can easily iterate through the array and set the value. The following code block refers to how you can apply only red color effects on an image stream by just not setting 0 for green and blue:

```
for (int i = 0; i < this.pixelData.Length; i += imageFrame.
BytesPerPixel)
{
  this.pixelData[i] = 0; //Blue
  this.pixelData[i + 1] = 0; //Green
}
```

As every pixel is represented by an array of length four, which is nothing but `imageFrame.BitsPerPixel` (32 bpp), we are increasing the loop with the same number. Similar to changing the red value, you can set the values for green and blue; you can even give a combination of these three values to apply some more color effects on the images.

You can apply the effects from the **Effects** drop-down box of the KinectCam settings, which holds the **Red**, **Green**, and **Blue** values. Changing these values will result in the application of the effect. If you don't want any effects, set it to **None**, which is set by default:

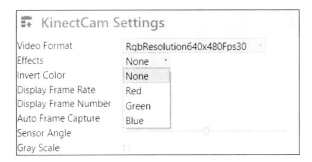

Making grayscale effects

Similar to RGB effects, you can apply grayscale effects on an image stream. To apply the grayscale, you need to apply the same values for all the bytes of the array for a single pixel, and the value should be the maximum byte of that pixel returned by the sensor. The following code snippet shows how to apply grayscale effects on the incoming image stream:

```
for (int i = 0; i < this.pixelData.Length; i += imageFrame.
BytesPerPixel)
{
  var data = Math.Max(Math.Max(this.pixelData[i], this.pixelData[i +
1]), this.pixelData[i + 2]);
  this.pixelData[i] = data;
  this.pixelData[i + 1] = data;
  this.pixelData[i + 2] = data;
}
```

Inverting the color

Another interesting effect that you can try, which even KinectCam does, is inverting the color values. The following code refers to how you can invert color pixel values:

```
for (int i = 0; i < this.pixelData.Length; i += imageFrame.
BytesPerPixel)
{
  this.pixelData[i] = (byte)~this.pixelData[i];
  this.pixelData[i + 1] = (byte)~this.pixelData[i + 1];
  this.pixelData[i + 2] = (byte)~this.pixelData[i + 2];
}
```

> The ~ operator performs a bitwise complement operation on the pixelData value, which has the effect of reversing each bit with the array value.

In the KinectCam application, ViewModel holds the two properties IsInvertColorEffectsEnabled and IsGrayScaleEnabled, and the value of these two properties is set from the UI checkboxes. When the value of these properties is true, the respective processing on the image frame is performed.

> Similar to RGB, grayscale, and color inverting, you can apply different additional effects on the image stream by just playing around with the pixel data. The only thing you should keep in mind while processing with a color pixel is the application performance. This is because the loop for changing the color pixel will run for each and every byte of each image frame.

Applying more effects to the camera

Well, this is not the end! Similar to other cameras, you can also apply several common effects, such as changing the brightness, contrast, hue, gamma, sharpness, white balance, gain, and saturation. The `ColorImageStream` class has the `CameraSettings` property of the type `ColorCameraSettings` class that takes care of all these effects very easily.

You can set the values of all these properties and fine-tune the camera capture as per your needs. The SDK provides another set of properties to get the maximum and minimum range for all of them. For example, the `MaxBrightness` and `MinBrightness` properties of the `ColorCameraSettings` class return the maximum and minimum values for the camera brightness.

Consider an application where you are applying the camera settings by changing the value's controls. At first, set the maximum and minimum values for the slider by getting the maximum and minimum values for the corresponding settings, and set the current property setting to the slider value. As shown in the following code snippet, we have set it for a slider control that controls the brightness:

```
this.sliderBrightness.Maximum = this.sensor.ColorStream.
CameraSettings.MaxBrightness;
this.sliderBrightness.Minimum = this.sensor.ColorStream.
CameraSettings.MinBrightness;
this.sliderBrightness.Value = this.sensor.ColorStream.CameraSettings.
Brightness;
```

This serves two purposes:

*   The slider range is bounded between the maximum and minimum values
*   The slider holds the default value initially

Now you must handle the changes to the camera setting properties in an asynchronous mode, such that it does not freeze the actual UI while updating the image frames as well as the slider control values:

```
private void sliderBrightness_ValueChanged(object sender, RoutedProper
tyChangedEventArgs<double> e)
{
  Dispatcher.Invoke(DispatcherPriority.Normal,
  new Action(
  delegate()
  {
```

```
    this.sensor.ColorStream.CameraSettings.Brightness =
    e.NewValue;
  }
  ));
}
```

As shown in the previous code snippet, you can use the `BeginInvoke` pattern in the `Dispatcher` thread to make sure the UI thread affinity is maintained, yet calling the code asynchronously to update the setting's values.

> To set the camera's `WhiteBalance` manually, you have to set `AutoWhiteBalance` to `false`.

Applying the backlight compensation mode

All in-camera light follows the basic fundamental that only reflected light can be measured. This means the best one can do is guess how much light is actually reflecting from the object. When the object background is too bright or/and when the object is too dark, backlight compensation takes the action of **auto exposure** of the camera to make the object appear clearer.

The `CameraSettings` class has the `AutoExposure` property, which is by default set to `true`. When the `AutoExposure` is `true`, you can change the backlight compensation mode of the color data by doing the following:

```
this.sensor.ColorStream.CameraSettings.BacklightCompensationMode =
BacklightCompensationMode.CenterOnly;
```

`BacklightCompensationMode` is an enumeration, and you can select any of the following values:

- AverageBrightness
- CenterPriority
- LowlightsPriority
- CenterOnly

> `AverageBrightness` is the default value for `BacklightCompensationMode`.

Applying slow motion effects

By changing the values of the FrameInterval property, you can apply slow motion effects by delaying the frames. Frame intervals and frames rates are inversely proportional, which means if you increase the frame interval, you will see drops in the frames rates.

Kinect Camera Effects – application

Kinect Camera Effects is an application that is built on the basis of whatever we have discussed as a part of applying camera effects on the camera. The following screenshot shows the application screen with different settings applied. This application is available for download from the book resources location.

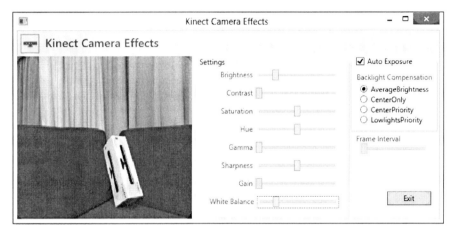

Seeing in low light

As we all know, IR is invisible to the human eye as it has a longer wavelength than the highest wavelength that a human eye can see in a spectrum. This same disadvantage of human beings is used as an advantage by using an IR light to see in the dark. The Kinect SDK provides an API that can help us read the same data.

Capturing IR stream data is as simple as capturing a color image stream, as the SDK returns the infrared stream as a part of the color image stream data. The only changes are ColorImageFormat and PixelFormats. You can simply change the following two sections in the code block that we have discussed in the *Capturing color image from the Kinect camera* section.

1. Enable the `ColorStream` with `InfraredResolution640x480Fps30`:

   ```
   this.sensor.ColorStream.Enable(ColorImageFormat.
   InfraredResolution640x480Fps30);
   ```

2. Set the `PixelFormats` to `Gray16` while creating the bitmap source as assigning it to image control:

   ```
   this.VideoControl.Source = BitmapSource.Create(
   imageFrame.Width, imageFrame.Height, 96,96,
   PixelFormats.Gray16,
   null, pixelData, stride);
   ```

That's all! After all the previous changes are done, run your application; you will find the video stream data full of IR dots. It will be quite fun if you do this testing in a dark room, because the IR will still help to capture the grayscale image:

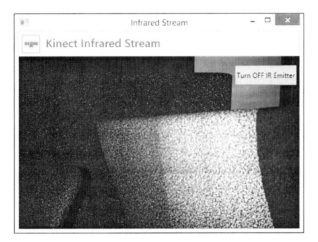

 Apart from using the infrared stream to capture images in low light, you can use this to calibrate the cameras while you are using multiple Kinect sensors or using the Kinect camera with other camera devices.

Making your application perform better

You have seen that image processing happens up to 30 frames per second. This means that memory allocation and clean-up is happening around 30 times per second. This makes performance trail, though it does not matter for a small application; but for a more complex application where there is major work involved other than only a color camera, it could be a big concern.

To make your application perform better, the alternative way is to process images using the `WriteableBitmap` object, which serves the purpose of frequently updating the image pixel. You can find this `WriteableBitmap` object in the `System.Windows.Media.Imaging` namespace. The `WriteableBitmap` object works in a different way than `BitmapSource`. The `WriteableBitmap` object allocates the memory at once and updates only the pixel data on frame change. `WriteableBitmap` improves the performance by reducing the memory consumption as well as memory allocation and deallocation.

The overall implementation approach for `WriteableBitmap` can be performed very easily. First create the `WriteableBitmap` object:

```
private WriteableBitmap writeableBitmap;
```

Then enable the `ColorStream` channel and initialize the `writeableBitmap` object with the frame width, height, and pixel formats. Then assign the `writeableBitmap` object to the source property of image control. Then attach the `ColorFrameReady` event:

```
if (this.sensor !=null & this.sensor.IsRunning && !this.sensor.
ColorStream.IsEnabled)
{
  this.sensor.ColorStream.Enable();
  this.writeableBitmap = new
  WriteableBitmap(this.sensor.ColorStream.FrameWidth,
  this.sensor.ColorStream.FrameHeight, 96, 96,
  PixelFormats.Bgr32, null);
  VideoControl.Source = this.writeableBitmap;
  this.sensor.ColorFrameReady += sensor_ColorFrameReady;
}
```

Use the following code block for the `ColorFrameReady` event handler. The only difference you will find in this event handler is the `WritePixels()` method, which is being updated with the pixel data for every frame.

```
void sensor_ColorFrameReady(object sender,
ColorImageFrameReadyEventArgs e)
{
  using (ColorImageFrame imageFrame = e.OpenColorImageFrame())
  {
    if (imageFrame != null)
    {
```

```
        byte[] pixelData = new byte[imageFrame.PixelDataLength];
        imageFrame.CopyPixelDataTo(pixelData);
        int stride = imageFrame.Width * imageFrame.BytesPerPixel;
        this.writeableBitmap.WritePixels(
        new Int32Rect(0, 0, this.writeableBitmap.PixelWidth,
        this.writeableBitmap.PixelHeight),
        pixelData,
        stride,
        0);
    }
  }
}
```

You can see that with the `WritePixels()` method, the reference to `writeableBitmap` is getting updated with the new frame from the sensor. This is just updating the frame's pixels and keeping other things unchanged.

Using the Coding4Fun toolkit

The Kinect Coding4Fun toolkit provides a set of extension methods and samples that helps the developer develop applications much faster and in an easier way. You can download the Kinect Coding4Fun toolkit from `http://c4fkinect.codeplex.com/`. This toolkit provides both the WPF and WinFrom versions.

Installing the Coding4Fun Kinect toolkit

Using the Coding4Fun toolkit for Kinect is pretty easy and straightforward. There are two ways that you can start with the Coding4Fun toolkit.

Using assembly

First, download the toolkit and add `Coding4Fun.Kinect.Wpf.dll` or `Coding4Fun.Kinect.Winfrom.dll` as a reference assembly for your application.

Using the NuGet package

On the other hand, you can install it as a NuGet package, which is already published at the following location:

```
http://www.nuget.org/packages/Coding4Fun.Kinect.Wpf
```

Follow these steps to install it as a NuGet package:

1. Start a new project or open an existing project where you want to use the Coding4Fun toolkit.

2. Navigate to **View** | **Other Window** | **Package Manager Console**. This will open the NuGet package manager consoles.

3. To install the toolkit for the WPF application, run the following command from the package manager:

```
PM> Install-Package Coding4Fun.Kinect.Wpf
```

This will successfully install the NuGet package and add the `Coding4Fun.Kinect.Wpf.dll` as a reference assembly with the project, as shown in the following screenshot:

Using Coding4Fun Kinect libraries in your application

To start using the toolkit, first of all you need to include the following namespace with your application:

```
using Coding4Fun.Kinect.Wpf;
```

And then? Everything will turn out like magic. Well, see how this makes things easy. You have already seen how to put an image frame in a stream and display it in an image control. So let's have a look at how the Coding4Fun toolkit does the same task:

```
using (ColorImageFrame imageFrame = e.OpenColorImageFrame())
{
  if (imageFrame == null)
  {
    return;
  }

  this. VideoControl.Source = imageFrame.ToBitmapSource();
}
```

Well, this is just a matter of one line. What it does to `ToBitmapSource()` is nothing but an extension method that is actually doing the same thing that we used to do step by step. So when we are using the Coding4Fun toolkit, we really don't need to take care of all these things. Yes, this is very simple to use. Similarly, you can use the following code snippet to save an image frame as an image by just using the `Save()` extension method of `BitmapSource`.

```
imageSource.Save(string.Format("{0}.Jpg", imageFrame.FrameNumber.
ToString()), Coding4Fun.Kinect.Wpf.ImageFormat.Jpeg);
```

You can clearly see that this approach causes a drastic reduction in the number of lines required to save images from an image frame, in contrast to the earlier section where we have seen how to save images without using the Coding4Fun toolkit.

Additional downloads

Along with the KinectCam application, this chapter has several projects for downloading that show the individual features that we have explored over the chapter. The Kinect Camera Effects and Infrared Stream applications are also available for download.

Summary

This chapter deals with the Kinect camera and the handling of the color image streams with multiple image formats that are supported by the Kinect SDK. We have meticulously covered aspects such as image frame processing, changing the stream resolution at runtime, capturing standalone images, and playing around with individual color pixels, by building a complete KinectCam application. You have also learned how you can fine-tune color images by applying different settings on the Kinect camera, and you have seen how the infrared streams help capture images in low lights. You have also seen how to change the sensor angle via code, and in the end you have seen how using the Coding4Fun toolkit can make your job easy. Throughout this chapter, you have also learned many small tips and tricks; these often play a vital role in big composite applications, and knowing them will stand you in good stead as you embark upon the journey of developing bigger and more functional applications. If you are comfortable with what we have covered, it's time to proceed to the next chapter where we will study depth image.

5
The Depth Data – Making Things Happen

In the previous chapter you have seen how the Kinect camera works, how you can capture color image data from the sensor, and played around with the three basic color components: *red*, *green*, and *blue*. In a similar fashion, you can capture the data from the Kinect depth sensor; however, the working principle of the depth sensor and information returned by the depth sensor are totally different than that of the color camera. Each color frame consists of numbers of pixel values, which give the values of red, green, and blue color components; whereas each pixel information in the depth data represents the distance of an object from the sensor. Not to mention, the depth data is one of the most important aspects of the Kinect device.

The basic depth data is really important for building any useful Kinect application. If you are going to build an application that detects you, your computer table or chair, or an application that controls a robot, or more, the depth data is what you need to work with. In this chapter you will learn the fundamentals of how the **IR depth sensor** and **IR emitter** work together to produce depth information of objects in front of the sensor. This chapter also covers some basic concepts of depth data processing and different techniques for using depth data in your applications. We will also learn how to identify the distance of an object/user as well as how to generate a 3D view of objects. At the end of this chapter you will be well-versed on how to work with the depth data of Kinect. A brief overview of the different aspects of this chapter is as follows:

- Understanding the depth data stream
- Depth data – behind the scenes
- Capturing and processing depth data
- Depth data and distance

- Understanding player index
- Tracking objects in Near Mode
- A 3D view of depth data

Understanding the depth data stream

The Kinect sensor returns the depth stream data as a succession of the depth image frame. The Kinect sensor returns raw depth with 16-bit grey scale format with a viewable range of 43 degrees vertical and 57 degrees horizontal. Well, this is not just an image; behind the scenes the Kinect sensor runs a series of algorithms on the captured data to give you more than an image, which tells you how far each pixel in that frame is. The depth pixel contains the distance between the Kinect device and the objects in front of the device, in millimeters. The data is represented based on the X and Y coordinates in the depth sensor view. For example, if a pixel coordinate is 200 x 300, the depth data for that pixel point contains distance in millimeters from the Kinect device (refer to the following image):

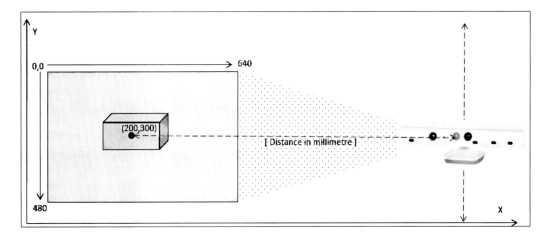

 The viewable angle range will remain the same with the change of sensor elevation angle, as the change is considered as a change on the base of the Kinect sensor.

The following resolutions are supported by the depth data stream with 30 frames per second (FPS):

- 640 x 480 pixels
- 320 x 240 pixels
- 80 x 60 pixels

The Kinect device can capture the data approximately 13.1 feet (4.0 meters) away from the sensor as well as a very close range of 40 cm in front of the device without losing accuracy or precision. The Kinect sensor also tracks objects beyond 4.0 meters, but in such cases quality will be compromised because of the noise.

Depth data – behind the scenes

The Kinect device consists of an IR emitter and an IR depth sensor. Both the components have to work together to produce the desired output. To the naked eye, the IR emitter may look like a camera, but in reality it's an IR projector that emits infrared light in a pseudorandom dot pattern constantly in front of the device.

 These dots are invisible to us, as the wavelength of the IR radiations are longer than the wavelength of visible light for human eyes.

The second element is an IR depth sensor that reads the dots in the scene, processes the data, and sends the depth information from which they were reflected. The following illustration shows how the IR emitter and IR depth sensor work to produce depth data:

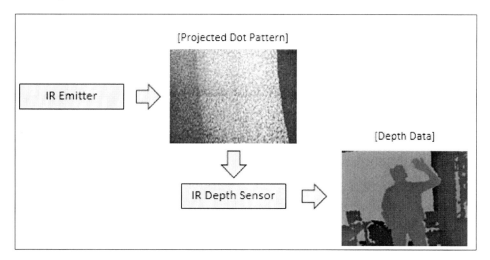

At this point, you might think, how does a single IR camera provide the depth information? How does the sensor get point information? There is an interesting concept behind this, which is known as stereo triangulation.

Stereo triangulation

Stereo triangulation is an analysis algorithm for computing the 3D position of points in an image frame. In general stereo triangulation, two images are used to obtain the two different views on a scene, in a similar fashion to human binocular vision. By comparing these two images, the relative depth information is calculated.

 To learn more about stereo vision, you can refer to the following URL:
`http://en.wikipedia.org/wiki/Computer_stereo_vision`

When it comes to Kinect, there is only one image, which is captured by the IR depth sensor; then how does the stereo triangulation work? Actually, there are two images instead of one. The second image is invisible – it's a pattern of the IR emitter that is already defined with the IR laser. The IR laser is not modulated. All that the laser does is project a pseudorandom pattern of specs on the Kinect environment. These two images are not equivalent as there is some distance between the IR emitter and IR depth sensor. These two images are considered as correspondence to the different camera, and allow you to use stereo triangulation to calculate depth as shown in the following image. It demonstrates how x1 and x2 are getting measured using stereo triangulation for a point X in the scene:

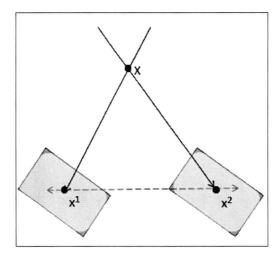

 Depth data depends on the IR lights, so the measuring of depth data can be impacted if you are placing the Kinect in direct sunlight or with any other device that interferes with IR lights.

Capturing and processing depth data

To capture the depth data from the Kinect sensor, the program should use exactly the same flow as we used to read the color data stream in the previous chapters.

1. Enable the depth stream channel with the type of depth image format.
2. Attach the event handler to the stream channel.
3. Process the incoming depth frames.
4. Render the frames on UI.

To start with, you can build a basic WPF application that can capture the raw depth stream and display it. We will extend this application, going forward to explore other features of depth data such as calculating distance and finding player indexes. Perform the following steps to set up a blank project for your DepthCam application:

1. Start a new instance of Visual Studio.
2. Create a new project by navigating to **File | New Project**.
3. You will see the **New Project** dialog box. Choose **Visual C#** as your development language, select **WPF Application Template**, and type the name as DepthCam.
4. From **Solution Explorer**, right-click on the **References** folder and select **Add References**.
5. Include a reference of the Microsoft.Kinect assembly.

Enabling the depth stream channel

Identify the connected Kinect sensor and enable the depth stream channel. The following code snippet finds the Kinect sensor and then enables the depth stream channel:

```
this.sensor = KinectSensor.KinectSensors[0];
this.sensor.DepthStream.Enable();
```

By default Enable() does not accept any arguments. You can simply call this method with the Depthstream property of the current sensor, as follows:

```
this.sensor.DepthStream.Enable();
```

The `ImageStream` class has an overloaded method for `Enable()`. By default, the sensor enables the depth stream with the `Resolution640x480Fps30` depth image format. If you want to initialize the depth stream with a different image format, use the overloaded method that accepts `DepthImageFormat` as an argument as shown in following snippet:

```
this.sensor.DepthStream.Enable(DepthImageFormat.
Resolution320x240Fps30);
```

 Only one depth stream channel can be activated at a time and you can select any type from the `DepthImageFormat` enumeration. If you are trying to enable multiple times with different `DepthImageFormat` enumerations, the latest one will take precedence.

You can use the `IsEnabled` property before enabling the stream channel or at any point of time to check if the channel is open for the depth stream or not. Following is the code snippet using the `IsEnabled` property before enabling the depth stream:

```
if (!this.sensor.DepthStream.IsEnabled)
{
this.sensor.DepthStream.Enable(DepthImageFormat.
Resolution640x480Fps30);
}
```

 To disable the stream channel, you can call the `Disable()` method, which just closes the connection channel for the current open stream irrespective of the `DepthImageFormat` enumeration that you have specified. `IsEnabled` is automatically set to `false` internally when you call the `Disable()` method or stop the sensor.

Attaching the event handler

Once the sensor is identified and the depth stream is enabled, attach the `DepthFrameReady` event handler to an event that is raised each time a new depth frame is available:

```
sensor.DepthFrameReady += new EventHandler<DepthImageFrameReadyEventAr
gs>(sensor_DepthFrameReady);
```

As shown in the previous snippet, each time a new depth frame is available, the method `sensor_DepthFrameReady()` will be invoked, where you need to process the raw depth data.

Processing the depth frames

The `DepthFrameReady` event handler invokes with
`DepthImageFrameReadyEventArgs,` which has the `OpenDepthImageFrame()`
method to return the current depth image frame sent by the sensor.

The default method stub for `DepthFrameReady` will look as follows:

```
void sensor_DepthFrameReady(object sender,
DepthImageFrameReadyEventArgs e)
{
}
```

To retrieve the depth image frame, you need to follow the step similar to the one we
followed for the color image stream process. The following code block shows the
depth image frame ready handler:

```
using (DepthImageFrame depthimageFrame = e.OpenDepthImageFrame())
{
    if (depthimageFrame == null)
    {
        return;
    }
    short[] pixelData = new short[depthimageFrame.PixelDataLength];
    int stride = depthimageFrame.Width * 2;
    depthimageFrame.CopyPixelDataTo(pixelData);
    depthImageControl.Source = BitmapSource.Create(depthimageFrame.
Width, depthimageFrame.Height, 96, 96, PixelFormats.Gray16, null,
pixelData, stride );
}
```

In the previous code block, we retrieve the depth image frame using the
`OpenDepthImageFrame()` method. This will return the raw depth data from the
sensor. `pixelData` creates the buffer size for the incoming depth image frame.

 For depth data, pixel data size is a type of `short []`
array, because it's a 16-bit data.

Like the color image frame, the depth frame has similar properties that copy the pixel data to the newly created buffer. CopyPixelDataTo() is used to copy the byte[] array of pixel data from the currently received image frame to the newly created buffer. Before copying the pixel data, you have to first calculate the buffer size using the PixelDataLength property, and then copy the same byte[] array image as DepthImageFrame. As the raw depth image frame is a 16-bit grayscale image, we have specified PixelFormats as Gray16 while creating the bitmap source for depth image control.

> You must have noticed the value of stride used here is depthimageFrame.Width * 2, where 2 is nothing but the value of BytesPerPixel (2 bytes) of the depth image frame.

Finally, we created the BitmapSource object and assigned it to the image control depthImageControl, which is defined in the XAML to display the stream data, as follows:

```
<Image Name="depthImageControl" Stretch="Fill" />
```

Depth data at first look

That's all; run the application and you will be able to see the depth image data from the sensor in your application:

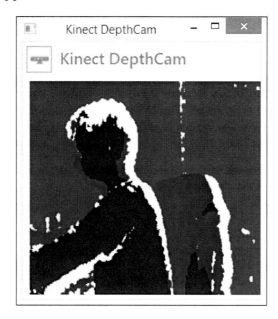

If you come closer or bring some object closer to the sensor, you will find yourself or the object disappear and the color becoming white (*second window in the screenshot*), and if you move backwards you will find everything changing back into black (*third window in the screenshot*):

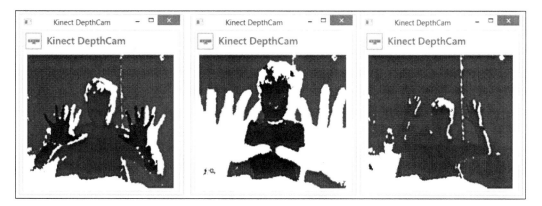

That was all about capturing the basic raw depth data from the Kinect sensor. So far you have enabled the depth stream and attached the event handler, which will invoke automatically whenever there is a depth frame. The frame will have the raw depth data that you need to handle within the depth frame ready event handler. So, let's have a look at the other properties and methods for the depth stream, which help to capture and process the data.

> The `DepthImageStream` class has a public method, named `OpenNextFrame()`. Using the `OpenNextFrame()` method, you can request a depth image frame from the sensor. This is how the **polling** model works for retrieving the image frame. This works in a similar fashion to capturing streams on demand. We have discussed these details in *Chapter 4, Getting the Most Out of the Kinect Camera*.

Looking inside depth image stream helpers

`DepthImageFrame` and `DepthImageStream` are the two classes that actually take care of all the depth data processing.

The following class diagram is a representation that will help you quickly understand the overall depth image frames and their associations, which we have discussed earlier. Each individual depth frame is represented by the DepthImageFrame class. The DepthImageFrame class is a sealed class and is derived from an ImageFrame base class. Whenever there is a frame from the sensor, DepthFrameReady events fire up with DepthImageFrameReadyEventArgs, which has the OpenDepthImageFrame() method exposed. OpenDepthImageFrame() returns the type of DepthImageFrame with the DepthImageFormat type that was specified during stream channel initialization. The data that is returned from the sensor can be processed further inside the DepthFrameReady event handler.

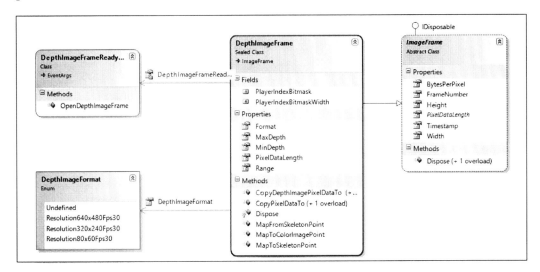

The depth image stream represents the succession of the depth image frame coming from Kinect devices. DepthImageStream is nothing but a stream of DepthImageFrame objects. The DepthImageStream class is derived from an ImageStream base class. This class defines the properties and methods for working with the depth image stream, such as to enable or disable the stream and setting the range and mode of the depth data. The following image shows the overall class diagram of the DepthImageStream class, along with its associations:

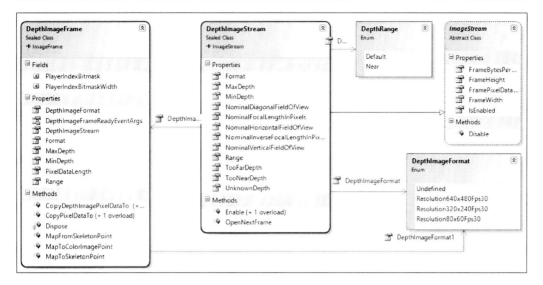

You have noticed that based on your movement, or by changing objects in front of the sensor, depth data is changing; so there is something that depends on the distance of the objects, which is being captured by the sensor. So let's have a look at how to play around with distance and depth data.

Depth data and distance

The depth vision for the Kinect sensor ranges from around 800 mm to approximately 4000 mm (2.6 feet to 13.1 feet), which is the default range for the depth stream. However, the sensor can capture the information beyond 4000 mm, in which case the quality of data will be compromised as the sensor is not built for that.

> The DepthImageStream and DepthImageFrame classes have the MaxDepth and MinDepth properties, which return the maximum and minimum depth ranges for that particular stream or captured image frame, in millimeters. This range value returns the best range where distance can be measured properly. Keep in mind, these are read-only properties; these values will change automatically based on the selection of DepthRange for the stream.

The following image shows the default depth range for a Kinect sensor where the sensor can track the objects and measure the distances:

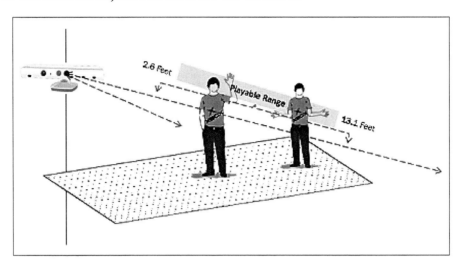

The Kinect depth sensor calculates distance based on the straight distance between the object and sensor. When there is a pixel in any of the diagonal views of the sensor, it internally draws a line that is perpendicular to the sensor and then calculates the distance directly from there, as shown in the following image:

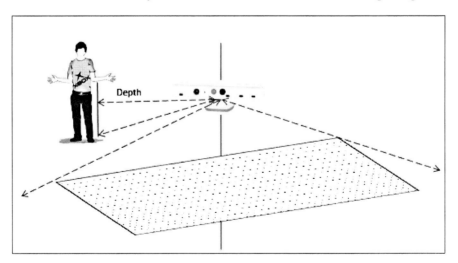

How the distance is calculated

The Kinect sensor returns 16-bit raw depth frame data. The first three bits are used to represent the identified players and the remaining 13 bits give you the measured distance in millimeters. We will discuss player index (first three bits) more in a later part of this chapter. Let's focus on the upper 13 bits, which represent the actual distance of the pixel value from the sensor.

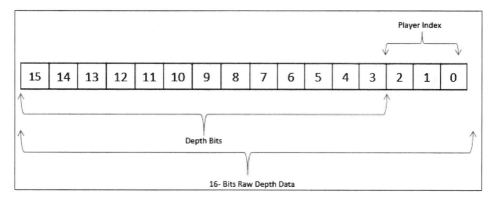

From the available 16-bit data, we need the upper 13 bits to get the distance. So, first of all we need to perform a **bitwise shift operation** (>>) to move the bits to their correct position.

 The DepthImageFrame class has a defined constant field PlayerIndexBitmaskWidth with a value of 3 to use during the logical shift operation.

Here is the generic formula for the distance calculation with depth data, where depthFrame is a short[] array:

```
int depth = depthFrame[depthIndex] >> DepthImageFrame.
PlayerIndexBitmaskWidth;
```

For example, consider in a particular frame, one of the pixel values is 20952. Now look at the following diagram, which explains how the depth in millimeters is calculated from a particular pixel value by applying bit shifting:

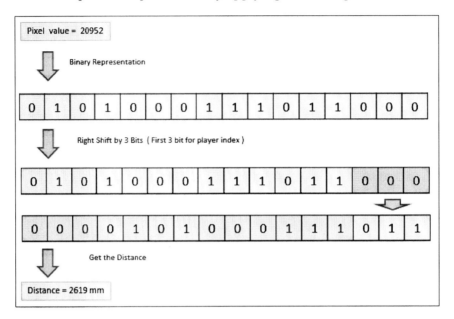

The easiest and most straightforward way to get your hands dirty with distance calculation is to calculate the distance of a particular pixel index from screen positions.

Getting the distance from a particular pixel

To get the distance from a particular pixel, first of all you need to calculate `pixelIndex` from the current selected position. Add a new event handler for `depthImageControl_MouseDown`, which will handle the distance calculation. Get the selected position by using the following code:

```
Point currentPoint = e.GetPosition(depthImageControl);
```

In the next step, calculate `pixelIndex` from the X and Y coordinates of the selected position:

```
int pixelIndex = (int)(currentPoint.X + ((int)currentPoint.Y * this.frame.Width));
```

And finally, get the distance by using bit masking:

```
int distancemm = this.pixelData[pixelIndex] >> DepthImageFrame.PlayerIndexBitmaskWidth;
```

The following screenshot shows the distance information of a particular position selected using the mouse cursor:

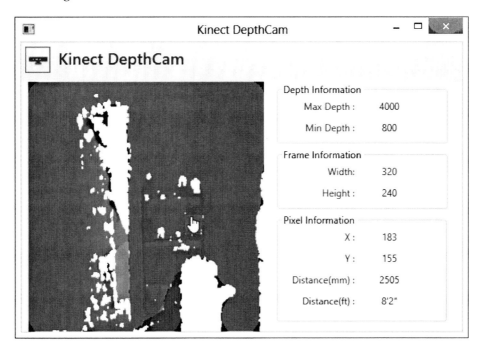

Accessing the range of distance

In the previous section you saw how to get the depth for a particular pixel. Here you will learn how to take control over a range of distance. The easiest way to learn this is by changing the bit values within a specific range of distances and seeing the effects.

As shown in the following snippet, a bitwise (~) complement operation is performed on bits whose values fall between 1500 mm and 3500 mm. The `ReversingBitValueWithDistance()` method accesses `depthImageFrame` and `pixelData` and reverses the bit values for the selected range:

```
private short[] ReversingBitValueWithDistance(DepthImageFrame
depthImageFrame, short[] pixelData)
{
    short[] reverseBitPixelData = new short[depthImageFrame.
PixelDataLength];
    int depth;
    for (int index = 0; index < pixelData.Length; index++)
    {
```

```
        depth = pixelData[index] >> DepthImageFrame.
PlayerIndexBitmaskWidth;
        if (depth < 1500 || depth > 3500)
        {
            reverseBitPixelData[index] = (short)~pixelData[index]; ;
        }
        else
        {
            reverseBitPixelData[index] = pixelData[index];
        }
    }
    return reverseBitPixelData;
}
```

Colorize depth data processing

To enhance the 16-bit raw depth data and identify the range of distances with different colors, you can convert the raw data into a 32-bit RGB frame where each pixel can represent an RGB color value based on the distance.

We have created one custom method GetColorPixelDataWithDistance() as follows, which accepts the raw depth data from the sensor and converts it into a 32-bit byte[] array:

```
private void GetColorPixelDataWithDistance(short[] depthFrame)
{
    for (int depthIndex = 0, colorIndex = 0; depthIndex < depthFrame.
Length && colorIndex < this.depth32.Length; depthIndex++, colorIndex
+= 4)
        {
        int distance = depthFrame[depthIndex] >> DepthImageFrame.
PlayerIndexBitmaskWidth;
        if (distance <= 1000)
        {
            depth32[colorIndex + 2] = 115;
            depth32[colorIndex + 1] = 169;
            depth32[colorIndex + 0] = 9;
        }
        else if (distance > 1000 && distance <= 2500)
        {
            depth32[colorIndex + 2] = 255;
            depth32[colorIndex + 1] = 61;
            depth32[colorIndex + 0] = 0;
        }
        else if (distance > 2500)
```

```
        {
            depth32[colorIndex + 2] = 169;
            depth32[colorIndex + 1] = 9;
            depth32[colorIndex + 0] = 115;
        }
    }
}
```

In the previous code block, we iterate through each and every pixel and calculate the distance by using bit shifting. `depth32` is the placeholder for the color depth image with a size of `new byte[depthImageFrame.PixelDataLength * 4]`. For every depth array, `0`, `1`, and `2` represent blue, green, and red respectively, and the 4th bit represents the values of alpha, which is not assigned here. This is the main reason behind increasing the color index by `4`.

 Distance and color values are given just as an example; you can change them as per your application's requirements.

Place a checkbox in XAML in the Kinect DepthCam application and on selection, call `GetColorPixelDataWithDistance()` from the depth frame ready event handler:

```
depth32 = new byte[depthimageFrame.PixelDataLength * 4];
this.GetColorPixelDataWithDistance(pixelData);
depthImageControl.Source = BitmapSource.Create(
depthimageFrame.Width, depthimageFrame.Height, 96, 96, PixelFormats.
Bgr32, null, depth32, depthimageFrame.Width * 4
);
}
```

 To colorize the depth data, you have to specify the `PixelFormats` type as `Bgr32` (highlighted in the previous code block), as pixel information for color image frames holds 32-bit data.

Run the same application, and select the **Enable Color Data** checkbox to see the colorized depth data:

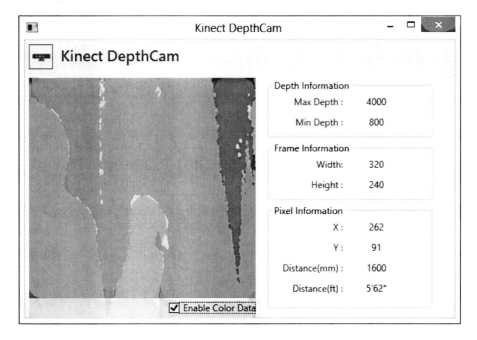

Colorizing the data based on distance is just for making it clear how the distance can be used. This type of calculation is tremendously helpful when you deal with some object detection within a specific range of distance.

Working with depth range

The Kinect sensor captured data within a certain range of distance, which is specified by the Range property of the DepthStream class. The Range property sets the viewable range for the Kinect sensor, which is a type of DepthRange enumeration.

A DepthRange enumeration has the following two values:

- Default
- Near

By default, DepthRange is set to Default and the range varies from 800 mm to 4000 mm. You can change the range of the depth data stream as follows:

```
sensor.DepthStream.Range = DepthRange.Near;
```

The **Near Mode** feature helps us track a human body within a very close range (approximately 40 centimeters), and the range varies from 400 mm to 3000 mm. The following image shows the reliable range for both the default and Near Modes:

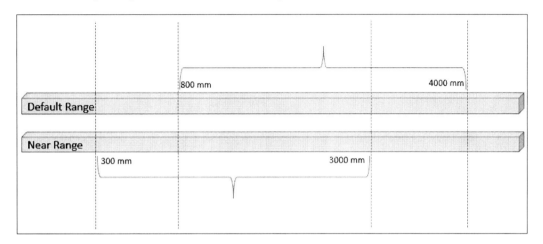

 This feature is limited to only the Kinect for Windows sensor. If you are using the Xbox sensor, you won't be able to work with Near Mode and the application will throw `InvalidOperationException`.

To play around with different modes, let's extend our existing application by adding a combobox that has two values, **Default** and **Near**, and set the `DepthRange` property on selection change:

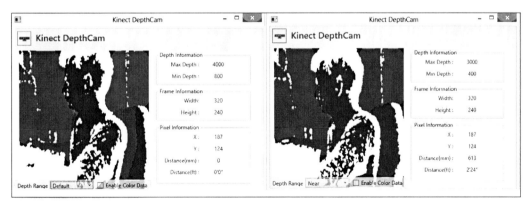

As shown in the previous screenshot, you can see that for the same pixel value, we are getting a distance in Near Mode but not in the default mode.

Special depth range values

`DepthImageStream` defines three additional read-only properties named `TooFarDepth`, `TooNearDepth`, and `UnknownDepth`, which help us have better control over distance by providing a range where getting the depth values is not possible:

- `TooFarDepth`: It provides the depth point where the object is beyond the range of the sensor
- `TooNearDepth`: It provides the depth point where the object is too close to the sensor
- `UnknownDepth`: There are instances when a depth is completely indeterminate; this can be considered as an unknown depth, and the value will be zero

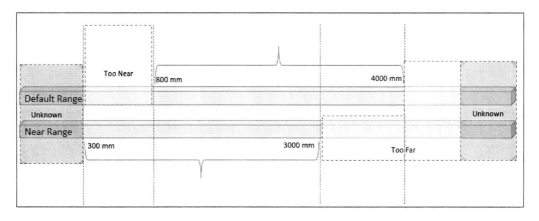

Depth data distribution

One of the best ways to graphically represent distribution of data is the histogram. Histograms visually tell how the current data values are distributed for a given data set. From a histogram, we can identify how frequently and how well data is distributed.

Depth values contain distances for the different possible ranges, shadows, or even unknown depth information. With histogram representation, the following is made possible:

- Identifying the depth data range for filtering data
- Occurrence of a certain range of values

- Probability distribution for a specific range of data
- Defining the range for capturing data

Generating a histogram is very easy, as the representation is as simple as a bar chart. You can simply use any .NET Chart Control and assign the depth value for every pixel to the chart control elements; alternatively, you can use basic WPF controls such as `StackPanel` to represent or draw the depth data as a bar chart.

Player index with depth data

So far, we have seen how to work with the raw depth data from the sensor and manipulate the data based on the distance. In this section you will learn how Kinect returns the player information and how to deal with the player who is standing in front of the Kinect sensor.

While we were discussing depth data and distance, you have seen that for a 16-bit raw depth data, the first three bits represent the player index and the higher 13 bits represent the distance. You have already learned how the distance calculation works with those higher 13 bits; let's have a look at how those first three bits represent a player.

> Player tracking requires the skeleton stream to be enabled. If you have enabled only the depth stream, the sensor won't be able to return the player information. The sensor returns the player index values within the depth pixel bits only if the skeleton stream is enabled. We will discuss skeleton tracking in the upcoming chapters.

How player index works

A Kinect sensor can detect up to six players, numbered one to six. A pixel with a player index value of 0 means there is no player recognized. For calculating the player index value, we do a logical AND operation with the pixel value and `PlayerIndexBitmask`. `PlayerIndexBitmask` is a constant defined in the `DepthImageStream` class, which represents a fixed value 7. So, there is a logical AND operation between these two values.

The following diagram shows the player index calculation with a pixel data value 10001010011110 (pixel value 8862) along with the player index:

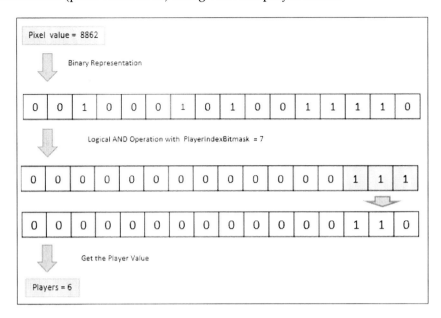

Well, that was all about the theoretical concepts of the player index calculation. Let's have a look at how to work with the player index using code.

Identifying players

To get the player index and change the color values, you need to perform an operation similar to the one you did for the colorization of depth data. The only difference is the way `PlayerIndexBitmask` is calculated, and highlighting the player pixels with different colors.

```
private void TrackPlayer(short[] depthFrame)
{
    for (int depthIndex = 0, colorIndex = 0; depthIndex < depthFrame.
Length && colorIndex < this.depth32.Length; depthIndex++, colorIndex
+= 4)
    {
        int player = depthFrame[depthIndex] & DepthImageFrame.
PlayerIndexBitmask;
        if (player > 0)
        {
            depth32[colorIndex + 2] = 169;
            depth32[colorIndex + 1] = 62;
```

```
            depth32[colorIndex + 0] = 9;
        }
    }
}
```

This will change the value of all the pixels associated with a player to brown and will set the background as black as we haven't set any colors for other pixels. The following screenshot shows the output of this code:

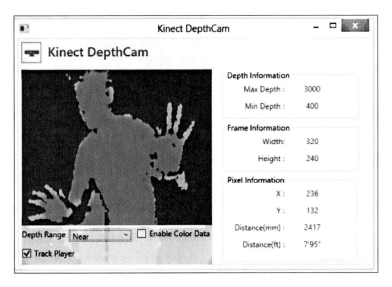

As per the previous code, it will set the same color to all the tracked players. You can track different players based on the player index, which will be covered in the next chapter.

Capturing color and depth data together

You can build an application that can enable both the color and the depth stream at the same time, which means you can capture both the color and the depth data at the same time. If you want to use both the cameras, we just have to enable both streams:

```
sensor.DepthStream.Enable();
sensor.ColorStream.Enable();
```

Then you can just attach the event handler for the stream and process the data inside the event handler:

```
sensor.ColorFrameReady += sensor_ColorFrameReady;
sensor.DepthFrameReady +=sensor _DepthFrameReady;
```

Though using color and depth data streams is usually very common and most of your applications would require that, here is one interesting scenario where you can use both of them very nicely. Consider you are a building a home security solution and you are using Kinect as an intrusion detector. You can track the intruder by identifying the player index values, and based on the distance, check how far the intruder is; if it's coming near the sensor, capture a color photo and save it. You can also take advantage of the infrared stream, if you want to track the same in low lights.

Getting the depth and player index automatically

You have seen how the Kinect sensor returns the raw depth data and how you can calculate the depth and player index by applying bit masking. You can get the depth and player index automatically as well from the depth data with the help of Kinect for Windows SDK. The SDK provides a structure named `DepthImagePixel`, which represents the individual pixels in `DepthImageFrame`. The `DepthImagePixel` structure holds the information about each individual pixel such as depth and player index. Different properties of the `DepthImagePixel` structure are listed in the following table:

Name	Description
Depth	Directly returns the depth for the current pixel, in millimeters. So, there is no bit masking required on pixel values.
IsKnowDepth	IsKnownDepth indicates if the depth value is a known value. This is similar to validating with the UnknownDepth property of the DepthImageStream class. This means, if the depth information is not UnknownDepth, it will return true, otherwise false.
PlayerIndex	Similar to depth information, this property returns PlayerIndex for the current pixel value.

Overall implementation will remain the same as the ones you are already familiar with. To work with `DepthImagePixel`, you need to perform the following steps:

1. First, define the storage for the pixel data; you can define the size with the `FramePixelDataLength` property of the `DepthImageStream` class:

```
private DepthImagePixel[] depthImagePixels;
depthImagePixels = new DepthImagePixel[ sensor.DepthStream.
FramePixelDataLength];
```

2. This will create a buffer to store the pixel information. Then, in the `DepthFrameReady` event handler, use the `OpenDepthImageFrame()` method to access the depth frame returned from the sensor. Once you have the frame, use the `CopyDepthImagePixelDataTo()` method to copy the data to `depthImagePixels`. `CopyDepthImagePixelDataTo()` copies each individual frame to the created buffer by calculating the depth and player index information.

```
using (DepthImageFrame depthimageFrame = e.OpenDepthImageFrame())
{
    if (depthimageFrame == null)
    {
        return;
    }
    depthimageFrame.CopyDepthImagePixelDataTo(this.
depthImagePixels);
}
```

3. You can display the pixels in UI using the earlier approach, which you are already familiar with. The thing you might be interested in is the depth values for individual pixels. To quickly check that, use the **debugger visualizer** by just adding a break point as shown in the following screenshot:

```
depthFrame.CopyDepthImagePixelDataTo(this.depthImagePixels);
```

⊞ ●	this.depthImagePixels[163]	{Microsoft.Kinect.DepthImagePixel}
	this.depthImagePixels[163].Depth	1360
	this.depthImagePixels[163].IsKnownDepth	true
	this.depthImagePixels[163].PlayerIndex	0

4. To get access to the individual pixel information, you can iterate through each of them:

```
for (int i = 0; i < depthImagePixels.Length; i++)
{
    short depth = depthImagePixels[i].Depth;
    short playerIndex = depthImagePixels[i].PlayerIndex;
}
```

The `DepthImagePixel` array size must be equal to the `PixelDataLength` or `FramePixelDataLength` property.

A 3D view of depth data

So far, you have seen the display and rendering of the depth data on a 2D surface, but there are more interesting and useful things we can do using the depth data. Our screen is only two dimensional; the camera takes a picture of an object in front of it and then projects it on a plane surface. We can construct a 3D view of the depth data returns by the Kinect sensor, with the help of the 3D rendering engine. In this section you will learn how to leverage the 3D functionality in Windows Presentation Foundation to give a 3D view to the depth data.

3D functionality enables the developer to represent complex illustrations of the data. Working with 3D graphics requires very good knowledge of the coordinate system, understanding of Mesh, Modeling, Materials, and Camera projections. If you are new to 3D graphics, please refer to the following URL: http://msdn.microsoft.com/en-us/library/ms747437.aspx (*3-D Graphics Overview*), which covers details on using 3D graphics in WPF.

The basic idea behind creating a 3D view on an object is to have a three-dimensional model. We can render the 2D projection into a bitmap using the 3D rendering engine. The engine defines what object to draw, color of the objects, camera projection, and the lights of the surface area.

The basics of the coordinate system

The most important thing to keep in mind is that the WPF 3D uses a different coordinate system, as shown in the following figure:

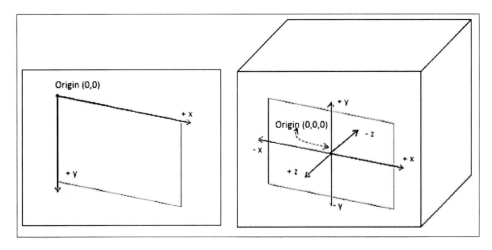

This representation of the coordinate system mostly helps you for interacting with the object, applying modeling, setting up the camera view, and performing coordinate conversions.

Basic elements of 3D graphics

To build any kind of 3D application, there are a few basic elements that are required. They are the following:

- **3D Model**: This is defined by the mesh objects (representation of 3D surface) and materials (represent the appearance of 3D objects). The geometry model of the 3D rendering engine creates the 3D object from the mesh and the materials.

- **View Port**: This takes care of rendering of data (3D Model) in the 3D coordinate system.

- **Camera**: Every 3D scene should have one camera. Without the camera view, we won't be able to render the objects. The camera defines the `Position`, `LookDirection`, and `UpDirection` properties of the view area.

Apart from that, you can apply light effects on 3D scenes, and also different rotations and animations on the view port.

To know more about *3-D Graphics How-to Topics*, refer to `http://msdn.microsoft.com/en-us/library/ms746607.aspx`.

Let's start building a simple application that reads the depth information from the Kinect sensor and renders it as 3D. The 3D display will change automatically as and when there is a new frame provided by the sensor. We will also apply some camera effects on the rendered object.

Setting up the project

Setting up the project is quite easy, just create a new **WPF Application** project in Visual Studio and name it `Depth3DView`. And then from the solution explorer, include the reference for `Microsoft.Kinect`.

Open `MainWindow.xaml.cs`. Along with `Using Microsoft.Kinect`, you have to add `using System.Windows.Media.Media3D`, which supports the 3D graphics in the WPF application.

Give it a 3D effect

We have discussed the basic elements of 3D elements and their uses.
Let's put the elements together and see how they work to represent a 3D object.

Creating the ViewPort

First of all, we need an instance of the `ViewPort3D` object as it takes care of rendering the element's overall 3D components on the UI. For building the application layout, we'll use a grid with two rows. The first row will have one `Viewport3D` object, and in the second row we will have a scrollbar to control the camera.

Open the `MainWindow.xaml` file and add a `Viewport3D` control in XAML and also specify the grid row, height, and width:

```
<Viewport3D x:Name="viewport" Grid.Row="0" Width="300" Height="300">
</Viewport3D>
```

Using the camera

The camera allows the views for a 3D scene. You can use either `PerspectiveCamera` or `OrthographicCamera` for viewing the scene. In this exercise, we will be using `PerspectiveCamera` by just adding the following below the XAML snippet inside `Viewport3D`:

```
<Viewport3D.Camera>
  <PerspectiveCamera x:Name="camera" FarPlaneDistance="5000"
NearPlaneDistance="100"
LookDirection="0,0,1" UpDirection="0,-1,0" Position="120,110,-1000"
FieldOfView="10" />
</Viewport3D.Camera>
```

`LookDirection` is what the camera looks at and `Updirection` is the vertical axis of the camera. `FarPlaneDistance` and `NearPlaneDistance` represent the range of the display area for the elements within the viewport that the camera will display. `Position` represents the X, Y, and Z positions for the view.

Controlling the camera position

To give some additional effects on the view area, you can apply some changes to the position of the camera. Add three different sliders for controlling the X, Y, and Z positions of camera. Below the XAML snippet place a slider control that controls the Y axis of the camera:

```
<StackPanel Orientation="Horizontal">
    <TextBlock Text="Y :" />
```

```
    <Slider Width="250" x:Name="YSlider" ValueChanged="YSlider_
ValueChanged" TickFrequency="1" SmallChange="1" LargeChange="1"
Minimum="100" Maximum="180" Value="120" />
</StackPanel>
```

Similar to the previous slider, you can add two more for controlling the X and Z axes, and set the minimum and maximum values as per the display range.

On the slider's `ValueChanged` event, you need to handle the position value. The following snippet shows the changing of the Y axis for the camera:

```
Dispatcher.Invoke(DispatcherPriority.Normal,
new Action(
    delegate()
    {
        perspectiveCamera.Position = new Point3D(
        e.NewValue,
        camera.Position.Y, Camera.Position.Z);
    }
));
```

Similar to the previous code block, you can easily implement the slider's `ValueChanged` event handler that controls the values for the X and Y axis of the camera.

Creating the 3D Model

We are done with setting up the viewport and the camera. Now we need to define the content for the viewport, which will be the instance of the `ModelVisual3D` element. This `ModelVisual3D` object will contain the mesh object, brush information, lighting, and so on. As of now, we don't have the mesh object ready, but at this point of time, we can define `ModelVisual3D` in XAML:

```
<ModelVisual3D x:Name="model">
    <ModelVisual3D.Content>
        <Model3DGroup x:Name="modelGroup">
            <AmbientLight Color="Gray"/>
            <DirectionalLight Color="Gray" Direction="-1,-3,-2"/>
            <DirectionalLight Color="Gray" Direction="1,-2,3"/>
        </Model3DGroup>
    </ModelVisual3D.Content>
</ModelVisual3D>
```

`ModelVisual3D.Content` holds the actual elements for `viewport`. We have content inside the `Mode3DGroup` element as we have defined multiple lights, and of course, we have to add the mesh objects in `model`.

Building the mesh object

Mesh is a representation of a surface of a 3D object, built using different triangles. Each triangle will have 3D vertices. The vertices are joined together to define the triangle with a front and a back side; only the front side will be rendered:

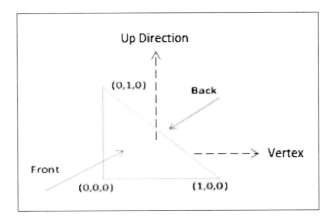

We can create the mesh object that consists of triangles using the `MeshGeometry3D` object, and then wrap up it using the `GeometryModel3D` object. First, add a new private member to the class:

```
private GeometryModel3D geometryModel;
```

We have created a method `CreateTriangleModel()`, which accepts three points for each triangle and constructs the `GeometryModel3D` object by applying `Material` as `SolidColorBrush`:

```
private GeometryModel3D CreateTriangleModel(Point3D p0, Point3D p1,
Point3D p2)
{
    MeshGeometry3D mesh = new MeshGeometry3D();
    mesh.Positions.Add(p0);
    mesh.Positions.Add(p1);
    mesh.Positions.Add(p2);
    mesh.TriangleIndices.Add(0);
    mesh.TriangleIndices.Add(1);
    mesh.TriangleIndices.Add(2);
    Material material = new DiffuseMaterial(new
SolidColorBrush(Colors.Dark));
    geometryModel = new GeometryModel3D(mesh, material);
    return geometryModel;
}
```

Setting up the initial data points

To create the basic 3D points, consider the image frame we will be receiving from the sensor with the resolution of 320 x 240. Hence, we have defined the array of `GeometryModel3D` with the same size:

```
private GeometryModel3D[] modelPoints = new GeometryModel3D[320 *
240];
```

 Here, you can choose a higher resolution as well, but you have to be careful about the performance of the application, as the same object is going to be rendered for each and every frame pixel.

Once you have defined the array, create the basic data points by calling the `SetData()` method as shown in the following code. Consider `PosZ` as `0` at this point, as currently we don't have its value. Once we have data from the sensor, this value will be updated by the pixel depth value:

```
int pixelHeight = 240;
int pixelWidth = 320;

private void SetData()
{
    int i = 0;
    int posZ = 0;
    for (int posY = 0; posY < pixelHeight; posY += 2)
    {
        for (int posX = 0; posX < pixelWidth; posX += 2)
        {
            modelPoints[i] = CreateTriangleModel(new Point3D(posX,
posY, posZ), new Point3D(posX, posY + 2, posZ), new Point3D(posX + 2,
posY + 2, posZ));
            modelPoints[i].Transform = new TranslateTransform3D(0, 0,
0);
            modelGroup.Children.Add(modelPoints[i]);
            i++;
        }
    }
}
```

When we call this method, all the objects will be automatically added into the child element of `model`.

Getting the depth data from Kinect

The final task of this exercise is getting the depth data from the sensor and creating the mesh data out of it. The basics of starting the sensor, enabling the data stream, and getting the depth data from the sensor are already known to you; the only area you have to focus on is updating the position of mesh object Z (PosZ) by updating the translation transformation. The Z value, here, is nothing but the depth of that particular pixel:

```
void sensor_DepthFrameReady(object sender,
DepthImageFrameReadyEventArgs e)
{
    using (DepthImageFrame depthImageFrame = e.OpenDepthImageFrame())
    {
        if (depthImageFrame == null)
        {
            return;
        }
        short[] pixelData = new short[depthImageFrame.
PixelDataLength];
        depthImageFrame.CopyPixelDataTo(pixelData);
        int translatePoint = 0;
        for (int posY = 0; posY < depthImageFrame.Height; posY += 2)
        {
            for (int posX = 0; posX < depthImageFrame.Width; posX +=
2)
            {
                int depth = ((ushort)pixelData[posX + posY *
depthImageFrame.Width]) >> 3;
                if (depth == sensor.DepthStream.UnknownDepth)
                {
                    continue;
                }
```

```
((TranslateTransform3D)modelPoints[translatePoint].Transform).OffsetZ
= depth;
            translatePoint++;
            }
        }
    }
}
```

As shown in the previous code block, we are calculating the depth for every pixel value on every incoming depth frame, and updating the mesh object transformation. You have also noticed that we have discarded the unknown depth value while processing the frames.

 We have also moved two pixels in each iteration of the depth frame. You can just increase it by one to get the 3D view of every pixel, but this requires lots of CPU processing and can decrease the performance of the application. If you are getting bad performance with even moving two pixels, you can change to three or four.

 If you are comfortable with WPF 3D graphics and prefer to do stuff using C# code rather using XAML, you can refer the *3D Point Cloud with the Kinect* post showcased at the Coding4Fun Kinect gallery at the following URL: http://channel9.msdn.com/coding4fun/kinect/3D-Point-Cloud-with-the-Kinect. Refer the details of this post for more information on designing a 3D Point Cloud.

Project Information URL: http://www.i-programmer.info/ebooks/practical-windows-kinect-in-c/4126-kinect-sdk1-a-3d-point-cloud.html

Have a look at 3D depth

That's all! On the `Windows_Loaded` event, enable the depth data start, start the sensor, and then call the `SetData()` method.

And finally, run the application and move the Kinect sensor around. You will be able to view constructed 3D points of depth data representations, as shown in the following screenshot. Change the camera position to see the changes in the view of the display view port area.

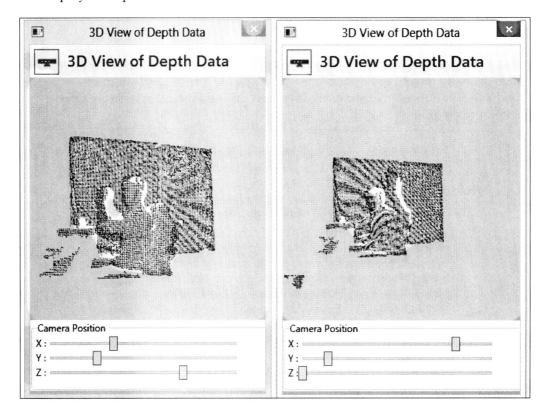

In the example, we discussed the basics of 3D data processing with the Kinect sensor. With this fundamental knowledge of 3D, you can go forward and try to build some real-life applications such as constructing 3D images from objects and marking/identifying 3D objects.

One amazing use of 3D data with the Kinect sensor is **KinectFusion**. KinectFusion is a real-time 3D surface constructor using Kinect sensor. It can quickly create a highly detailed 3D model of people, objects, or even a complete room. Check out the video demo available on the Microsoft Research website, at `http://research.microsoft.com/apps/video/dl.aspx?id=152815`. Another detailed paper is available at `http://research.microsoft.com/pubs/155416/kinectfusion-uist-comp.pdf`.

Summary

In this chapter we discussed one of the most important aspects of the Kinect sensor and the Kinect for Windows SDK; that is, depth data processing. We have taken a closer look inside depth data, how the Kinect sensor processes depth data, and how the pixel values are used to calculate the distance. We have also seen how the player index is calculated from the depth data. We have explored several demo applications throughout this chapter, which give you a clear understanding of what depth data is, how it works, and what its uses are. You have also learned how you can get depth and pixel information directly from pixel data instead of performing bit masking. In the last section, we have discussed a 3D representation of depth data. An in-depth knowledge of depth data is very important going forward, because most of the complex applications depend on depth data processing and skeleton tracking. In the next chapter we will explore the skeleton tracking features of the Kinect for Windows SDK.

6
Human Skeleton Tracking

The Kinect sensor returns the raw depth data, where each pixel contains a value that represents the distance between the sensor and the object. In the previous chapter we explored depth image processing techniques, how depth sensors work, how we can measure the distances, and how each pixel value represents the player information. The depth data gives us unlimited possibilities to play around with Kinect. To build an interactive application and enable a rich user experience, we need to gain control over the application using our body motion. When we talk about how to build an application that interacts with human body motion, first of all we need to capture the information about the users standing in front of the Kinect, and from then on the skeleton tracking comes into the picture.

The complete skeleton-tracking feature is built on the depth data processing, internal machine learning, and color vision algorithms. Using skeleton tracking, the Kinect sensor can track the human body with various joint points. Using the Kinect for Windows SDK, you can track up to six players and up to 20 joints for each skeleton. Only two users can be tracked in detail, which means the sensor can return all the twenty tracked joint points information; whereas, for reset users, it just gives the overall position. This is because it would require a lot of processing to track joint information for all the six users.

In this chapter we will start with the fundamentals of skeleton tracking, events, and the skeleton object model. We will learn how to work with skeleton joints and bones. Detailed information on each of the topics listed below will be provided. We will also develop a few applications that harness these features. In the end, we will have an integrated solution that showcases different features of skeleton tracking:

- How skeleton tracking works
- Skeleton tracking with Kinect for Windows SDK
- Start tracking joints, and looking inside skeleton stream helpers
- Building an intrusion-detection camera

- Learn how to track a skeleton in seated mode
- Choosing a skeleton for your application
- A deep look inside skeleton joints and bones hierarchy
- Providing live feedback to users based on their positions
- Making the skeleton movement softer
- Advanced Skeleton Viewer – a tool for viewing skeleton data
- Debugging skeleton applications

How skeleton tracking works

The Kinect sensor returns raw depth data from which we can easily identify the pixels that represent the players. Skeleton tracking is not just about tracking the joints by reading the player information; rather, it tracks the complete body movement. Real-time human pose recognition is difficult and challenging because of the different body poses (consider; a single body part can move in thousands of different directions and ways), sizes (sizes of humans vary), dresses (dresses could differ from user to user), heights (human height could be tall, short, medium), and so on.

To overcome such problems and to track different joints irrespective of body pose, Kinect uses a **rendering pipeline** where it matches the incoming data (raw depth data from sensor) with sample trained data. The human pose recognition algorithm used several base character models that varied with different heights, sizes, clothes, and several other factors. The machine learned data is collected from the base characters with different types of poses, hair types, and clothing, and in different rotations and views. The machine learned data is labeled with individual body parts and matched with the incoming depth data to identify which part of the body it belongs to. The rendering pipeline processes the data in several steps to track human body parts from depth data.

The Kinect sensor can identify the pixel range of a player from the depth data. In the initial steps of the rendering pipeline process, the sensor identifies the human body object, which is nothing but raw depth data that is similar to another object captured by the sensor. In the absence of any other logic, the sensor will not know if this is a human body or something else. The following image shows what a human body looks like when it is represented with depth data; the sensor recognizes it as a big object:

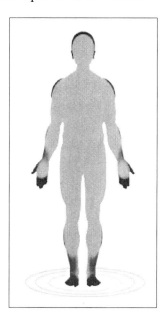

To start recognizing a human body, the sensors start matching each individual pixel of incoming depth data with the data the machine has learned. This match is done within the sensor with very high speed of processing. The data each individual machine has learned is labeled and has some associated values to match with incoming data. This complete matching is based on the probability that the incoming data matches with the data the machine has learned.

The immediate next step in pose recognition is to label the body parts by creating segments. This segment creation is done by matching similar probable data. Kinect uses a trained tree structure (known as a **decision tree**) to match the data for a specific type of human body. This tree is known as a **Decision Forrest**.

 A Decision Forrest is a collection of independently trained decision trees.

All the nodes in this tree are different model character data labeled with body part names. Eventually, every single pixel data passes through this tree to match with body parts. The complete process of matching data is run over and over. Whenever there is matched data, the sensor starts marking them and starts creating **body segments**, as shown in the following image:

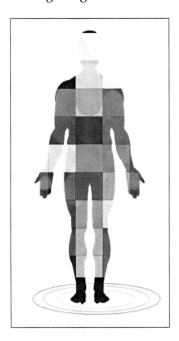

Once the different body parts are identified, the sensor positions the joint points with the highest probable matched data. With identified joint points and the movement of those joints, the sensor can track the movement of the complete body. The following image shows the tracked joints of different body segments:

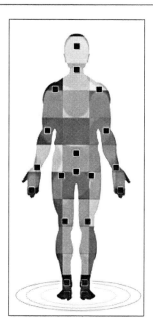

The joint positions are measured by three coordinates (X, Y, and Z), where X and Y define the position of the joint and Z represents the distance from the sensor. To get the proper coordinates, the sensor calculates the three views of the same image: front view, left view, and top view, by which the sensor defines the 3D body proposal. The three views are shown in the following screenshot:

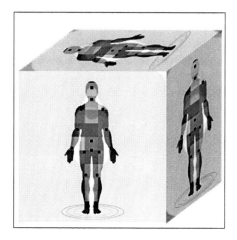

Steps to remember

The following are steps you need to remember:

1. Depth data is processed in the rendering pipeline process and matches with decision forrest labeled data and generates the inferred body segments.

2. Once all parts are identified based on the labeled data, the sensor identifies the body joints.

3. The sensor then calculates the 3D view from the top, front, and the left of the proposed joints.

4. Then the sensor starts tracking the human skeleton and body movement based on the proposed joint points and the 3D view.

The following image shows the overall process flow that creates joint points from raw depth data:

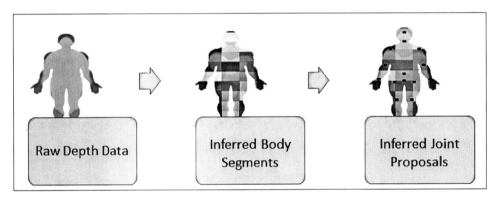

 To get an insight on how skeleton tracking works, please refer to the following URL: http://research.microsoft.com/apps/pubs/default.aspx?id=145347

Skeleton tracking with the Kinect SDK

The Kinect for Windows SDK provides us with a set of APIs that allow easy access to the skeleton joints. The SDK supports the tracking of up to 20 joint points. Each and every joint position is identified by its name (head, shoulders, elbows, wrists, arms, spine, hips, knees, ankles, and so on), and the skeleton-tracking state is determined by either `Tracked`, `Not Tracked`, or `Position Only`. The SDK uses multiple channels to detect the skeleton. The default channel tracks all 20 skeletal joint positions with the `Tracked`, `Not Tracked`, or `Inferred` tracking mode. The following diagram represents a complete human skeleton facing the Kinect sensor, shaped with 20 joint points that can be tracked by the Kinect for Windows SDK:

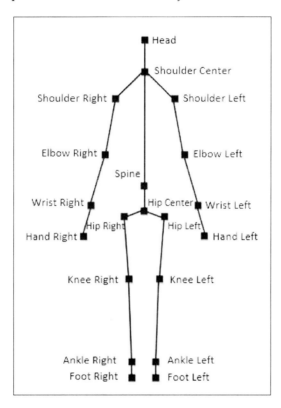

Kinect can fully track up to two users, and can detect a maximum of six users within the viewable range; the other four are known as **proposed skeletons**. You can only get the complete 20 joints for the fully tracked skeletons; for the other four people, you will get information only about the hip center joint. Among the two tracked skeletons, one will be active and the other will be treated as passive based on how we are using the skeleton data. If a skeleton is tracked fully, the next successive frames will return the full skeleton data, whereas for passively tracked skeletons, you will get only proposed positions. The following image shows the fully tracked skeletons for two users:

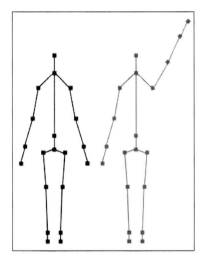

The Kinect for Windows SDK also supports tracking of a **seated skeleton**. You can change the tracking mode to detect a seated human body that returns up to 10 joint points, as shown in the following image:

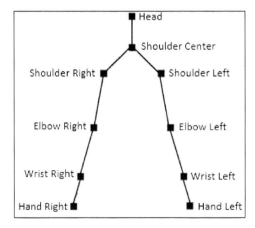

So far we have covered how skeleton tracking works and the different types of joints returned by skeleton tracking. Our ultimate goal is to be able to write an application that detects a human standing in front of the Kinect and getting the joint movements. To start with, we first walk through the basic options available for skeleton tracking and see how to get skeleton data.

Start tracking skeleton joints

Kinect returns skeleton data in the form of `SkeletonStream`. We can set up either the **default tracking** or the **seated tracking** mode using the `SkeletonTrackingMode` enumeration during the initialization of the skeleton stream. The process flow for capturing skeleton data will remain the same as the one we used for the color and depth data streams. We can capture the data by using either **event model** or **polling model**. The `KinectSensor` object has an event named `SkeletonFrameReady`, which fires each time new skeleton data becomes available from the sensor. Each frame of `SkeletonStream` produces a collection of `Skeleton` objects. Each `Skeleton` object contains the data for a series of `Joint` points, which are wrapped inside the `JointCollection` object. Each joint has its own type of tracking mode and additional information to represent the positions.

Our initial focus is to write an application that can leverage the skeleton tracking APIs provided in the Kinect for Windows SDK.

Tracking the right hand

In this section, we are going to create a simple application that will track our right hand joint position and display the hand movement in our application screen. Throughout this exercise, we will also learn various steps such as enabling and disabling the skeleton, skeleton event handling, processing skeleton frames, and tracking joints. This is going to be really fun and interesting, as you will be able to see the real joint movements in your application.

Setting up the project

Following are the steps for implementing the code as we did for other applications:

1. Start a new instance of Visual Studio.
2. Create a new project by navigating to **File** | **New Project**.

3. You will see the **New Project** dialog box. Choose **C#** as your development language, select **WPF Application Template**, and type the name as `TrackingHand`.

4. From **Solution Explorer**, right-click on the **Reference** folder and select **Add References**.

5. Include a reference of the `Microsoft.Kinect` assembly.

Creating a joint placeholder

The very first thing we will do here is create a placeholder that will represent the joint on our application's screen. To start with, open the `MainWindow.Xaml` file from **Solution Explorer**. To display the joint, replace the default `Grid` control with a `Canvas` control, and add an `Ellipse` control inside it and name it as `righthand`. The following XAML snippet describes how `Ellipse` is placed inside `Canvas`:

```
<Canvas>
    <Ellipse Canvas.Left="0" Canvas.Top="0" Fill="Blue" Height="15"
Name="righthand" Width="15" />
</Canvas>
```

`Canvas` represents the overall view area, whereas `ellipse` represents the single joint point. For this application it will represent the right-hand joint.

 The ellipse control name is given based on the mapping of the joint so that you can easily recall which ellipse represents which joint. You are free to choose any name, but make sure you are doing the right mapping in your code.

Get Kinect running and instantiate skeleton tracking

To retrieve the skeleton data, first of all you need to get the reference of the currently connected sensor and then enable the skeleton stream channel. Write the following code block for enabling and instantiating the skeleton stream in the `MainWindow.xaml.cs` file:

```
KinectSensor sensor;
void MainWindow_Loaded(object sender, RoutedEventArgs e)
{
    this.sensor =  KinectSensor.KinectSensors.Where(item => item.
Status == KinectStatus.Connected).FirstOrDefault();
    if (!this.sensor.SkeletonStream.IsEnabled)
    {
```

```
        this.sensor.SkeletonStream.Enable();
        this.sensor.SkeletonFrameReady += sensor_SkeletonFrameReady;
    }
    this.sensor.Start();
}
```

The code block is written inside the `MainWindow_Loaded` event handler, which is invoked when `MainWindows` loads. First, we have created an instance of the `KinectSensor` class and taken the reference of the connected Kinect device. Once you have the reference of the sensor, enable `SkeletonStream` by calling the `Enable()` method. Then attach the `SkeletonFrameReady` event for the skeleton stream, which will invoke the `sensor_SkeletonFrameReady()` method automatically whenever the sensor returns a new skeleton frame.

Enabling and disabling the skeleton stream

We know Kinect uses a multichannel pipeline to process the data stream, hence we need to enable the proper channel to get the desired data from the sensor. `SkeletonStream` has a method named `Enable()`, which needs to be invoked before raising the `SkeletonFrameReady` event handler to capture skeleton frame data.

You can simply call the `Enable()` method with the `SkeletonStream` property of the current sensor as follows:

```
    this.sensor.SkeletonStream.Enable();
```

We can apply smoothing to the skeleton data with `TransformSmoothParameters`. You need to pass `TransformSmoothParameters` during the enabling of the stream data. `SkeletonStream` has an overloaded method for `Enable()`, which accepts the smoothing parameter as shown in the following code:

```
    this.sensor.SkeletonStream.Enable(TransformSmoothParameters
    smoothParameters);
```

 We will discuss more about smoothing skeleton data in a later part of this chapter.

The `SkeletonStream` class also includes an `IsEnabled` property, which is read-only. `IsEnabled` returns the current status of the skeleton stream channel. You can use the `IsEnabled` property before enabling the stream channel or at any point in time to check if the channel has an open skeleton stream or not. Here's the code snippet using the `IsEnabled` property before enabling the `SkeletonStream` stream:

```
if (!this.sensor.SkeletonStream.IsEnabled)
{
    this.sensor.SkeletonStream.Enable();
}
```

SkeletonStream also has a Disable() method that disables the channel for skeleton data.

 IsEnabled is automatically set to false internally when you stop the sensor or call the Disable() method for SkeletonStream.

We have seen that the Disable() method is associated with all the data streams (color, depth, and skeleton). Disabling stream data is very rare and depends on the kind of application we are building. For the skeleton stream, we might need to call the disable methods explicitly in some scenarios.

- Skeleton data needs a good amount of processing, so it's always good to disable it when we don't need it. For example, if you are developing a security-based solution using the Kinect sensor and you want to track the human body only when it's required (during a specific time period); in such a scenario you can enable the stream when needed and disable it when it's not required. On the other hand, you can keep your color or depth stream running.

- Another scenario could be developing an application using multiple Kinect sensors. Even though you can track a skeleton on multiple Kinect sensors at the same time, you need enough CPU processing power, or you might want to do a context switching for skeleton tracking (stop one sensor skeleton tracking and start another one). In this case you can use skeleton stream disabling.

At this point of time, we have our basic screen to display the joint movements, we have attached the event handler for the skeleton, and enabled the skeleton stream channel. Let's explore what is happening inside the frame ready event handler.

Processing the skeleton frames

Whenever there is a new skeleton frame readied by the sensors, the sensor_SkeletonFrameReady() method will be invoked as it is registered with the SkeletonFrameReady event. When the method is called, it will give an argument of type SkeletonFrameReadyEventArgs. The event argument has a method called OpenSkeletonFrame() that reads the current SkeletonFrame object from the sensor.

The default method stub for the `SkeletonFrameReady` event handler will look as follows:

```
void sensor_SkeletonFrameReady(object sender,
SkeletonFrameReadyEventArgs e)
{
}
```

To retrieve the skeleton frame, you need to follow some basic steps similar to the ones used for capturing the color or depth image frame. The following code block shows the `SkeletonFrameReady` event handler, which processes the individual frames:

```
void sensor_SkeletonFrameReady(object sender,
SkeletonFrameReadyEventArgs e)
{
    using (SkeletonFrame skeletonFrame = e.OpenSkeletonFrame())
    {
        if (skeletonFrame == null)
        {
            return;
        }
        skeletonFrame.CopySkeletonDataTo(totalSkeleton);
        Skeleton firstSkeleton = (from trackskeleton in totalSkeleton
        where trackskeleton.TrackingState == SkeletonTrackingState.
Tracked
        select trackskeleton).FirstOrDefault();
        if (firstSkeleton == null)
        {
            return;
        }
        if (firstSkeleton.Joints[JointType.HandRight].TrackingState ==
JointTrackingState.Tracked)
        {
            this.MapJointsWithUIElement(firstSkeleton);
        }
    }
}
```

In the previous code block, the first step of the skeleton frame ready event handler is to retrieve the current skeleton frame using the `OpenSkeletonFrame()` method and store it into the `skeletonFrame` object. Once we have the skeleton frame information for the currently captured frame, we copy the complete set of data into the array `totalSkeleton` using the `CopySkeletonDataTo()` method. `totalSkeleton` is a class-level array that is defined as follows:

```
Skeleton[] totalSkeleton = new Skeleton[6];
```

The reason behind creating this array of length six was to create a placeholder for individual skeletons as the sensor can track up to six skeletons.

 You can also use the `FrameSkeletonArrayLength` property of `SkeletonStream` instead of directly specifying the array length as 6; however, `FrameSkeletonArrayLength` is nothing but a read-only property with a value 6 defined inside the Kinect SDK library.

For this example, we are considering capturing data for a single skeleton. The method uses a LINQ statement to work through each of the skeletons and looks for those skeletons that are `Tracked`, and finally selects the first one from the `totalSkeleton` array. The `firstSkeleton` variable holds the joint points of the skeleton selected first.

Our immediate next step will be to map the joint point with the UI element that we have already created as part of the XAML design. To do that, we invoke a method named `MapJointsWithUIElement()` from the `sensor_SkeletonFrameReady()` method:

```
this.MapJointsWithUIElement(firstSkeleton);
```

This mapping is required for individual skeleton joints. This is because by mapping every frame's data we will able to get the joint's movement with each frame. That's the whole reason behind calling `MapJointWithUIElement()`. Let's have a look at what is happening inside this method to map UI elements with the joint points.

Mapping the skeleton joints with UI elements

Mapping and scaling is another aspect of skeleton tracking and this is more relevant in terms of representing and displaying the skeleton joint points in the UI. The `MapJointWithUIElement()` accepts the skeleton details, which contains joint positions. The following code snippet shows the mapping between the ellipse and the joints. As we are tracking only the right hand, we mapped with the `JointType.Handright` point for this example:

```
private void MapJointsWithUIElement(Skeleton skeleton)
{
    Point mappedPoint = this.ScalePosition(skeleton.Joints[JointType.
HandRight].Position);
    Canvas.SetLeft(righthand, mappedPoint.X);
    Canvas.SetTop(righthand, mappedPoint.Y);
}
```

To understand mapping in a better way, have a look at the following image that represents the mapping between a right hand joint from the `Tracked` skeleton data and the UI ellipse element named `righthand`.

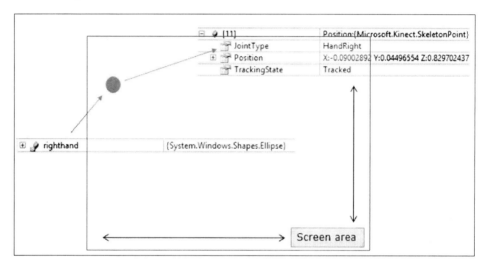

The overall representation of the skeleton data within global space is known as **skeleton space**. The origin of the skeleton space is the depth images that return the skeleton data with a set of joint positions. In the end, each joint position is represented with (x,y,z) coordinates. The `ScalePosition()` method, shown as follows, converts `SkeletonPoint` to `DepthImagePoints`, which is used as a mapping coordinate for the UI elements:

```
private Point ScalePosition(SkeletonPoint skeletonPoint)
{
    DepthImagePoint depthPoint = this.sensor.CoordinateMapper.
MapSkeletonPointToDepthPoint(skeletonPoint, DepthImageFormat.
Resolution640x480Fps30);
    return new Point(depthPoint.X, depthPoint.Y);
}
```

`depthPoint` will return the X and Y points corresponding to the skeleton points. The mapping conversion is taken care of by the Kinect SDK internally.

There are several ways you can use to display joints on the UI, such as drawing the elements at runtime and assigning the joint values to predefined elements. Here we have used the second approach, where we mapped UI elements with skeleton joint positions. In a later part of this chapter we will explore the first approach, where we display the joints directly on the UI rather than map them through elements.

Running the application

The application will provide us output similar to that shown in the following screenshot when you stand in front of the Kinect sensor and it tracks your right hand. The dot in the screenshots represent the positions of the right hand. So, just stand and wave your hand to see the movement of the dot.

Adding more fun

You can even make this application more interesting by displaying images rather than dots and showing the position of joints as shown in the following screenshots. The three images show the three different positions of the hand joint that is tracked by the Kinect sensor:

If you really liked what you have seen in the previous screenshots and if you want to implement it right away, it's very straightforward. You just need to modify the XAML a little bit; just replace the earlier ellipse control with the following snippet:

```
<StackPanel Canvas.Left="0" Canvas.Top="0" Name="righthand" >
    <Image Source="/myhand.png" Height="48" Width="55" />
    <Label x:Name="myhandPosition" Content="" Background="#F7F7F7"
FontSize="16" Foreground="Black" Canvas.Left="0" Canvas.Top="0" />
</StackPanel>
```

Now `StackPanel` is the parent container, named `righthand`, and it contains an `Image` control that shows the hand image (you can get the hand image from the book's resources; add the image to this solution), and a `Label` control named `myhandPosition` to display the current position of the joint.

Now, add the highlighted line within the `MapJointsWithUIElement()` method, which will display the joint's position:

```
private void MapJointsWithUIElement(Skeleton skeleton)
{
    Point mappedPoint = this.ScalePosition(skeleton.Joints[JointType.
HandRight].Position);
            myhandPosition.Content = string.Format("X:{0},Y:{1}",
mappedPoint.X, mappedPoint.Y);
    Canvas.SetLeft(righthand, mappedPoint.X);
    Canvas.SetTop(righthand, mappedPoint.Y);
}
```

If you run this application now and move your hand in front of the sensor, once the sensor tracks your hand you will able be able to see the movement of your hand image as per the current position, as shown in previous images.

The sample project Hand Tracking with Joint Position Display is available for download in the book's resource location. The application tracks your right hand and displays the hand movement and joint position.

You can easily extend the application and display all the joint points in a similar way as we have done for a single joint. You have to add other elements to represent joints in the UI and then you need to do a proper mapping.

Flow – capturing skeleton data

The following image represents the overall process flow for capturing skeleton data. This is just to give you a quick overview of what we have covered till now. First check if there is a sensor connected to the system or not. In the next step, enable the skeleton stream, attach the event handler for skeleton tracking, and then start the sensor. Once the sensor returns any skeleton data, read the skeleton frame and map it with UI elements.

An intrusion detector camera application

With the knowledge you have gained so far in this chapter on the basics of skeleton tracking, you can build a small and interesting application – an intrusion detector camera. Kinect will be used as a watchdog at home or any other place where you want to monitor. The application will capture a photo and store it in your system whenever there is a human intrusion detected.

To build this application, you need to know how to capture the color stream from the sensor and save it in the system. We have already discussed capturing and saving image frames in *Chapter 4, Getting the Most out of Kinect Camera*.

Set up a new project and perform the basic and common tasks for identifying and getting a reference for the sensor. Once the sensor is identified, enable both the ColorStream and SkeletonStream channels and attach the event handler for both in the Loaded event of the application, as shown in the following code block:

```
this.sensor.ColorStream.Enable();
this.sensor.SkeletonStream.Enable();
this.sensor.ColorFrameReady += sensor_ColorFrameReady;
this.sensor.SkeletonFrameReady += sensor_SkeletonFrameReady;
```

This code will enable both the color and skeleton stream channels and register the sensor_ColorFrameReady and sensor_SkeletonFrameReady event handlers, which will fire when the sensor returns the data.

You handle the color image processing and display the color stream data with the `sensor_ColorFrameRead()` method. How do you do that? It's already discussed in the *Capturing color image from Kinect camera* section in *Chapter 4, Getting the Most out of Kinect camera*.

Once you have implemented the color frame ready event handler, and if you run the application at this point, you will be able to view color camera data on the application screen.

Now, add a `SaveImage()` method to the application, which will save the image frame. You can use this method from the *Capturing and saving images* section in *Chapter 4, Getting the Most out of Kinect camera*. Once this is done, call the `SaveImage()` method from the `sensor_ColorFrameRead()` method.

Now run the application again; the application screen will still display the color camera data, but if you open the application execution directory specified by the save image path, you will find that every frame is captured and saved.

So far, what we have implemented is working. But this is not what we are looking for. We want our camera to capture only when it detects some human intrusion. This can be done within the `sensor_SkeletonFrameReady()` method. You are already familiar with how to track the skeleton and check the joint tracking state. What you need to do here is remove `SaveImage()` from `sensor_ColorFrameRead()` since we are no longer calling it from here. Then add the following lines of code in the `SkeletonFrameReady()` method after the line where we are getting the skeleton data from the sensor:

```
if (firstSkeleton.Joints[JointType.Head].TrackingState ==
JointTrackingState.Tracked)
{
    this.SaveImage();
}
```

Whenever the sensor detects a skeleton, we just make sure that the head joint is being tracked and then call the `SaveImage()` method.

Now, if you run the application it will capture the image only when the skeleton is tracked and the head joint is visible to Kinect.

Adding night vision

Skeleton tracking uses IR lights to track a human skeleton, hence it can recognize human intrusion even in dark or low light. However, at night the color camera will capture either low light or dark images. You can extend this application one step further and allow night vision using infrared stream data. Refer the *Seeing in low lights* section in *Chapter 4*, *Getting the Most out of Kinect camera*, to see how it works and how to implement it.

The following screenshots show three different modes (full light, low light, and dark light) of the application. The skeleton and the head joint can be tracked and saved in the application's directory location.

At present this application has a limitation; we are capturing images for each and every frame once the sensor starts recognizing a human. That's not desirable because the application will create hundreds of images within a few seconds. We can smartly handle this by capturing images only when the skeleton is detected the first time, and start tracking again once the sensor loses the currently tracked skeleton. We will discuss more about this and extend the application in a later part of this chapter.

The sample project Intrusion Detector Camera is available for download in the book's resource location. The application will capture images and store the application's execution directory (/bin) when a new skeleton is tracked.

Looking inside skeleton stream helpers

The SDK provides an ample amount of APIs to interact with the sensors and play around with skeleton data. There are several classes and structures associated with skeleton tracking. SkeletonFrame and SkeletonStream are the two classes that actually take care of skeleton data processing. They are the core of skeleton stream data. Unlike color and depth streams, these two classes are not derived from ImageFrame and ImageStream because the skeleton data is not an image frame. Let's focus on the individual class members and their uses.

The skeleton frame

The SkeletonFrame class is a sealed class and contains the individual skeleton information that is tracked by the sensor. This class defines the properties and methods for working with skeleton frames. Like ImageFrame for color and depth images, SkeletonFrame represents a single frame from SkeletonStream. The OpenSkeletonFrame() method of SkeletonFrameReadyEventArgs returns the current SkeletonFrame from SkeletonStream. You can also use OpenNextFrame() to get a skeleton frame while using the polling model instead of the event model. The following screenshot shows the class diagram for the SkeletonFrame class and its association:

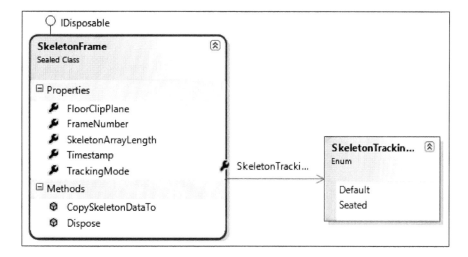

The skeleton stream

The skeleton frame information is represented as SkeletonStream. The SkeletonStream class defines the properties and methods for working with skeleton data and enables us to take control over all the skeleton data. The SkeletonStream class also defines the properties for setting up TrackingMode for Skeleton and allows us to choose the right skeleton for the application using the AppChooseSkeletons() method. The following screenshot shows the overall class diagram of the Skeleton class along with its association:

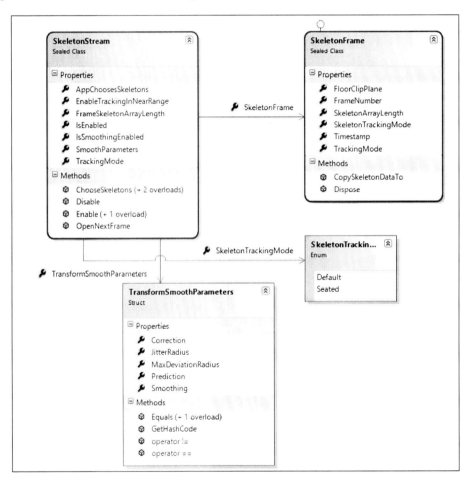

As you can see from the previous screenshot, the skeleton stream consists of skeleton frames and every skeleton frame has the information about individual skeletons.

We have covered details of these properties and methods in a later part of this chapter.

Skeleton-tracking mode

The fundamental purpose of skeleton tracking is to track the body's joint points, and so far what we have seen is tracking skeleton joints for a complete body when a player is standing in front of the sensor. This is what the skeleton-tracking engine tracks by default. We can control the selection mode of skeleton tracking programmatically by using the `TrackingMode` property of the `SkeletonStream` class. `TrackingMode` is a type of the `SkeletonTrackingMode` enumeration, which has the following values:

- Default
- Seated

 You can use only one tracking mode at a time. The tracking-mode selection can be done during the enabling of the skeleton stream or on the fly when required. If you are applying both, the latter one will take preference.

Default skeleton tracking

When you enable the skeleton stream, the SDK sets `TrackingMode` to `Default` automatically. So, you really don't need to set the `Default` mode explicitly. In this tracking mode, the Kinect sensor can track a maximum of 20 joint points and the root joint for default tracking is the hip joint. If you want to set the tracking mode explicitly, you can use the following line of code:

```
sensor.SkeletonStream.TrackingMode = SkeletonTrackingMode.Default;
```

Seated skeleton tracking

Consider you are building some application where the player is seated on a chair or elsewhere; in this case, most of the body joints below the hip are not visible to the sensor. We can also argue that if we are building an application that needs to track only the user's hands, why do we need to track all the joint points?

The seated-skeleton tracking mode is specially designed to serve the purpose of capturing seated people in front of the sensor. The Kinect for Windows SDK can track up to 10 joint points (joints from the upper body part) by ignoring all the leg joints including hip joints.

It can also track the same set of joint points while the user is standing. The only difference is it will not track the lower body's joint points. While tracking the skeleton in seated mode, you have to make sure the head and torso are visible to the sensor. This will ensure that the sensor starts tracking the skeleton in seated mode.

To enable seated skeleton tracking, you have to set `TrackingMode` to `Seated` as follows:

```
sensor.SkeletonStream.TrackingMode=SkeletonTrackingMode.Seated;
```

Using seated-skeleton tracking

This really helps the developer to write optimized code by tracking specific skeletons for seated scenarios. Following are a few scenarios where you can use seated-skeleton tracking:

- A paint application to draw using your hand movements
- Moving some objects using hands
- Developing some application that involves exercise of the hands, the head, and shoulders
- Developing a musical instrument playing application

For all the above mentioned scenarios, we really don't need to track complete skeletons. We can just track the upper body part and easily access the tracked joints as we did earlier.

Points to be considered with seated-skeleton tracking

A seated skeleton brings lots of opportunities for developers to develop applications with a seated posture. This section highlights a few key facts that we really need to know when dealing with a seated skeleton:

- For a seated skeleton, the default or root joint is the Shoulder Center.
- The seated-skeleton mode uses the same underlying classes, objects, and structures as the `Default` mode does. The only difference is you will get the `NotTracked` status for all the lower body parts' joints, including Hip Center and Spine.

- This will also work while the player is standing.

- The `Seated` mode delivers lower frames per second than the `Default` mode; also, the data is noisier than the default mode skeleton. This is because the tracking skeleton with seated mode is more challenging than standing-body tracking.

- You can use the near-mode range for seated-skeleton tracking if your application is intended to track a player from a close range.

Skeleton tracking in near mode

The Kinect for Windows SDK provides support for tracking a skeleton while the depth data range is set to near as well. In *Chapter 5, The Depth Data – Making Things Happen*, we have discussed about the near mode and we have seen how the sensor can give a player range that is very small (40 cm) using depth near range.

The SDK leverages the near-range features for skeleton tracking as well. Both the default and seated skeleton can be tracked using the near range.

Enabling skeleton tracking in near mode is straightforward. First of all make sure near mode is enabled for `DepthDataStream`. You can set it using the following code:

```
this.sensor.DepthStream.Range = DepthRange.Near
```

Once the near mode is set properly, we can just set `EnableTrackingInNearRange` as `true` for the skeleton data stream as follows:

```
this.sensor.SkeletonStream.EnableTrackingInNearRange = true;
```

The `EnableTrackingInNearRange` property has both the get and set accessories; so you can use this property to check if the tracking is already enabled for near range or not.

> By default `EnableTrackingInNearRange` is set to `false`, which means even if the `DepthRange` is set to `Near`, the sensor won't be able to return the skeleton data when the player is within near range. So, it must be explicitly set as `true` to enable the tracking.

The following image illustrates the important steps for enabling skeleton tracking within near range:

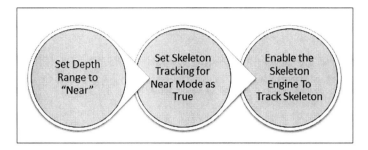

When we set the tracking range to Near, it is intended to track a player within a very close range. If you are building an application that tracks people very close to the Kinect, the best combination is seated-skeleton tracking with near mode tracking enabled.

The Skeleton

Skeleton is the unit of SkeletonStream. It contains the information about joints, tracking states, current positions, and the identification ID for the skeleton. The following screenshot shows the overall representation of the Skeleton class and its association with the SkeletonPoint and SkeletonTracking states:

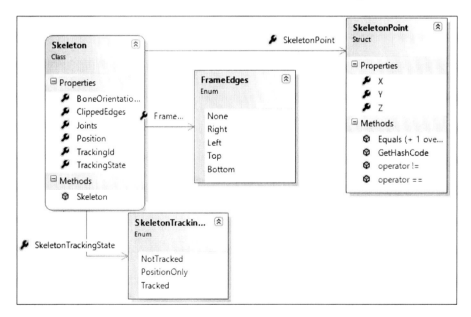

Skeleton-tracking state

The tracking state determines if the skeleton is being tracked by the Kinect sensor or not. The SDK provides a `SkeletonTrackingState` enumeration to check associated values. The following table lists the details of the `SkeletonTrackingState` enumeration:

Name	Description
NotTracked	The SDK will return NotTracked when the sensor does not have any information about the skeleton. In this case, all the skeleton's joint points will have a value of zero.
PositionOnly	PositionOnly is returned when the skeleton is detected, but the sensor does not have complete information about the skeleton or it is not tracked completely.
Tracked	The status Tracked means the skeleton is tracked with the position and joint details.

Counting the number of tracked skeletons

Consider that the `skeleton` object holds the reference of the tracked skeleton; in this case, you can get the number of total joints tracked for that particular skeleton by using the following snippet:

```
int totalTrackedJoints = skeleton.Joints.Where(item => item.
TrackingState == JointTrackingState.Tracked).Count();
```

 While interacting with skeleton data, it's always recommended to check the skeleton-tracking state before accessing the skeleton data, especially for the `Tracked` state. This will ensure you are processing the data that has skeleton information.

Choosing which skeleton to track

Kinect for Windows can track more than one skeleton, hence it is important to identify which skeleton is being tracked or which skeleton is to be used by the application. Each and every skeleton is identified by a unique identification number. The skeleton-tracking engine assigns each skeleton a unique integer identifier to track the skeleton. You can get access to the tracking ID as the `Skeleton` class has a property `TrackingId` that returns the unique ID for the skeleton.

Skeleton-tracking ID

A `TrackingId` property of value zero means an empty skeleton, or that the skeleton is not being tracked. The application uses a collection to store the skeleton information. The collection size is six, as the sensor can track up to six skeletons. When there is a skeleton tracked by the sensor, the skeleton-tracking engine assigns the `TrackingId` for that tracked skeleton and pushes the skeleton information within a collection. This `TrackingId` will remain the same unless there is a new skeleton being tracked for that particular position within the collection. From the next time, if the sensor loses track of the player for that `TrackingId`, the skeleton-tracking engine will remove the entry from the collection.

 `TrackingId` is a positive integer value and represents the attempt at which the sensor tracked the skeleton. The ID of the skeleton that was tracked last should always be greater than the previously tracked skeleton's ID.

We can use `TrackingId` to specify which skeletons are to be tracked or used by the application. For that, you have to first inform the skeleton stream that you want to choose the skeleton on your own, instead of the pipeline returning you the skeleton. To enable this you have to use the following code block:

```
sensor.SkeletonStream.AppChoosesSkeletons = true;
```

After setting `AppChoosesSkeletons` to `true`, you need to call the `ChooseSkeletons()` method of the `SkeletonStream` object. The `ChooseSkeletons()` method will give you control over choosing the skeleton. The `ChooseSkeletons()` method has two overloads where you can pass the `TrackingId`. So, if you have identified which skeleton is to be used for your application, you can do the following:

```
sensor.SkeletonStream.AppChoosesSkeletons = true;
sensor.SkeletonStream.ChooseSkeletons(skeleton.TrackingId);
```

This will ensure that the skeleton tracking engine tracks only the skeleton that you have identified and ignores the others.

The `TrackingID` property is extremely important and can be used in many real-life applications to track skeleton changes. For example, you are developing a health care application where a patient is doing exercise in front of the Kinect and it measures how the user is performing the exercises. Now, if the patient moves out and someone else started exercising, your application can easily alert the end user that the earlier patient got changed and the exercise will start again. Even if the first patient comes back after the sensor loses tracking, the application will get a new `TrackingId` value; the application can issue a notification about this as well.

Monitoring changes in the skeleton

You can use the `TrackingID` property of the `Skeleton` class object to check if the previously tracked skeleton got changed or not. To do so, you can use a local variable to store the currently tracked ID. Let's consider the variable defined as follows:

```
public int CurrentSkeletonID =0
```

Now, when the skeleton has been tracked, assign the ID only when there is a difference between the tracking ID and the previously stored ID.

```
if (skeleton != null && this.CurrentSkeletonID != skeleton.TrackingId)
{
    this.CurrentSkeletonID = skeleton.TrackingId;
}
```

Now, the current ID will only update when there is a new skeleton tracking ID. You can easily compare these two values:

```
if (skeleton != null && this.CurrentSkeletonID != skeleton.TrackingId)     skeleton.TrackingId 55
{
    this.CurrentSkeletonID = skeleton.TrackingId;     this.CurrentSkeletonID 2
}

⬇

if (skeleton != null && this.CurrentSkeletonID != skeleton.TrackingId)     skeleton.TrackingId 68
{
    this.CurrentSkeletonID = skeleton.TrackingId;     this.CurrentSkeletonID 55
}
```

Refer to the previous image; you can clearly identify the change in the tracking ID. Initially the tracking ID was 2, then when the skeleton changed the first time (tracked again after the sensor loses track of player) the ID became 55 and similarly for the second time the ID became 68.

These IDs are not sequential in nature. However, Kinect sends a request to the skeleton engine to track the skeleton sequentially, but the skeleton tracking ID updates only when the sensor tracks the skeleton.

The sample project Monitoring Skeleton Change is available for download in the book's resource location. The application shows the list of skeleton tracking IDs, tracked time along with the total number of joints tracked for the skeleton. The list updates only when there is a new skeleton tracked by the sensor for the first skeleton position.

Limiting tracking for the intrusion-detector camera

When we built the intrusion detector camera we found that the camera was capturing photos continuously from the time the skeleton was tracked. But we wanted to capture the picture only when the skeleton was tracked for the first time, or when the skeleton changed. Using `TrackingId` we can easily implement this. You can use the skeleton tracking method we detailed in the previous example, but here we will do something different and more interesting.

Once the sensor tracks the skeleton, we will capture a photo using a color frame and store the tracking ID in a local variable. Then we will force the skeleton engine to track that particular skeleton as long as the sensor has information about it. Till that time the sensor won't be sending information about any other skeleton. This also demonstrates how you can choose a particular skeleton and force the skeleton tracking engine to focus on it.

You need to use the following piece of code in the `sensor_SkeletonFrameReady` event:

```
Skeleton skeleton;
if (CurrentSkeletonID != 0)
{
    skeleton = (from trackSkeleton in totalSkeleton
    where trackSkeleton.TrackingState == SkeletonTrackingState.Tracked
&& trackSkeleton.TrackingId == CurrentSkeletonID
    select trackSkeleton).FirstOrDefault();
    if (skeleton == null)
    {
        CurrentSkeletonID = 0;
        this.sensor.SkeletonStream.AppChoosesSkeletons = false;
```

```
        }
    }
    else
    {
        skeleton = (from trackSkeleton in totalSkeleton
        where trackSkeleton.TrackingState == SkeletonTrackingState.Tracked
        select trackSkeleton).FirstOrDefault();
        if (skeleton == null)
        {
            return;
        }
        else
        {
            CurrentSkeletonID = skeleton.TrackingId;
            this.sensor.SkeletonStream.AppChoosesSkeletons = true;
            his.sensor.SkeletonStream.ChooseSkeletons(CurrentSkeletonID);
        }
        if (skeleton.Joints[JointType.Head].TrackingState ==
JointTrackingState.Tracked)
        {
            this.SaveImage();
        }
    }
```

In the first section of the code block, what we are doing is matching the currently tracked skeleton ID with the previously saved ID. This will ensure that the skeleton object returned by the application is always the same person, that is, the ID that was saved in CurrentSkeletonID. If the skeleton is returning null, it means the player is no longer present. At this time, we are asking the skeleton engine to track the skeleton automatically by setting AppChooseSkeleton back to false and setting the CurrentSkeletonID to 0, so that next time when the skeleton is tracked it will track a new skeleton with a new tracking ID. This is where we capture the photo (as shown in the highlighted code).

The sample project Intrusion Detector Camera is available for download in the book's resource location. The extended version of this application will capture images only when the Kinect sensor tracks a new skeleton. The application will force the skeleton tracking engine to send information about that skeleton as long as it is available. If the sensor loses track of it, the application will capture the photo once again when there is a new skeleton.

The building blocks – Joints and JointCollection

Joints and JointCollection are the building blocks of Skeleton. Each Skeleton object has a property named Joints, which is a type of JointCollection and contains all the traceable joints. JointCollecton contains a set of Joints and can be accessed by specifying the index value. When you pass JointType to get the Joint point, it will return the Joint object.

Let's consider you have an object of a tracked skeleton as follows:

```
Skeleton skeleton = (from trackskeleton in totalSkeleton
where trackskeleton.TrackingState == SkeletonTrackingState.Tracked
select trackskeleton).FirstOrDefault();
```

In the previous code, the skeleton object now contains Joints in the form of JointCollection. Now to get the reference of a particular joint type, you need to pass the type within the collection as shown in the following example for the Head JointType:

```
Joint headJoint= skeleton.Joints[JointType.Head]);
```

headJoint now refers to HeadJoint of the skeleton object, with tracking state and position.

In general we can represent the joints with any shape because they are totally based on the coordinate system, and we can understand where the position is. We must be clear about the basic definitions of the skeleton joint coordinate systems. All the joints are represented as three dimensions (x, y, z) and the right-handed coordinate system is used by convention, meaning that the z axis is the positive cross product of the x and y axes, with x pointing to the right, y pointing up, and z pointing at the viewer.

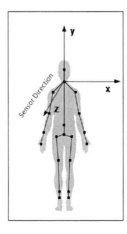

Each individual position represents using a well-defined structure `Joint` within the SDK. The structure of every joint is represented using three main properties:

- JointType
- Positions
- TrackingState

The `JointType` property is a value in the `JointType` enumeration, which has the names of all 20 joints. Each and every joint position represents an object of `SkeletonPoint`. The `Position` property is a type of `SkeletonPoint`, which represents the x, y, and z values of `Joint`.

It may happen that all the joints are not visible to the sensor due to some obstacle or human position. Once the sensor has tracked the skeleton and a couple of joints thatare clearly visible to the sensor, it will try to infer the location for the rest of the joints. If it fails to infer, then they will be marked as `NotTracked`. The `JointTrackingState` property describes if the joint is being tracked, inferred, or not tracked.

Joint-tracking state

All the skeleton joints are associated with the property `JointTrackingState`, which returns the tracking state for the current joint. `JointTrackingState` is an enumeration defined in the SDK library.

JointTrackingState Enumeration

Name	Description
Tracked	When the tracking state is Tracked, the sensor has a clear vision of the joint position and all the three coordinates (x, y, z) are captured properly.
NotTracked	Joint tracking state returns NotTracked when the joints are not visible to the sensor and the sensor is not able to track.
Inferred	When the tracking status is Inferred, the Kinect sensor does not have the actual joint position data, but it has made some calculations for the joint points based on other tracked joints.

Steps to be followed for joint tracking

Before playing around or accessing the joint information such as `Position`, `JointType`, and `TrackingState`, it's important to make sure that you have a tracked joint to work with. So, before proceeding to work with joints, the tracking first checks whether the skeleton is being tracked or not using `SkeletonTrackingState`. Once the skeleton is being tracked by the sensors, pass that skeleton data to the next step for processing. And in the next step check for the joint tracking status. As discussed in the previous section, joint tracking also has three different states that allow you to determine what action to take. To make sure you are on the right path, you have to keep in mind the following steps while developing an application using skeleton and joints:

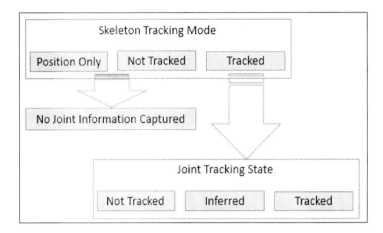

 You can't add or remove any item from the joint collection. because `JointsCollection` in `Skeleton` does not implement an `Add()` or `Remove()` method . This is because it must always contain exactly 20 elements, corresponding to the 20 trackable body joints.

Create your own joints data point

As we discussed, `JointCollection` is limited to a maximum of 20 joints as the Kinect for Windows SDK can support a maximum of 20 joints tracks. But if you want to create your own data point (not new joint) for a skeleton joint you can use the following approach where you can first create a skeleton point with respective positions for the x, y, and z axis:

```
SkeletonPoint position;
position.X = 1.1f;
position.Y = -1.1f;
position.Z = 1.8f;
```

Once the position is defined, create a joint point and assign the joint position with the previously created joint point:

```
Joint joint;
joint.Position = position;
joint.JointType= JointType.Head;
joint.TrackingState = JointTrackingState.Tracked;
```

In the end assign the joint the value of the respective joint type. As per this example we have assigned the position for the Head joint within `collection`:

```
JointCollection collection = new JointCollection();
collection[JointType.Head] = joint;
```

You can use this approach to set a joint point to a specific location and then use the same joint once the sensor tracks the skeleton.

Bones – connecting joints

Bones are the visual representation between joints. They don't have any physical presence and that is why we are calling them virtual. The complete hierarchy of a skeleton is composed of a series of bones, which is the connection of all the tracked joints with the joint collection of that skeleton.

The skeleton representation is a hierarchical representation of a bone and each bone in a skeleton hierarchy has a **parent joint** and a **child joint**. This also implies that every joint can be a parent and child joint unless it is a leaf joint, such as Head Joint, Hand Joints, and so on. Parent joints are always above child joints in the hierarchy.

For example, consider the Right Leg of a skeleton which consists of Hip Center, Hip Right, Knee Right, Ankle Right, and Foot Right joints. Now for a bone between Hip Center and Hip Right, Hip Center is the parent and Hip Right is the child. Similarly, for another bone between Hip Right and Knee Right, Hip Right is a parent joint and Knee Right is a child joint. As shown in the following diagram, for every hierarchy we will have a set of bones with parent and child joints:

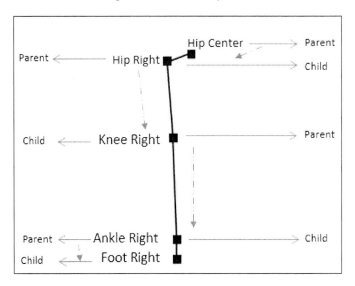

Parent joints drive the transformations of their respective child joints. Thus, when we translate or rotate a parent joint, we also need to translate or rotate all of its related child joints. For example, when one moves a knee joint, the child joint, that is, the knee also moves. However every joint has a degree of freedom, for example, a knee can only move in one direction, whereas a head can move in all directions.

With the Kinect for Windows SDK we don't have any direct API that can draw bones between joints, but we can easily draw them using few lines of code. Let's have a look at how it works.a

Bone sequence

The highest joint in a skeleton is known as a **root joint** and every skeleton can have only one root joint. For a default skeleton the root joint is Hip Center and for a seated skeleton it is Shoulder Center. As the root joints are different for both tracking modes, they have different bone sequences as well.

Bone sequence for a default skeleton

By considering the Hip Center as root, there could be five different sequences as shown in the following diagram:

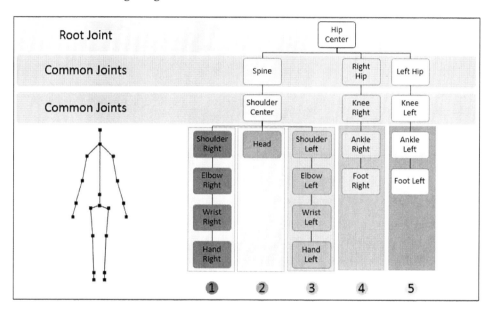

As shown in the previous diagram we can have a total five sequences of bones (1 to 5). We can move and orient the entire skeleton in the skeleton space by translating and rotating the root joint.

Bone sequence for a seated skeleton

The following diagram shows the hierarchical bone sequence for a seated skeleton with Shoulder Center as root joint:

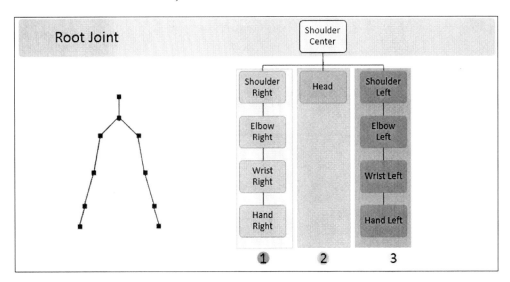

 Note that the sensor does not track Spine Joint in seated mode as well.

Drawing bones between joints

In this section we will learn how to draw a bone between two joints in the simplest way. As we have already seen, the approaches for drawing bones totally depends on us; the main thing is the underlying backend logic. Bones are the visual representation between joints and can be represented by a line or any other object. One of the simplest approaches to draw bones is by just connecting joints by a line. The following code snippet shows the same:

```
void drawBone(Joint trackedJoint1, Joint trackedJoint2)
{
    Line skeletonBone = new Line();
    skeletonBone.Stroke = Brushes.Black;
    skeletonBone.StrokeThickness = 3;
    Point joint1 = this.ScalePosition(trackedJoint1.Position);
    skeletonBone.X1 = joint1.X;
```

```
    skeletonBone.Y1 = joint1.Y;
    Point joint2 = this.ScalePosition(trackedJoint2.Position);
    skeletonBone.X2 = joint2.X;
    skeletonBone.Y2 = joint2.Y;
    myCanvas.Children.Add(skeletonBone);
}
```

The `drawBone()` method accepts two tracked joints and draws a line between them. If you pass a sequence of joints one by one that constructs one complete bone sequence, it will draw the bone sequence completely. `myCanvas` is a `Canvas` control that draws the bone elements. The `ScalePosition()` method does the mapping between `SkeletonImagePoint` (3D) and `DepthImagePoint` (2D).

The sample project Drawing Bones is available for download in the book's resource location. This solution tracks all the joints that construct the complete right hand bone sequence. This will work in both the seated and default skeleton tracking modes.

Adjusting the Kinect sensor automatically and giving live feedback to users

If you are familiar with playing games with the Xbox console and Kinect sensor, you must have noticed that before starting many of the games the game start screen gives you live feedback on where you are standing and also notifies you if there is a need to change your position.

The Kinect sensor can track all the joints when the player is completely visible to the sensor. If any of the joints are not visible, the sensor returns the status of the joints as either `Skeleton` class `Not Tracked` or `Inferred`. You can make your application smart enough to tell your end user which part of the body is going out of the Kinect view area, and sometimes you can change the sensor elevation angle to adjust the sensor as per the user's position.

The `Skeleton` class has a property named `ClippedEdges`, which is of type `FrameEdges`, that describes which parts of the skeleton are out of the Kinect's view. `FrameEdges` is a `Flag` enumeration with the following flags:

- None
- Right
- Left
- Top
- Bottom

All the values are self-explanatory. They indicate which portion of the body is getting cut off from the Kinect sensor view area. Based on this value you can provide live feedback to users on standing properly. You can call the following CheckForClippedEdges() method from the SkeletonFrameReady event handler, where you can pass the individual skeleton frame to check if any body area is getting cut off.

```
private void CheckForClippedEdges(Skeleton skeleton)
{
    switch (skeleton.ClippedEdges)
    {
        case FrameEdges.Bottom:
            GiveLiveFeedback(FrameEdges.Bottom);
            break;
        case FrameEdges.Left:
            GiveLiveFeedback(FrameEdges.Left);
            break;
        case FrameEdges.None:
            GiveLiveFeedback(FrameEdges.None);
            break;
        case FrameEdges.Right:
            GiveLiveFeedback(FrameEdges.Right);
            break;
        case FrameEdges.Top:
            GiveLiveFeedback(FrameEdges.Top);
            break;
        default:
            break;
    }
}
```

The CheckForClippedEdges() method accepts the tracked skeleton and checks the ClippedEdges property if any of the FrameEdges flags have been set. Depending on the flag values, call the GiveFeedBack() method, where you can write your own implementation to notify the user.

For FrameEdges Bottom and Top, you can make real use of the Kinect motor by changing the sensor elevation angle automatically to adjust. We have discussed this in the *Changing sensor elevation angle* section in *Chapter 4, Getting the Most out of the Kinect Camera*.

The sample project Live Feedback to User is available for download in the book's resource location. The application will give an indication of the direction in which the user needs to move so that the Kinect can track properly. You can also explore how the sensor elevation change works when it's required to move up. The application output is given in the following screenshot. This works for both, the seated and default mode of skeleton tracking.

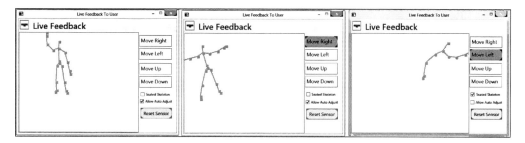

Skeleton smoothing – soften the skeleton's movement

At the beginning of this chapter we have discussed that skeleton processing is one of the most complex features because of its internal algorithm, data structures, joints representation, and data processing. Over this chapter you have gained a good understanding of skeleton data and while playing around with the applications you must have realized that the joint movements are not that smooth and there is some jitter present. Overall, this shaky movement of skeleton data does not provide a good end user experience and we need to overcome this problem to enable a rich user experience.

What causes skeleton jitters

Though the skeleton jitters could be caused by the application performance due to both software and hardware, there are several internal possible reasons for skeleton joints jittering. One of the main reasons is processing large amounts of data over a period of time during skeleton tracking. Because of the processing of large data, it's very difficult to calculate the accuracy of the joint movements.

Making skeleton movement softer

The Kinect for Windows SDK exposes some APIs for smoothing and filtering out the skeleton data. We can set smoothing parameters while setting up the skeleton stream data. The smoothing parameters solve the jittering problem by filtering the skeleton data and applying a smoothing algorithm to it. We have already seen that the `SkeletonStream` class has an overloaded `Enable()` method. This method accepts `SmoothParameters` as a parameter, which is a type of `TransformSmoothParameters` structure.

For example, the following code enables a skeleton stream using `TransformSmoothParameters`.

```
// create the smooth parameters
var smoothParameters = new TransformSmoothParameters
{
    Correction = 0.1f,
    JitterRadius = 0.05f,
    MaxDeviationRadius = 0.05f,
    Prediction = 0.1f,
    Smoothing = 1.0f
};
// Enable the skeleton stream with smooth parameters
this.sensor.SkeletonStream.Enable(smoothParameters);
```

Smoothing parameters

`TransformSmoothParameters` is a public structure defined in the `Microsoft.Kinect` assembly. It has five public properties that enable the overall smoothing of skeleton data. The following table lists out the properties:

Name	Description
Correction	The `Correction` parameter specifies the amount of correction needed for the raw data. The value must be within the range of 0 to 1.0 and the default value is 0.5. With lower values more correction is applied, the raw data is corrected, and the data looks smoother.
Smoothing	The `Smoothing` parameter determines the amount of smoothing applied while processing. The value must be within the range of 0 to 1.0 and the default value is 0.5. If you increase this value you will get smoother skeleton data, however, it increases the latency. With the smoothing value as zero, you will get the raw skeleton data.

Name	Description
JitterRadius	Using JitterRadius we can limit the radius value for jittery data. This is measured in meters and the default value is 0.5. If the position of a jitter is outside the set radius, it is corrected to be positioned at the radius.
MaxDeviation Radius	This is the max limit of the deviation that is allowed to be considered for determining a jitter. If any of the points fall outside of the MaxDeviationRadius range they are not considered as jitter. Out of this range, the value is considered as a valid position.
Prediction	As the complete process of smoothing depends on statistical data analysis, sometimes we need the predicted values. Prediction returns the number of frames predicted into the future. The property is a float value with a default value of 0.5. The prediction value must be greater than or equal to zero.

How to check if skeleton smoothing is enabled

The SkeletonStream has a read-only property IsSmoothingEnabled to check if the smoothing is enabled. For example, you can use the property as follows:

```
bool isSmoothingEnable = this.sensor.SkeletonStream.
IsSmoothingEnabled;
```

The IsSmoothingEnabled property is automatically set to true when the stream is enabled with TransformSmoothParameters and false when the default Enable() method is used.

 If a sensor is already running and returning the skeleton data, enabling smoothing will reset or reinitialize the stream data.

Exponential smoothing

The Kinect for Windows SDK exposes an API to apply the smoothing parameter while enabling the skeleton stream and once it's applied, all the joint positions returned by the skeleton tracking engine will be smooth. The smoothing parameters are applied to the data returned by the skeleton engine over time. The overall smoothing process uses statistical analysis to generate a moving average of joints, which reduces the noise. The Kinect for Windows SDK uses the **Holt double exponential smoothing** procedure to reduce the jitters from skeletal joint data. The exponential smoothing is applied to a series of time-based data to make a forecast.

The skeleton engine returns the skeleton frame in a regular time interval. The smoothing algorithm applies to each set of data and calculates a moving average based on the previous set of data. During the calculation of moving average, it uses the values passed by the smoothing parameter. For example, from the following sample chart you can see the difference between the raw skeleton and smoothed data. If you noticed, the trend of data movement always remains the same as the original data but the deviation is less.

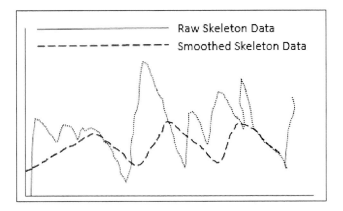

 To learn more about exponential smoothing, please refer to the following link: http://en.wikipedia.org/wiki/Exponential_smoothing

Applying smoothing on skeleton data could be very expensive in terms of application performance. This is because the skeleton stream data itself is massive, and applying smoothing filtering on it makes data processing slow and this highly depends on the parameters you are using.

There are no such standard values for smoothing for any application. This could vary based on the application and the type of user experience you need, which you can test and apply during your development phase.

Skeleton space transformation

The Kinect sensor represents the skeleton data in a 3D coordinate system. With respect to the Kinect sensor and human body points, the x axis and y axis define the position of the joint and z axis represents the distance from the sensor. The overall representation of the skeleton data within global space is knows as **skeleton space**. The origin of the skeleton space is the depth images, which return the skeleton data with the set of joint positions. In the end, each joint position is represented with (x, y, z) coordinates.

With only the skeleton data, it is difficult to directly interact with the user. This is because the user's coordinate space is different than the skeleton joint information. So we need some approach to transform the skeleton joint's coordinate system into a global space where both the users and the application understand each other's coordinate system.

The Kinect for Windows SDK provides us with a set of APIs that allows us to easily translate the skeleton space to either depth space or color space and vice versa. The `CoordinateMapper` property of the `KinectSensor` class takes care of the image's space transformation. The `CoordinateMapper` property is of type `CoordinateMapper` class, which has several methods that convert `SkeletonPoint` to either `DepthImagePoint` or `ColorImagePoint`.

For example, the `ScalePosition()` method that we wrote about earlier was taking the skeleton joint positions (`SkeletonPoint`), which have values for all three coordinates, as input. Within the `ScalePosition()` method we called the `CoordinateMapper.MapSkeletonPointToDepthPoint()` method, which takes `skeletonPoint` as an argument and maps it with the specified `DepthImageFormat` value.

```
private Point ScalePosition(SkeletonPoint skeletonPoint)

{
    DepthImagePoint depthPoint = this.sensor.CoordinateMapper.
MapSkeletonPointToDepthPoint(skeletonPoint, DepthImageFormat.
Resolution640x480Fps30);
    return new Point(depthPoint.X, depthPoint.Y);
}
```

The Kinect SDK handles this coordinate transformation internally and returns `DepthImagePoint` (with only X, Y) with respect to the current space.

The `CoordinateMapper` class also has a set of methods that can map frame to frame, such as mapping color frame to depth frame or skeleton frame.

The Advanced Skeleton Viewer application

Advanced Skeleton Viewer is built on the overall concepts that we have discussed so far. We can say this is an integrated solution to explore skeleton tracking in a better way. This application has the following features:

- Enable near range while tracking the skeleton in both default and seated mode
- Display the tracked joints, joint names, and drawing bones
- Visualize different bone sequences for both tracking modes
- Visual indication for total tracked skeleton
- Record and play a fixed set of skeleton collections
- Select a specific frame and display

The following screenshot shows the overall application. Click on **Start Tracking** to initiate skeleton tracking. Then, you can click on **Record**, which will store the skeleton information and the frame number of the collection. You can use the collection later to play the recorded skeletons. The collection element is also displayed in a list from which you can select any skeleton for viewing. Also, by selecting different bone sequence options, you will be able to view the specific bone sequence for the skeleton in the display area. The progress bar shows the total number of skeletons tracked.

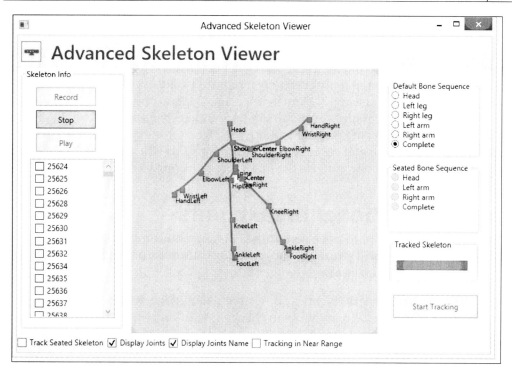

The sample project Hand Tracking with Joint Position Display is available for download in the book's resource location. This will work for both the seated and default modes and you see different bone sequences by selecting bone options. Record and playback is available for a fixed number of frames (limited to 1000 skeleton frames). Click on **Start Tracking** to start tracking the skeleton.

Debugging the applications

Debugging an application with skeleton tracking is difficult and time consuming. This is because to test or debug the application you have to stand or sit in front of the sensor properly, so the sensor can detect required joints. We use breakpoints to pause the execution of the application in a specific location and continue with further debugging. The sensor returns approximately 30 frames per second, so all the frames may not have the right data you are looking for. Hence, you have to go back and track the skeleton again and come back. To overcome this situation and to make your debugging faster, you can use the following two approaches.

Using conditional breakpoints

Visual Studio allows you to put a conditional breakpoint at any particular line of code. The application will pause the program's execution at the breakpoint only when the given condition is satisfied.

Now, think about a scenario where you want to debug your application only when the Head joint is tracked. So, rather than checking with every frame for a Head joint, put a condition in the break point condition, so that execution will pause only when a Head joint is tracked. To do this, first of all you need to put a breakpoint on the line where you want to pause execution. Then just right-click on the red breakpoint icon. From the context menu you just click on **Condition**, and specify the condition in the **Condition** textbox as shown in the following screenshot:

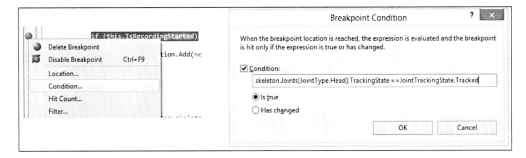

Click on **OK** and start executing your application. Now, the application execution will only pause on the specified line when the Head joint is tracked.

You can also use the conditional breakpoint to see if some value has changed. For example, you want the application to hit the breakpoint only when a particular skeleton tracking ID has changed; in this case you can use the breakpoint condition for the **Has changed** option. Refer to the following screenshot, where we have specified the condition with the **Has changed** option selected:

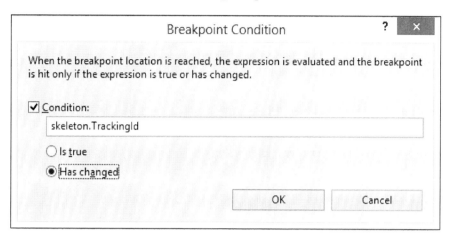

 Visual Studio supports IntelliSense within the **Condition** textbox as well.

Using Kinect Studio

You will get this tool as a part of the Kinect Developer Toolkit. In *Chapter 2*, *Getting Started*, we talked a little bit about Kinect Studio. It's a tool which can record and sense data streams. This tool is really helpful for debugging applications where skeleton tracking is involved. Before you start debugging your application, you can record your body movement using Kinect Studio. Then use the same stream to debug your application as long as you want. You can save the recorded data for future use as well.

First launch Kinect Studio and connect the application you want to debug to it:

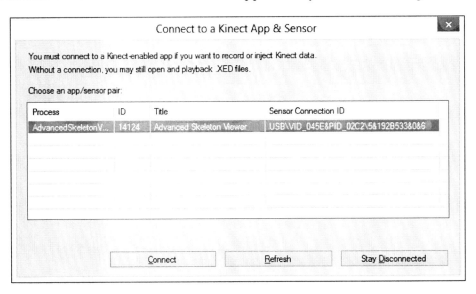

Click on **Connect**, and then click on the **Record** button to start recording. Perform the necessary operations that you want to do for your application, and when done, stop the recording in Kinect Studio. Now you can play the stream within Kinect Studio to see what was recorded and the data can be sent to your application when it's in the debug mode by selecting the **Play in Application** option.

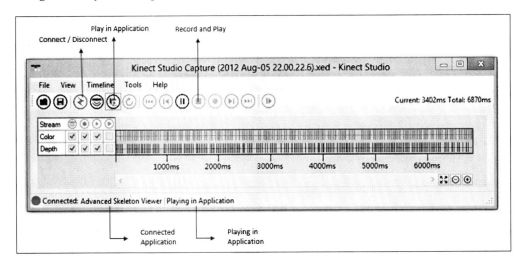

From then on you just need to connect your application with Kinect Studio and play it from there. You will receive the same data stream from your application as recorded earlier. This will make your job much easier while debugging applications.

Getting data frames together

We have covered three (color, depth, skeleton) types of data streams that are returned by the sensor. One of the common things we have noticed is the frame ready events with each of the streams (`ColorFrameReady` for `ColorStream`, `DepthFrameReady` for `DepthStream`, and `SkeletonFrameReady` for `SkeletonStream`). We had to subscribe to the events individually for different stream data and every corresponding event argument has a method that pulls the frames from stream data (`OpenColorImageFrame`, `OpenDepthImageFrame`, and `OpenSkeletonFrame`). The application raises the appropriate type of handler only when the subscribed stream data is ready. For example, `SkeletonFrameReady` will only be invoked when the sensor returns the skeleton data.

For a real application, we have seen that most of the time we need all three types of data streams. Rather than using different event handlers for different streams, we can use a single event `AllFramesReady`, which will do the job for all three of them. The `AllFramesReady` event fires when new frames are available for the color, depth, and skeleton streams.

 Even if we are subscribing to the single event handler `AllFramesReady`, we have to enable the proper data stream to get the data from the sensor. For example, if you want to enable color and depth streams, you have to explicitly call the `Enable()` method for both the streams as we did for individual streams.

You can register the `AllFramesReady` event handler as follows:

```
this.sensor.AllFramesReady+=sensor_AllFramesReady;
```

With the help of the `AllFrameReady` event we can get access to all frames by subscribing to a single event handler with `AllFramesReadyEventArgs`:

```
void sensor_AllFramesReady(object sender, AllFramesReadyEventArgs e)
{

}
```

The AllFramesReadyEventArgs class has support for accessing all kinds of data. As shown in the following screenshot, the event argument has three different methods for different stream channels; we have already used them in individual frame ready events.

```
void sensor_AllFramesReady(object sender, AllFramesReadyEventArgs e)
{
    e.
}
        Equals
        GetHashCode
        GetType
        OpenColorImageFrame
        OpenDepthImageFrame
        OpenSkeletonFrame
        ToString
```

The following screenshot illustrates the mapping of AllFramesReady with individual event handlers for data subscription:

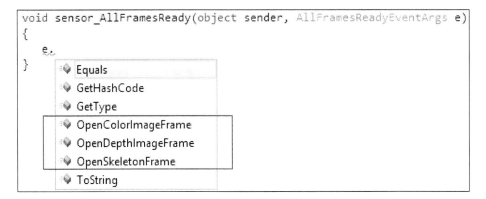

```
void sensor_AllFramesReady(object sender, AllFramesReadyEventArgs e)
{
    using (ColorImageFrame imageFrame = e.OpenColorImageFrame())
    {
        void sensor_ColorFrameReady(object sender, ColorImageFrameReadyEventArgs e)...
    }

    using (DepthImageFrame depthimageFrame = e.OpenDepthImageFrame())
    {
        void sensor_DepthFrameReady(object sender, DepthImageFrameReadyEventArgs e)...
    }

    using (SkeletonFrame skeletonFrame = e.OpenSkeletonFrame())
    {
        void sensor_SkeletonFrameReady(object sender, SkeletonFrameReadyEventArgs e)...
    }
}
```

Using AllFramesReady does not necessarily mean that you have to use all three types of data, you can use it for any single data stream as well.

Summary

This chapter primarily explores the skeleton tracking capability of the Kinect for Windows SDK. In order to completely grasp the different facets of human body movement and their implications on developing motion-oriented applications, it's essential to get a thorough understanding of human skeleton tracking. In this chapter we have delved deep into the functioning of Kinect skeleton tracking, not only in terms of the API, but we have also explored one of the most interesting parts of how Kinect sensors work internally to track human skeletons. Our approach towards covering the intricacies of the various APIs that support skeleton tracking has been even more comprehensive and detailed. The relevant text is richly supplemented with well labeled schematic diagrams, especially those pertaining to the body segments, joints, and bone direction. This chapter has also touched on the topic of tracking skeletons for both default and seated human bodies, and we have also seen how we can track a skeleton within near mode range. We have also discussed a number of tips and tricks that can help you during development of applications. Additionally, we have discussed different features like smoothing and tracking a particular skeleton, debugging skeleton applications, and so on. This chapter is also supported with different sample projects that harness the skeleton tracking features. It is essential that you thoroughly understand the information presented in this chapter before proceeding and experimenting with applications that need human interaction.

7
Using Kinect's Microphone Array

The Kinect device consists of a microphone array that supports a multitude of audio features. The Kinect device has four separate downward-facing microphones that are placed at the bottom of the Kinect device in a linear fashion.

The microphone array allows the following:

- Capturing better quality sound and providing inbuilt signal processing, including noise suppression and echo cancellation
- Identifying the source direction of the incoming sound
- Based on the sound to each microphone in the array, it can automatically find out the direction that the sound is coming from and listen to a specific microphone by suppressing the other noises

Once the direction of the sound source is set, the Kinect sensor is intelligent enough to change the direction as and when the source moves. One of the common examples of such a scenario is playing a game using voice commands. If the player moves, the sound source's direction moves automatically.

The Kinect sensor has an inbuilt audio-processing pipeline that takes care of the complete audio-processing capabilities. Another important aspect of the Kinect microphone array is speech recognition. The microphone array helps to recognize human speech very clearly by focusing only in a particular direction and canceling noises in the environment.

This chapter digs deep into the understanding of Kinect audio data processing using the microphone array and playing around with the Kinect SDK Audio APIs. The major areas we will cover in this chapter are as follows:

- Verifying the Kinect audio configuration
- The Kinect SDK architecture for audio
- How Kinect processes audio signals
- Inside Kinect's microphone array
- Capturing and playing audio
- Processing audio data by suppressing and canceling noise
- Understanding sound source localization and beam formation.

Verifying the Kinect audio configuration

Before starting development with the Kinect Audio API, the very first thing you must check is whether your system is recognizing the Kinect microphone array as an audio device and can listen to it.

To make sure the audio devices are set up properly, navigate to **Control Panel | Device Manager**, look for the **Kinect for Windows** node, and there you will find **Kinect for Windows Audio Array Control** (refer to the following screenshot), which indicates that the Kinect microphone array is installed and recognized by your system properly:

In addition to the **Kinect for Windows** node, the SDK installs audio driver components under the **Sound, video and game controllers** node:

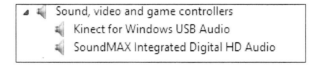

The **Kinect for Windows USB Audio** component has the sound drivers for the microphone array. If you change the **Device Manager** view from **Device by type** to **Device by Connection**, you will find that **Kinect for Windows Audio Array Control** and **Kinect for Windows USB Audio** are part of a USB composite device (refer to the following screenshot), which means on combining, these two will work together under a single USB root hub and do more than one job.

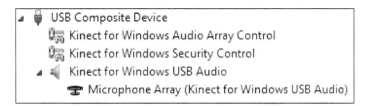

Troubleshooting: Kinect USB Audio not recognizing

If there is a problem during the installation of the SDK, you may encounter a problem with the audio drivers, and the Kinect USB Audio device displays a warning symbol in the **Device Manager** as shown in the following screenshot:

To overcome such scenarios, follow these steps:

- While installing the SDK make sure the Kinect device is unplugged
- Before using Kinect, restart your system once the installation is done

 The single USB controller, which shares many devices such as headphones, webcams, USB keyboard, and mouse along with the Kinect device, can be the main culprit causing the non-detection of the driver. It's always recommended to assign a dedicated USB Controller to the Kinect sensor.

Using the Kinect microphone array with your computer

Once the Kinect is connected and you have verified the installed drivers, you can identify the Kinect microphone like any other microphone connected to your PC in the **Audio Device Manager** section.

Navigate to **Control Panel | Sound** and switch to the **Recording** tab. You will find Kinect's **Microphone Array** as a recording device:

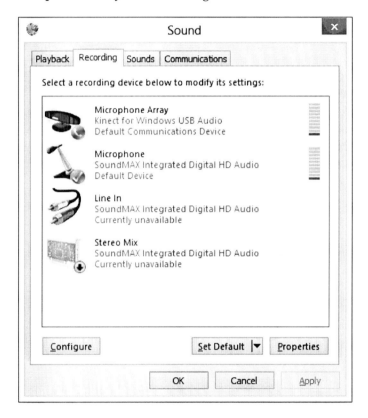

To test it out, set **Microphone Array** as the default microphone device.

Now, open the default Windows sound recorder; you will be able to start recording sound using the Kinect microphone array.

The Kinect SDK architecture for Audio

The SDK installs the Kinect USB Audio components that actually interact with the microphone array of the Kinect sensor and the SDK components. For speech recognition, Kinect uses the underlying speech API of the Windows operating system. Kinect has its own internal pipeline that processes the captured audio data; however, when it comes under the operating system level, the audio API is built on existing audio framework components. From the following diagram, you can see that the captured audio from the Kinect microphone array is passed to the application via the Kinect and Windows Audio Components:

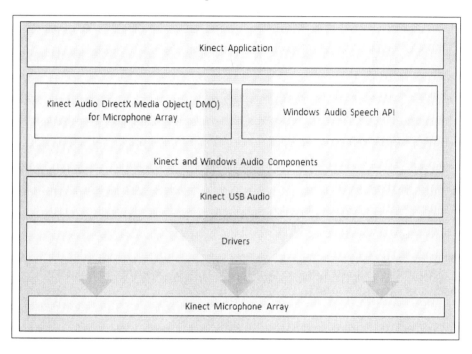

Along with the device drivers, the following are the two major components:

* DirectX Media Object (DMO)
* Windows Speech Recognition API (SAPI)

The majority of audio functionality, such as as **Noise Suppression** (**NS**), **Acoustic Echo Cancellation** (**AEC**), and **Automatic Gain Control** (**AGC**) is controlled by the DMO. However, these are not new functionalities for DMO; the SDK exposes a set of APIs that can control the previously mentioned features via the Kinect application. When there is a need to process some data using the Kinect application, you need to invoke those sets of methods from the Kinect SDK, and they internally call the existing DMO method to perform the action.

On the other side, the complete Kinect Audio Speech Recognition is based on the Windows Speech API. We will discuss speech recognition more in our next chapter.

Kinect microphone array

The microphone array is the heart of Kinect audio. Before we start talking about what a microphone array is and how it works, let's first have a quick look at what the major challenges and focus area of Kinect audio were.

The major focus area of Kinect audio

The major focus area of Kinect's audio processing was human speech recognition and recognizing the voice of the players when they are moving around and are in different positions.

- The first challenge was identifying audio with loud sound. Consider a situation where you are playing a game and a loud sound is coming from some different source, such as a TV. That creates difficulty in recognizing the player's voice because of the loud sound as well as the echo and noises in the room.

- The second major challenge was to identify the speech within a dynamic range of area. While playing, the player could change his position, or multiple players could be speaking from different directions.

To overcome all these problems and to provide one of the best solutions for speech recognition, Kinect has a microphone array to capture the voice and deal with high-quality sounds.

Why microphone array

The Kinect sensor has four microphones; three of them are on the right side and the other one on the left. The following screenshot shows how the microphones are positioned and the distance between the microphones within the Kinect device:

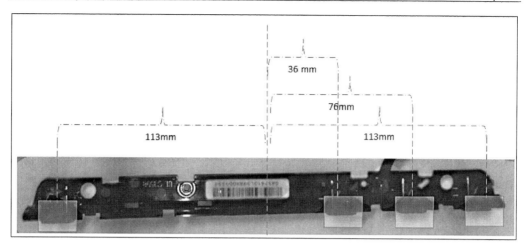

The logic behind placing microphones in different places is to identify the following:

- The origin of the sound
- The direction of the incoming sound

As all the microphones are placed in different positions, the sound will arrive at each of the microphones at different time intervals, which means there should be some delay in sound reception between each microphone. By this, the Kinect sensor can understand the direction from which the sound is coming. Kinect is also intelligent enough to calculate the approximate distance based on the wave and the time difference of sound from the actual source, similar to how our ears and brain work.

Having a longer distance (149 mm) between the first microphone and the second one allows the Kinect to see a difference between the inputs in terms of delay of sound as well as calculating the sound source's direction. There is a delay of the duration of up to seven samples between the left-most microphone and the next microphone, whereas there is a little less delay for the other three microphones.

Audio signal processing in Kinect

Kinect has its own inbuilt sophisticated audio-processing pipeline to filter the audio data. Once the source and position of the sound is calculated, the audio-processing pipeline merges the signals of all microphones and produces a signal with high-quality sound. Kinect can identify the sound within a range of +50 to -50 radians.

The range of angle within which Kinect can listen is called **source angle**.

As Kinect is responsible for *human* voice recognition, the audio-processing pipeline also applies a filter on the wave frequency by suppressing all the frequencies that go out of the frequencies of the human voice (between 80 and 1100 Hz). Along with that, the pipeline is also responsible for filtering out other noise, removing the echoes, and producing an amplified voice.

The Kinect audio-processing pipelines use several **digital signal processors (DSP)** that have all the complex algorithms to produce better voice recognition, irrespective of the circumstances.

 Combining different sound signals by identifying the sound source and listening to a particular direction is called **beamforming**.

The following are a few key components of the audio-processing pipeline:

- Acoustic Echo Cancellation (AEC)
- Beam Former (BF)
- Sound Source Localizer (SSL)
- Noise Suppression (NS)
- Automatic Gain Controller (AGC)

Combining the **Beam Former (BF)** and **Sound Source Localizer (SSL)** makes Kinect a highly directional microphone so that it can listen to a particular direction. BF changes the beam angle based on the response of the SSL.

 The process of changing beam angle automatically is called **Beam Steering**. The angle returned by the beam former is the **beam angle**, which is nothing but the angle in which Kinect is listening.

Just like other microphones in this domain, Kinect uses Acoustic Echo Cancellation (AEC) to remove the sounds that are coming from the loudspeaker. Noise Suppression (NS) is used to suppress the unwanted sounds that we don't need. Automatic Gain Controller (AGC) sits at the end of the pipeline and is used as an amplifier. This allows you to gain voice control as well as keep the captured audio level high while the player is moving around.

Taking control over the microphone array

The Kinect for Windows SDK exposes a set of properties and methods that help to capture audio from the Kinect microphone array and process the audio data. The SDK has a top level `KinectAudioSource` class that is primarily responsible for capturing and manipulating the audio data.

Kinect audio stream

The microphone array can supply four channels of 32-bit audio at 16 KHz. This isn't surprising since the Kinect is made up of four microphones.

To view the default format that the Kinect microphone array provides, navigate to the **Advanced** tab of the **Microphone Array Properties** dialog window from **Control Panel**:

Starting and stopping the Kinect audio stream

Kinect sensors return raw audio streams to our application. The audio channel needs to be enabled before the sensors start sending the audio stream. The `KinectAudioSource` class exposes a method called `Start()` to enable the audio channel and initiate the audio stream to capture audio:

```
// Start Kinect Audio Stream
Stream audioStream = this.sensor.AudioSource.Start();
```

> The Kinect sensor must be in the running state in order to start the audio stream. If you try to start the audio stream and the sensor is not running, the application will throw an `InvalidOperationException`. So, it is always good to check the `IsRunning` property of `KinectSensor` before starting the audio stream. If `IsRunning` returns `false`, start the sensor before the audio stream.

Once finished with the operation, you need to stop the channel by calling the `Stop()` method:

```
//Stop Kinect Audio Stream
this.sensor.AudioSource.Stop();
```

`AudioSource` is a property of the `KinectSensor` class, which is a type of the `KinectAudioSource` class; the `sensor` object represents the instance of the currently connected sensor.

Starting audio streaming after a time interval

The `KinectAudioSource` class has an overloaded method for starting the audio stream. The only difference in this method is that it takes a time span as an argument, which ensures the sensor will start capturing the audio stream only after the specified timeout period.

For example, if you run the following code block, the application will start capturing the audio stream after 10 milliseconds:

```
Stream audioStream = this.sensor.AudioSource.Start(TimeSpan.
FromMilliseconds(10));
```

 If you don't read the stream value within the specified time period, the DMO discards the buffer data and new data will be captured.

Once the audio stream is started, the sensor starts sending the audio stream, and then you can easily use the stream data.

 You can have only one running audio stream channel at a time from a Kinect device. If you are starting the audio stream and there is already an open audio stream, the SDK will first stop the existing running stream before starting the new stream channel.

Kinect sound recorder – capturing Kinect audio data

In this section you are going to learn how to record and play raw audio data streams from the Kinect microphone array. You will also learn how you can leverage the Kinect SDK Audio API's capability to process the captured audio stream data and apply noise suppression and echo cancellation.

Setting up the project

The very first thing you need to do is create and set up the project by adding the required assemblies that are required for accessing the sensor. Perform the following steps to set up a blank project for your `KinectSoundRecorder` application:

1. Start a new instance of Visual Studio.

2. Create a new project by navigating to **File | New Project**.

3. You will see the **New Project** dialog box. Choose **Visual C#** as your development language, select **WPF Application Template**, and type the name as `KinectSoundRecorder`.

4. From the **Solution Explorer**, right-click on the **References** folder and select **Add References**.

5. Include a reference of the `Microsoft.Kinect` assembly.

Designing the application – XAML and data binding

Open the **MainWindow.Xaml** file from **Solution Explorer**. The basic UI using XAML, as shown in the next screenshot, contains three button controls to start, stop, and play the recorded sound. We have placed a progress bar control just to display the amount of time the recording has been going on; the progress bar will also indicate how much time is remaining while playing. We have placed one additional label control, which will display the status message of the current operation. To play the captured audio, we have also used a WPF media element control.

```
<Button x:Name="buttonStart" IsEnabled="{Binding CanStartRecording}"
Content="Start" Click="buttonStart_Click" />
<Button x:Name="buttonStop" IsEnabled="{Binding CanStopRecording}"
Content="Stop" Click="buttonStop_Click" />
<Button x:Name="buttonPlay" IsEnabled="{Binding CanPlayback}"
Content="Play" Click="buttonPlay_Click" />
<ProgressBar x:Name="audioProgress" Maximum="10" Minimum="0" />
<Label VerticalAlignment="Center" Foreground="Blue"
x:Name="labelStatusMessage" Content="Status Message" />
<MediaElement Name="kinectaudioPlayer" />
```

Use the previous XAML snippet within WPF `Grid` container and specify the `Grid.Row` and `Grid.Column` properties to generate the UI as shown in the following screenshot:

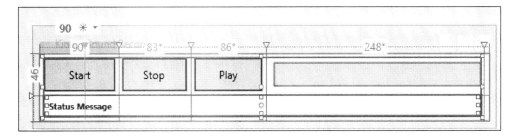

Add a new class named `MainWindowViewModel.cs`, which implements the `INotifyPropertyChanged` interface and has the properties, listed in the following screenshot, that call the `OnNotifyPropertyChanged()` method if there is any value change:

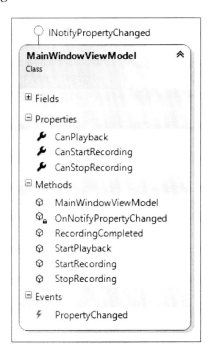

The `MainWindowViewModel` class also has a set of methods to enable and disable the UI buttons during start, stop, and playback of the recorded audio. For example, when we click on the **Start** button, it invokes the `StartRecording()` method, which sets the `CanStartRecording` and `CanPlayback` properties to `false`.

```
public void StartRecording()
{
    this.CanStartRecording = false;
    this.CanStopRecording = true;
    this.CanPlayback = false;
}
```

If you have noticed the XAML UI, we did the binding of all the controls with the `MainWindowViewModel` class properties. Now the property change will automatically take care of updating the UI controls. But, before the binding comes into action, you need to set the data context:

```
public MainWindowViewModel ViewModel { get; set; }
public MainWindow()
{
    InitializeComponent();
    Loaded += new RoutedEventHandler(MainWindow_Loaded);
    this.ViewModel = new MainWindowViewModel();
    this.DataContext = this.ViewModel;
}
```

We are done with the handling of controls for start, stop, and play. Now the remaining part is capturing and playing the audio.

Recording the Kinect audio

Recording is a very simple and straightforward process and can be done by performing the following steps:

1. Create a buffer for recording the audio.

2. Read the Kinect audio stream into the buffer.

3. Write the buffer data into the file system.

The main recording is done by the `RecordAudio()` method, which can record an audio from the Kinect source for 10 seconds at 16 KHz.

```
public void RecordAudio()
{
    int recordingLength = (int)10 * 2 * 16000;
    byte[] buffer = new byte[1024];

    using (FileStream fileStream = new FileStream("d:\\kinectAudio.
wav", FileMode.Create))
    {
        WriteWavHeader(fileStream, recordingLength);
```

```
        using (Stream audioStream = this.sensor.AudioSource.Start())
        {
            int count, totalCount = 0;
            while ((count = audioStream.Read(buffer, 0, buffer.
Length)) > 0 && totalCount < recordingLength)
            {
                fileStream.Write(buffer, 0, count);
                totalCount += count;
            }
        }
    }
}
```

Before writing the data into a WAV file, note that the WAV file requires a special header format. You can find out the details for the header format from the following URL:

`http://msdn.microsoft.com/en-us/library/windows/desktop/ee419050%28v=vs.85%29.aspx`

We have implemented the same in the `WriteWavHeader()` method.

Starting the recording

The next step for the sound recorder implementation is starting the recording. We have already created the view model that takes care of all the UI-related binding. So once we call the `StartRecording()` method, the recorder screen will disable the **Stop** and **Play** buttons in the UI unless the recording is finished. We have used a dispatcher timer over here just to show a timer progress during your recording. This progress will indicate the recording time as well as the time remaining while playing the audio. The line highlighted in the following code block is where we call the record audio from our helper class:

```
this.ViewModel.StartRecording();
this.PlugDispatcher();
var audioThread = new Thread(new ThreadStart(RecordAudio));
audioThread.SetApartmentState(ApartmentState.MTA);
audioThread.Start();
```

You have to use **multithreaded apartment** (**MTA**) to avoid the Interop layer exception. The managed Audio APIs run the DMO in a background thread, which requires an MTA threading model.

WPF requires **single-threaded apartment** (**STA**) to run an application, hence we have used an MTA thread to start recording the audio. This will be totally independent of the UI. This thread will invoke the `RecordAudio()` method, which will eventually start recording sound from the Kinect audio source for 10 seconds.

Playing the recorded audio

Once the recording is done, the **Play** button will be enabled automatically. In the UI, we have used the WPF media element to play the sound. The following highlighted code shows how we have loaded the recorded audio source into the media element and played the audio:

```
If (!string.IsNullOrEmpty("d:\\kinectAudio.wav") && File.Exists
("d:\\kinectAudio.wav"))
{
    this.PlugDispatcher();
    kinectaudioPlayer.Source = new Uri("d:\\kinectAudio.wav", UriKind.
RelativeOrAbsolute);
    kinectaudioPlayer.LoadedBehavior = MediaState.Play;
    kinectaudioPlayer.UnloadedBehavior = MediaState.Close;
    labelStatusMessage.Content = "Playing in Progress";
    playinginProgress = true;
}
```

Running the Kinect Sound Recorder

Now you are done with the development of the sound recorder and have gone through the major area of implementation. Let's have a look at the behavior once you run the application.

To run the application, press *F5* or select **Start Debugging** from the **Debug** menu. The following screen will appear:

Click on **Start** to start recording. The progress bar will indicate the time remaining for the recording to complete.

Once the recording is done, the **Play** button will be enabled automatically. Then click on **Play** to play the recorded audio from the Kinect sensor.

Processing the audio data

The KinectAudioSource class not only helps to capture the audio data from the sensors but also offers to take control over many aspects of audio data processing by interacting with the underlying DMO.

Echo cancellation

Echo cancellation helps to increase the sound quality. The Acoustic Echo Cancellation (AEC) component within the audio-processing pipeline is responsible for removing the echoes that we are sending to the microphone. To make the AEC work, you need to set the `EchoCancellationMode` property of `kinectAudioSource`.

`EchoCancellationMode` uses a set of enumeration values to set the type of echo cancellation as listed in the following table:

Name	Description
CancellationOnly	With the value of `CancellationOnly`, the audio DMO will perform only cancellation of acoustic echo.
CancellationAndSuppression	This enables the cancellation of echo as we perform the echo suppression using **AES** (**Acoustic Echo Suppression**).
None	No echo cancellation will be performed by AEC.

 By default, the value of `EchoCancellationMode` is set to `None`. So, if you are not setting this property explicitly, the DOM will neither be performing echo cancellation nor noise suppression.

Along with the `EchoCancellationMode` property, you will need to provide an integer value to `EchoCancellationSpeakerIndex`, which indicates the speaker, that is, from where the sound is coming. The following code snippet shows how to use the previously mentioned properties within your code:

```
this.sensor.AudioSource.EchoCancellationMode = EchoCancellationMode.
CancellationOnly;
this.sensor.AudioSource.EchoCancellationSpeakerIndex = 0;
```

Noise suppression

Noise is the sound that Kinect does not understand, or which we do not want to use. While playing around with audio, there could be different possibilities of sound; noise could be coming from different sources. The noise suppresser is used in the audio-processing pipeline and suppresses the unwanted audio signals and ignores them for further levels of processing. You can use the `NoiseSuppression` property to set the noise suppression of Kinect audio.

The following code snippet shows how to use `NoiseSuppression` with the Kinect audio source:

```
this.sensor.AudioSource.NoiseSuppression = true;
```

 The noise suppression is enabled by default.

Automatic gain control

The Kinect audio pipeline has an **Automatic Gain Controller** (**AGC**) placed at the end, which is used as an amplifier for the incoming sound source. This allows you to gain voice control irrespective of how far away the player is standing and the volume at which the sound is coming. With the Kinect SDK Audio API, you have some flexibility to control the gain control of DMO.

The `AutomaticGainControlEnabled` property of the `KinectAudioSource` class enables the automatic gain control. You can use `AutomaticGainControlEnabled` as shown in the following snippet:

```
this.sensor.AudioSource.AutomaticGainControlEnabled = true
```

 The default value of `AutomaticGainControlEnabled` is `false`. With the `AutomaticGainControlEnabled` set as `true`, if you record the sound, you will notice an improvement in the sound volume if you walk around the room during recording.

So far you have seen the different audio-processing APIs that are present in the Kinect for Windows SDK. Let's put them together with our existing Kinect sound recorder control and build a complete sound recorder with which you can record clear and good quality sound irrespective of the environment.

Audio data processing with the Kinect sound recorder

We will be extending our existing application by adding three checkboxes that control the noise suppression, automatic gain control, and echo cancellation capabilities from the UI. The following is the additional XAML code:

```
<Expander Header="Process Audio">
    <GroupBox Name="processingGroup" Margin="5" Height="57">
        <StackPanel>
```

```
        <CheckBox x:Name="checkNoiseSuppression" Content="Noise
Suppression" IsChecked="{Binding IsNoiseSuppression}"></CheckBox>
        <CheckBox x:Name="checkEchoCancelation" Content="Echo
Cancelation" IsChecked="{Binding IsEchoCancelation}"></CheckBox>
        <CheckBox x:Name="checkGainControl" Content="Automatic
Gain Control" IsChecked="{Binding IsGainControl}"></CheckBox>
      </StackPanel>
    </GroupBox>
</Expander>
```

With the additional checkboxes for audio processing, the Kinect sound recorder will look like the following screenshot:

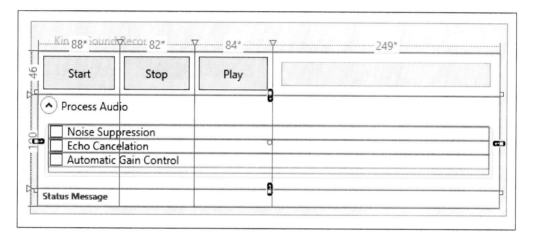

You have added an extra control that needs binding. Add the following three properties of type `boolean` in the `MainWindowViewModel` class:

Now you can bind these properties with the Kinect audio source to enable the noise suppression and automatic gain control:

```
this.audioSource.NoiseSuppression = ViewModel.IsNoiseSuppression;
this.audioSource.AutomaticGainControlEnabled = ViewModel.
IsGainControl;
```

For echo cancellation, you can first check if the echo cancellation is enabled or not; if it's enabled, set the mode along with the speaker index:

```
if (ViewModel.IsEchoCancellation)
{
    this.audioSource.EchoCancellationMode = EchoCancellationMode.
CancellationOnly;
    this.audioSource.EchoCancellationSpeakerIndex = 0;
}
```

Finally, run the application and select the required checkbox to enhance the audio quality of your sound recorder:

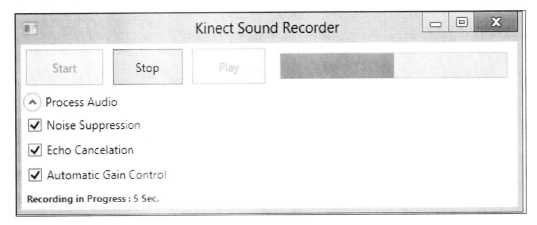

The easiest way to check is to record a piece and look at its visualization inside an audio editing tool; you can use a tool such as Audacity (`http://audacity.sourceforge.net/`).

The following image shows a short recorded audio using the Kinect Sound Recorder, where first one was recorded by disabling the noise suppression and second one was recorded by enabling noise suppression. From the visualization, you can easily identify the noise reduction in the second recording when the noise suppression was set to `true`.

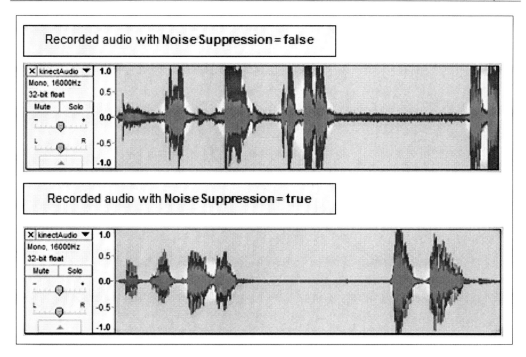

Sound source localization

The fundamentals of sound source localization are based on identifying the sound source angle and the beam angle, and the response to the changes as well.

Sound source angle

The source angle is the range area that Kinect can listen to and it's valid from +50 to -50 radians. The `KinectAudioSource` class has the `SoundSourceAngle` property, which returns the current source angle.

 Once we start the Kinect audio source, the `SoundSourceAngle` property starts updating automatically.

The Kinect source angle is calculated based on the current Kinect camera coordinates, where the x and y axes define the horizontal plane.

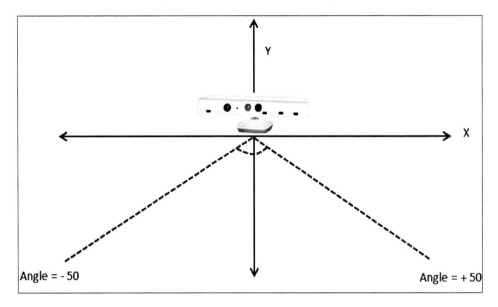

You can use the MaxSoundSourceAngle and MinSoundSourceAngle properties of the KinectAudioSource class to get the maximum and minimum values of the sound source angle.

The SDK raises the SoundSourceAngleChanged event if there is any change in the source angle. The SoundSourceAngleChangedEventArgs class contains two properties that return the current source angle and the confidence that the sound source angle is correct.

Confidence level

The confidence level of the sound source angle is used to determine the correctness of the sound that was captured by the sensor. The value of the confidence level ranges from 0.0 to 1.0, where 0.0 is no confidence and 1.0 is full confidence.

 The best scenario for using confidence level is speech recognition. You can accept or reject some speech based on the confidence level of the sound.

The KinectAudioSource class exposes the SoundSourceAngleConfidence property, which returns the confidence level of a particular source angle.

Beamforming

One of the novel features of the Kinect SDK is **beamforming**, which is the ability to determine the direction of an audio source by analyzing the audio streams captured by the microphone array.

A zero angle indicates that the sound is coming from the front of the sensor; a positive angle means that the sound is coming from the user's left, and from the right for a negative angle.

Beam angle mode

The SDK provides a property BeamAngleMode, by which we can set the mode of the beamforming. With this value of beam angle mode, the DMO level decides whether the application has to control the beamforming or DMO has to take care of it. The SDK has the following set of modes that can be set for the beam angle mode.

Name	Description
Automatic	This is the default beamforming mode, where the system calculates the beam angle based on the strongest incoming signal and sets the beam. Here, by system we mean that the underlying DMO will take care of beamforming.
Adaptive	With the Adaptive mode of beamforming, the beam angle is controlled by the internal algorithm of Kinect. It builds up a weighting function over time and then selects the strongest signal from the weighted values.
Manual	When the mode is set to Manual, the application has to take care of the beam angle change.

The KinectAudioSource class exposes the BeamAngle property, which returns the current beam angle irrespective of the mode we have used for changing the angle. BeamAngleChanged is invoked automatically whenever there is a change in the beam angle. To get the maximum and minimum beam angle, you can use the MaxBeamAngle and MinBeamAngle properties, which are exposed by the KinectAudioSource class. Both of these properties are read-only, and the maximum and minimum values are defined as constants.

Setting the beam angle manually

BeamAngle is a read-only property that cannot be used to set the beam angle directly. If you want to set the beam angle manually, you have to set the angle using the ManualBeamAngle property, and the BeamAngleMode property must be set to Manual.

The SoundSourceAngleConfidence property works only when BeamAngleMode is set to either Automatic or Adaptive.

Extending the Kinect Sound Recorder with sound source localization

In this section we are going to display the sound source angle, the beam angle, and the sound source confidence level while recording audio from Kinect.

Add the following properties in the MainWindowViewModel class and make sure all of them are notifying the property change, while setting the values:

Add three textblock controls in the UI and use the previously mentioned properties as binding values. For example, to display and bind the confidence level, use the following XAML snippet:

```
<StackPanel Margin="5" Orientation="Horizontal">
    <TextBlock Text="Confidence Level : "/>
    <TextBlock Text="{Binding SoundConfidenceLevel}"/>
</StackPanel>
```

The source of the sound, the source angle, and the beam angle can be identified during the capturing of audio from the Kinect device. You have to add the following highlighted code snippet within the RecordAudio() method to display the values for the source angle, the beam angle, and the confidence level.

```
public void RecordAudio()
{
    ...
    using (Stream audioStream = this.sensor.AudioSource.Start())
    {
        int count, totalCount = 0;
```

```
while ((count = audioStream.Read(buffer, 0, buffer.Length)) >
0 && totalCount < recordingLength)
{
    _fileStream.Write(buffer, 0, count);
    totalCount += count;
    this.ViewModel.SoundSourceAngle = this.sensor.
    AudioSource.SoundSourceAngle.ToString();
    this.ViewModel.SoundConfidenceLevel = this.sensor.
    AudioSource.SoundSourceAngleConfidence.ToString();
    this.ViewModel.SoundBeamAngle = this.sensor.AudioSource.
    BeamAngle.ToString();
}
    }
}
```

Whenever there is a change in the sound source angle, the
SoundSourceAngleChanged event is raised automatically. You need to register the
event handler before the sensor starts capturing audio:

```
// Attaching the event handler
this.sensor.AudioSource.SoundSourceAngleChanged+= AudioSource_
SoundSourceAngleChanged;
```

The event argument has two properties that hold the current source angle and the
confidence level:

```
// SoundSourceAngelChanged event handler
void AudioSource_SoundSourceAngleChanged(object sender,
SoundSourceAngleChangedEventArgs e)
{
    this.ViewModel.SoundSourceAngle = e.Angle.ToString();
    this.ViewModel.SoundConfidenceLevel = e.ConfidenceLevel.
ToString();
}
```

The BeamAngleChanged event handler is invoked when the beam angle of the
microphone array changes, and can be handled as follows:

```
Void AudioSource_BeamAngleChanged(object sender,
BeamAngleChangedEventArgs e)
{
    this.ViewModel.SoundBeamAngle = e.Angle.ToString();
}
```

Run the Kinect Sound Recorder once again; now, within a few seconds of audio capturing, you will able to see the changes in the sound source as well as the beam angle while recording the audio. Move around the room, you will able to see the changes in the source angle and the beam angle.

Summary

Exploring the audio capabilities of the Kinect sensor is the essence of this chapter. In order to fully grasp the expanse of the auditory abilities of this novel device, it is essential for us to have an understanding of the underlying hardware and how it functions. Hence, we have delved deep into the functioning of the Kinect microphone array and the need for it. You have learned the reason behind having four microphones and how the design makes the Kinect device a directional audio source detector. You have also learned about all the major terms relating to the Kinect microphone array, such as beamforming, source angle, and beam steering. You have also seen how data is processed in the Kinect audio-processing pipeline. The demo provided demystifies the exact technique of capturing and consequently using the captured audio data. In the next chapter we will raise the bar further by venturing into speech recognition of Kinect audio.

8
Speech Recognition

One of the key aspects of **Natural User Interface** (**NUI**) is *speech recognition*. The **speech recognition** application allows users to say any command in front of the microphone, and on the other side the computer executes a certain action depending on the recognized command. The Kinect microphone array works as an excellent input device for speech-enabled applications. This provides much better quality in audio capturing compared to a single microphone by providing *noise suppression*, *echo cancelation*, and by listening to a particular direction with the help of *sound source localization*.

In the previous chapter, you have seen how the Kinect SDK interacts with the microphone array and you can build an application by capturing the audio stream. While the `KinectAudioSource` class is envisioned primarily for streaming and processing audio, combining it with the `SpeechRecognitionEngine` class actually shows the power of using a Kinect microphone array.

In this chapter, you will be learning about speech recognition using a Kinect microphone array and we will build some speech-enabled drawing applications. The major areas that we will cover in this chapter are as follows:

- How speech recognition works
- Using Kinect with your Windows PC speech recognition
- Exploring Microsoft **Speech API** (**SAPI**)
- Creating your own grammar and choices for the speech recognition engine
- Draw What I Want – building a speech-enabled application

How speech recognition works

An application can have different types of **user interface** (**UI**), and controlling the UI using speech is one of the approaches of user interaction. Using the speech recognition system, users say what they want and the computer executes the command and the results are reflected on the UI.

We can categorize the patterns of speech recognition in the following two ways:

- **Command mode**: This is the mode where you say a command and the speech recognition engine recognizes the speech. As an example, you may want to start and stop a game by just saying "start" and "stop".

- **Sentence mode** or **diction mode**: This is the mode where you can say a sentence to perform an operation. As an example, to rotate a line you can say "rotate the line".

At the first glance, speech recognition looks like a simple matching logic, but indeed it is not. The speech recognition engine consists of the following two major modules:

- Acoustic model
- Language model

Each one of the modules has a sole responsibility for recognizing speech.

 Speech recognition is a pattern-recognition task, which is performed in different steps with the speech recognition engine.

The following is the list of operations performed for recognizing the user's speech:

1. Microphones capture the audio stream and in the first step they convert the analog audio data into a digital wave, which can be understood by the computer. This operation is actually done in the very first stage of the audio processing pipeline, as the audio needs a better acoustic representation to be further processed by the speech recognition engine.

2. In the next step, the audio sound signals are sent to the speech recognition engine to recognize the audio.

3. The **acoustic model** of the speech recognition engine analyzes the audio and converts the sound into a number of basic speech elements; we call them phonemes. The acoustic model is one of the major components of the speech recognition engine. This also includes internal learning algorithms.

 The **phonemes** are the units of speech, which are used to match with the voice.

4. The **language model** is the second major component of the speech recognition engine. The language model analyzes the content of the speech and tries to match the word by combining the phonemes within an inbuilt digital dictionary. So what it does is, it combines the phonemes created by the acoustic module with a word and compares that with the inbuilt digital dictionary.

5. If the word exists in the dictionary, the speech recognition engine recognizes the what you said.

 The speech recognition engine also uses the **lexicon** lists for a large number of words in the language, and provides information on how to pronounce each word. This helps in better recognition of voice, as far as the factor of pronunciation is concerned.

The speech recognition engine matches the context-sensitive patterns, which is extremely helpful for matching very similar words such as "their" and "there". Though these two words sound very similar, the meanings are totally different. As an example, if you say, "keep it there", only "keep it" will help the speech recognizer understand to select "there" or "their".

The following figure shows the basic speech recognition process using different modules of a speech recognizer:

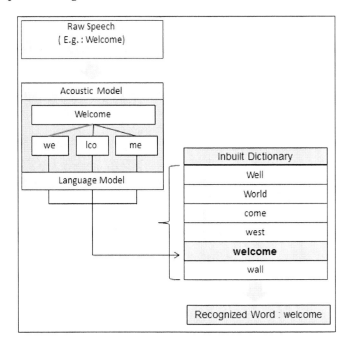

For example, the word *"welcome"*, which is captured by the microphone, is converted into a digital signal. The *acoustic model* of the speech recognition engine splits the word into phonemes that say *"we"*, *"lco"*, and *"me"*. Then the language model combines each one of them and tries to match them with the inbuilt dictionary. In the dictionary, there are several words that fall under a combination of the same set of characters. As we have already defined the word *"welcome"*, the speech recognition engine will return a success value with the matched word.

Using Kinect with your Windows PC speech recognition

Once your system detects the Kinect microphone array as an audio device, you can configure it for speech recognition to control your computer using the speech command. Let's have a look at how you can use the Windows speech recognition with the Kinect microphone array. To do so we have to perform the following steps:

1. Navigate to **Control Panel | Manage Audio Devices | Recording**. Set **Microphone Array** as the default audio device.

2. Right-click on the default device and select **Configure Speech Recognition** from the context menu as shown in the next screenshot:

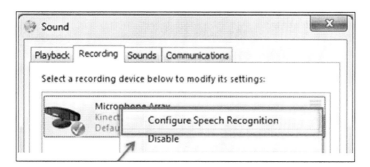

3. From the speech recognition configuration windows, you can start the speech recognition, but before that you need to link the microphone array with the speech recognition system. To enable that, first click on the **Set up microphone** option as shown in the next screenshot:

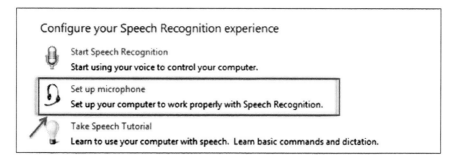

4. From the **Set up microphone** window dialog, select the **Other** option, as the Kinect microphone array does not fall under the rest two categories. Click on **Next** and follow the steps for detecting devices and voices.

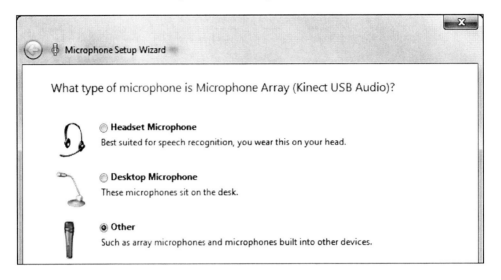

5. Once everything is set up, click on **Start Speech Recognition** from the speech configuration windows as shown in the next screenshot:

This will launch the default Windows speech recognition application and you can control your PC using voice commands and your Kinect sensor used as an input device as shown in the next screenshot:

Beginning with Microsoft Speech API (SAPI)

The Kinect SDK uses *Microsoft Speech Library* for speech recognition. The SDK Installer installs the *Microsoft Kinect Speech Recognition Language Pack (En-US)* along with all other required components.

The **Speech Application Programming Interface** (**SAPI**) works as a middleware and provides an interface between the application and speech recognition engine.

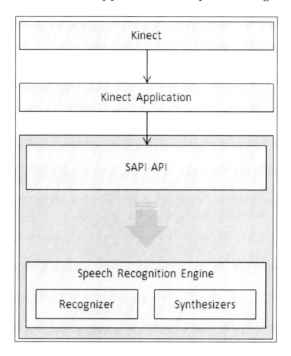

 While installing the SDK, you have to make sure you don't have any previous version of a speech language pack installed; if yes, then first uninstall it, otherwise the installation will not proceed.

Steps for building speech-enabled applications

To develop any speech-enabled application, you need to typically perform the following basic steps:

1. Enable the Kinect audio source.
2. Start capturing the audio data stream.
3. Identify the speech recognizer.

4. Define the grammar for the speech recognizer.

5. Start the speech recognizer.

6. Attach the speech audio source to the recognizer.

7. Register the event handler for speech recognition.

8. Handle the different events invoked by the speech recognition engine.

Microsoft Speech API provides the `SpeechRecognitionEngine` class, which works as a backbone for the speech-enabled application. The very first job to start with `SpeechRecognitionEngine` is to identify the recognizer itself.

 The **recognizer** is nothing but the installed runtime for speech recognition, which contains the *acoustic model, language model,* and all other essential information for speech recognition. Each and every recognizer is identified by their unique ID.

The `InstalledRecognizers` method of the `SpeechRecognitionEngine` class returns the lists of installed recognizers in the system, and we can filter them out based on the recognizer ID.

The `SpeechRecognitionEngine` class accepts an audio stream from the Kinect sensor and processes it. The `SpeechRecognitionEngine` class raises a sequence of events when the audio stream is detected. This sequence is as follows:

- First `SpeechDetected` is raised if the audio appears to be a speech.

- `SpeechHypothesized` then fires multiple times when the words are tentatively detected. This is when it tries to match them with the inbuilt dictionary.

- Finally `SpeechRecognized` is raised when the recognizer finds the speech.

The speech recognizer also provides all the information based on the confidence level of the sound source on the speech that was identified. If the speech is detected but does not match properly or is of very low confidence level, the `SpeechRecognitionRejected` event handler will fire.

Basic speech-recognition approach

The straightforward way to use speech recognition is to create an instance of the `SpeechRecognitionEngine` class. To use that class, first of all, you need to add the `Microsoft.Speech.dll` assembly as a reference assembly and then add the `Microsoft.Speech.Recognition` namespaces. You can then attach an event handler to the `SpeechRecognized` event, which will fire whenever the audio is internally converted into text and identified. The following code shows how you can create an instance of SpeechRecognitionEngine and register the Speech Recognized event handler.

```
SpeechRecognitionEngine speechRecognizer = new
SpeechRecognitionEngine();
speechRecognizer.SpeechRecognized += speechRecognizer_
SpeechRecognized;
```

Once the speech is recognized, you can perform the required operation using the SpeechRecognizedEventArgs.Result property as follows:

```
void speechRecognizer_SpeechRecognized(object sender,
SpeechRecognizedEventArgs e)
{
    Console.WriteLine("Recognized Text {0} ", e.Result.Text);
}
```

The SpeechRecognizer event handler has a Result property of type RecognitionResult class. The Result property contains what has been identified and the quality in terms of confidence level. The following table shows a few of the property names and their uses:

Name	Description
Text	This returns the text identified by the speech recognition engine.
Confidence	This is the value assigned by the recognizer on which the recognition engine accepts the command. This is a float value with ranges from 0 to 1.
Alternates	This returns the alternate matches for the input sound. The return value is the read only collection of RecognizedPhrase.
Audio	This property returns the original audio that is being used for the recognized commands. You can get hold of this audio with the help of the RecognizedAudio class.
Words	This returns the words generated by the speech recognizer. Words is a collection of the type RecognizedWordUnit class. This is quite useful when we deal with a sentence to match.

Building grammar

We have seen how speech recognition works and the events it raises when the speech is matched or rejected. But one thing is missing here, and that is, what to recognize? We want to perform an operation whenever speech is recognized; but what are those speeches or commands and with whom do we need to match? How do we define such commands in our application? How will the recognizer understand our voice command?

Well, this can be done by specifying grammar based on **Speech Recognition Grammar Specification (SRGS)**. **Grammar** is the set of commands that tell the speech recognition engine what to match. This could be a single word or a sentence. As for example, if you want to start or stop a game by just saying "start" or "stop", you need to define them as grammar so that the speech recognition engine looks into the set of grammars and returns the matched one that you were looking for.

Using Microsoft Speech API library, there are two ways by which you can build grammar commands explained in the sections ahead.

Using Choice and GrammarBuilder

The GrammarBuilder class helps us to build the grammars in a declarative way using the Choices class. The Choices class is responsible for providing a set of alternatives for speech recognition grammar. The GrammarBuilder class builds the grammar based on the Choices object provided as shown in the next figure:

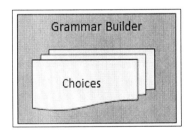

For example, you want to draw an object with a specific set of colors using a speech command. So first of all, we have to define the choices as follows:

```
Choices colorObjects = new Choices();
colorObjects.Add("red");
colorObjects.Add("green");
colorObjects.Add("blue");
colorObjects.Add("yellow");
```

In the next step, we have to build a grammar for the previously defined choices as follows:

```
GrammarBuilder grammarBuilder = new GrammarBuilder(colorObjects )
```

Appending new grammars

You can play around with the `GrammarBuilder` class to create a special type of sequence of grammar as per your requirement.

As shown in the following code, we are appending a set of choices for the object, which you want to draw by calling the `Append` method:

```
grammarBuilder.Append(new Choices("circle", "triangle", "rectangle",
"square"));
```

With the declaration of grammar in this code with the same `grammarBuilder` object, it constructs a declarative grammar that accepts a two-word input, where the first word has four possibilities of colors and the second word has five types of objects.

In such cases, the commands "red circle", and "green square" will be recognized, but "red diamond" won't be recognized.

 Also, you have to keep in mind that the sequences of choices need to be the same. As per the previous example, "red circle" will be recognized; however "circle red" will not.

Similarly, you can add multiple sets of choices in `GrammarBuilder` as shown in the next figure:

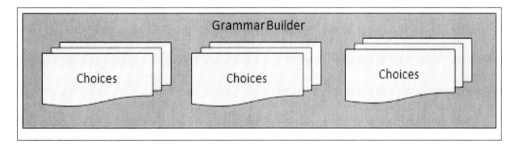

Grammar Wildcard

The grammar can also follow the rules of a normal wildcard, where the grammar element matches any input to the current sequence.

```
grammarBuilder.AppendWildcard();
```

With the wildcard, you can say anything for the current element. For instance, "draw red circle", and "need blue square" will be recognized if we are defining the first word as a wildcard.

Building grammar using XML

The alternative way to construct the grammar is to load it from an **Speech Recognition Grammar Specification (SRGS)** document. The **SRGS document** is nothing but an XML document with a set of rules to specify grammar as shown in the next figure:

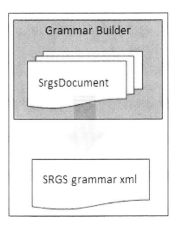

To do this, you need to use the srgsDocument class from the System.Speech. Recognition.SrgsGrammar namespace and load the same using the Grammar class into a speech recognizer as follows:

```
SrgsDocument grammarDoc = new SrgsDocument("mygrammar.xml");
```

The typical formats of the SRGS grammar XML file are shown in the following code where the highlighted area defines the set of colors:

```
<?xml version="1.0" encoding="UTF-8" ?>
<grammar version="1.0" xml:lang="en-US"
xmlns="http://www.w3.org/2001/06/grammar"
tag-format="semantics/1.0" root="Main">
  <rule id="color" scope="public">
```

```
      <one-of>
        <item>red</item>
        <item>green</item>
        <item>blue</item>
      </one-of>
    </rule>
  </grammar>
```

Creating grammar from GrammarBuilder

The `GrammarBuilder` object just builds the grammar; to use the grammar we need to create an instance of the `Grammar` class with the created instance of `GrammarBuilder` as follows:

```
Grammar grammar = new Grammar(grammarBuilder);
```

Similarly, you can create the grammar from an SRGS document as follows:

```
Grammar grammar = new Grammar(grammarDoc);
```

Loading grammar into a recognizer

Once you are done with defining the grammar, in the next step, you need to load the grammar to the speech recognizer. We need to load the instance of the `Grammar` class with the already created instance of `GrammarBuilder` into the speech recognizer as follows:

```
Grammar grammar = new Grammar(grammarBuilder);
speechRecognizer.LoadGrammar(grammar);
```

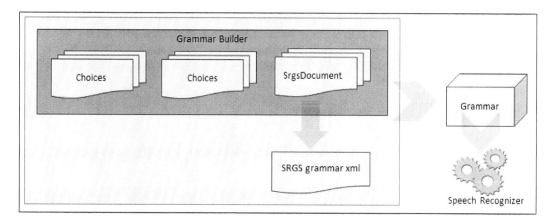

Loading multiple grammars

You can create different grammar builders and load them into a speech recognizer one by one (refer to the following figure). This helps you to create a versatile set of commands.

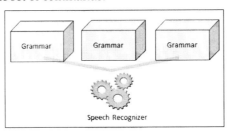

Unloading grammars

The `SpeechRecognitionEngine` class has the `UnloadGrammar` method. Using that you can unload the grammars when required. You can even use the `UnloadAllGrammars` method to unload all the grammars.

To unload a grammar, you have to pass the grammar name as an argument in the `UnloadGrammar` method. Once the grammar is unloaded, you have to load it again for further use.

Draw What I Want – a speech-enabled application

Draw What I Want is a cool demo application, which will draw a set of predefined objects with a specific color using your voice command. For example, if you say "draw red circle", the application will draw a red circle. Let's start building the application by applying the learning from whatever concepts we have covered.

Setting up the project

The steps for implementing the code are as follows:

1. Start a new instance of Visual Studio.

2. Create a new project by navigating through **File | New Project**.

3. You will see the **New Project** dialog box. Choose **C#** as our development language and select **WPF Application Template** and type the name as `DrawWhatIWant`.

4. From the **Solution Explorer** window, right-click on the **Reference** folder and select **Add References**.

5. Include a reference of the `Microsoft.Kinect` assembly.

6. As we are going to interact with Microsoft Speech API, include a reference to the `Microsoft.Speech` assembly.

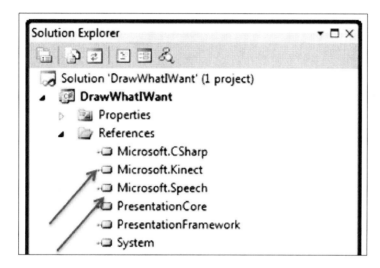

7. From **Solution Explorer** open the **MainWindow.xaml** file to design the required UI.

Designing the application – XAML and data binding

The XAML snippet shown in the following code is from the `MainWindow.xaml` file, where you can see a canvas to draw the color objects and a text block control for showing the command words.

```xml
<Canvas Grid.Row="0" Grid.Column="0" Height="322" Width="362"
x:Name="PlaceHolder" VerticalAlignment="Top" Margin="0">
</Canvas>
<StackPanel Background="GhostWhite" Grid.Row="0" Grid.Column="1" >
  <StackPanel Margin="5"
  Orientation="Horizontal">
  <TextBlock Text="Words : "  FontWeight="Bold" />
  <TextBlock Text="{Binding Words}"/>
</StackPanel>
<StackPanel Margin="10"
```

```
Orientation="Horizontal">
  <TextBlock Text="Say - Close The Application - to Quit"
Background="AliceBlue" FontWeight="Bold" Height="18" Width="217" />
</StackPanel>
```

Similar to the `TextBlock` control for displaying words, in the UI we have used multiple sets of `TextBlock` controls to display the various parameters such as source angle, beam angle, confidence level, and the hypothesized word. The design view of the application is shown in the next screenshot:

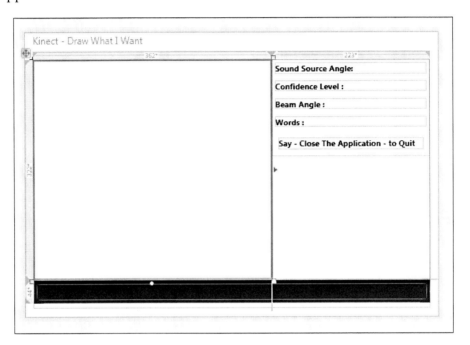

Data binding

Once we are done with the UI implementation, add a new class named `MainWindowViewModel` and inherit from `INotifyPropertyChanged` and implement the `OnNotifyPropertyChanged` method as shown in the following code:

```
using System.ComponentModel;
public class MainWindowViewModel : INotifyPropertyChanged
{
    public event PropertyChangedEventHandler PropertyChanged;
    private void OnNotifyPropertyChanged(string propertyName)
    {
        if (this.PropertyChanged != null)
```

```
        {
            this.PropertyChanged.Invoke(this, new PropertyChangedEvent
    Args(propertyName));
        }
    }
}
```

Add a new property `Words` in the `MainWindowViewModel` class as shown in the next code block:

```
private string words;
public string Words
{
    get { return words; }
    set
    {
        if (this.words != value)
        {
            this.words = value;
            this.OnNotifyPropertyChanged("Words");
        }
    }
}
```

Similar to the `Words` property, add the following properties that will notify a change whenever there is a change in the source angle, or the beam angle, or in the confidence level.

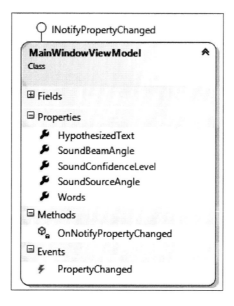

Set the data context for the UI with the newly created `ViewModel` in the `MainWindow.Xaml.cs` file. This will automatically bind up the UI with the properties when the application starts. If there are any changes on the property values, `ViewModel` will notify the UI and update the values accordingly as follows:

```
public MainWindowViewModel ViewModel { get; set; }
public MainWindow()
{
    InitializeComponent();
    Loaded += new RoutedEventHandler(MainWindow_Loaded);
    this.ViewModel = new MainWindowViewModel();
    this.DataContext = this.ViewModel;
}
```

Instantiating speech recognizer

To instantiate the speech recognition engine, first you have to identify the recognizer based on the recognizer ID.

The following code block shows how to start the recognizer for Kinect. The code blocks are very much generic like the other speech recognition applications; the only difference is the recognizer ID that you are defining for your application.

```
const string RecognizerId = "SR_MS_en-US_Kinect_11.0";
private void StartKinectRecognizer()
{
    RecognizerInfo recognizerInfo = SpeechRecognitionEngine.
InstalledRecognizers().Where(r => r.Id == RecognizerId).
FirstOrDefault();
    if (recognizerInfo == null)
    {
        MessageBox.Show("Could not find Kinect speech recognizer");
        return;
    }
    Thread newThread = new Thread(new ParameterizedThreadStart(BuildGr
ammarforRecognizer));
    newThread.Start(recognizerInfo);
}
```

If the `InstalledRecognizers` method finds the defined ID in the system, it will proceed further to deal with the speech recognizer, otherwise the application will show the defined message and return back.

Working with the speech recognition engine

We have now reached the main section where we need to create the speech recognition engine to handle everything. With the `StartKinectRecognizer` method, a new thread will span and invoke a method called `BuildGrammarforRecognizer`. In the `BuildGrammarforRecognizer` method, the first thing you need to configure is the Kinect audio source and then create the grammar for the speech recognition engine.

Configuring Kinect audio

You are already familiar with the following code block, where we have just taken the reference of the current sensor `AudioSource` and attached the required event handler:

```
private void EnableKinectAudioSource()
{
    source = sensor.AudioSource;
    source.BeamAngleChanged += new EventHandler<BeamAngleChangedEventA
rgs>(source_BeamAngleChanged);
    source.SoundSourceAngleChanged += new EventHandler<SoundSourceAngl
eChangedEventArgs>(source_SoundSourceAngleChanged);
    source.AutomaticGainControlEnabled = false;
    source.NoiseSuppression = true;
}
```

Creating grammar

In this demo, we are going to draw an object with a voice command, so our grammar needs to be declarative. As for example, if we say "draw red triangle", the application will draw a triangle in red. The following is the grammar definition:

```
var grammarBuilder = new GrammarBuilder { Culture = (recognizerInfo as
RecognizerInfo).Culture };

// first say Draw
grammarBuilder.Append(new Choices("draw"));

var colorObjects = new Choices();
colorObjects.Add("red");
colorObjects.Add("green");
colorObjects.Add("blue");
colorObjects.Add("yellow");
colorObjects.Add("gray");

// New Grammar builder for color
grammarBuilder.Append(colorObjects);
```

```
// Another Grammar Builder for object
grammarBuilder.Append(new Choices("circle", "square", "triangle",
"rectangle"));

// Create Grammar from GrammarBuilder
var grammar = new Grammar(grammarBuilder);

// Creating another Grammar and load
var newGrammarBuilder = new GrammarBuilder();
newGrammarBuilder.Append("close the application");
var grammarClose = new Grammar(newGrammarBuilder);
```

In this code block, you can also find that we have loaded two different types
of grammars and it's very much understandable that we are using that, as "close
the application" is a separate set of words, and can't be fitted with color choices or
object choices.

Start the speech recognizer

The final job is to run the speech recognizer and load the created grammar
as shown in the first highlighted block and then attach the required event handler:

```
using (var speechRecognizer = new SpeechRecognitionEngine((recognizerI
nfo as RecognizerInfo).Id))
{
    speechRecognizer.LoadGrammar(grammar);
    speechRecognizer.LoadGrammar(grammarClose);
    speechRecognizer.SpeechRecognized += SreSpeechRecognized;
    speechRecognizer.SpeechHypothesized += SreSpeechHypothesized;
    speechRecognizer.SpeechRecognitionRejected +=
    SreSpeechRecognitionRejected;

    using (Stream s = source.Start())
    {
        speechRecognizer.SetInputToAudioStream(s, new SpeechAudioForm
atInfo(EncodingFormat.Pcm, SamplesPerSecond, bitsPerSample, channels,
averageBytesPerSecond, blockAlign, null));
        while (keepRunning)
        {
        RecognitionResult result = speechRecognizer.Recognize
        (new TimeSpan(0, 0, 5));
        }
    speechRecognizer.RecognizeAsyncStop();
    }
}
```

Drawing an object when speech is recognized

Speech recognizer invokes the `SpeechRecognized` event handler whenever the speech is detected. The event handler has a property called `Result` that contains most of the information. Whenever the speech is recognized, we are invoking a method to parse the command. Here you can check the confidence level values before invoking the command parser. As shown in the following code block, the threshold value for confidence is set to `0.6`; you can change it as per your needs and the required clarity of the voice you want to capture.

```
private void SreSpeechRecognized(object sender,
SpeechRecognizedEventArgs e)
{
    ViewModel.SoundConfidenceLevel = e.Result.Confidence.ToString();
    float confidenceThreshold = 0.6f;
    if (e.Result.Confidence > confidenceThreshold)
    {
        Dispatcher.BeginInvoke(new Action<SpeechRecognizedEventArgs>
        (CommandsParser), e);
    }
}
```

The `CommandParser` method accepts the `SpeechRecognizedEventArgs` class, which has a property called `Result`. In the `CommandParser` method you have to parse each and every word to match.

For example, the first word we need to match is "draw" then "red", followed by the word "triangle". The `Words` property contains the individual word, which is recognized by the speech recognition engine. Our job is to perform an action against those words as follows:

```
private void CommandsParser(SpeechRecognizedEventArgs e)
{
    var result = e.Result;
    Color objectColor;
    Shape drawObject;
    System.Collections.ObjectModel.ReadOnlyCollection<RecognizedWordUn
    it> words = e.Result.Words;
    DisplayWords(result);

    if (words[0].Text == "draw")
    {
        string colorObject = words[1].Text;
        switch (colorObject)
        {
            case "red": objectColor = Colors.Red;
```

```
            break;
        case "green": objectColor = Colors.Green;
            break;
        case "blue": objectColor = Colors.Blue;
            break;
        case "yellow": objectColor = Colors.Yellow;
            break;
        case "gray": objectColor = Colors.Gray;
            break;
        default:
            return;
    }

    var shapeString = words[2].Text;
    switch (shapeString)
    {
        case "circle":
            drawObject = new Ellipse();
            drawObject.Width = 100;
            drawObject.Height = 100;
            break;
        case "square":
            drawObject = new Rectangle();
            drawObject.Width = 100;
            drawObject.Height = 100;
            break;
        case "rectangle":
            drawObject = new Rectangle();
            drawObject.Width = 100;
            drawObject.Height = 60;
            break;
        case "triangle":
            var polygon = new Polygon();
            polygon.Points.Add(new Point(0, 0));
            polygon.Points.Add(new Point(-169, 0));
            polygon.Points.Add(new Point(60, -40));
            drawObject = polygon;
```

```
            break;
                default:
                return;
        }

        PlaceHolder.Children.Clear();

        drawObject.SetValue(Canvas.TopProperty, 100.0);
        drawObject.SetValue(Canvas.LeftProperty, 120.0);
        drawObject.Fill = new SolidColorBrush(objectColor);
        PlaceHolder.Children.Add(drawObject);
    }

    if (words[0].Text == "close" && words[1].Text == "the" &&
words[2].Text == "application")
    {
        this.Close();
    }
}
```

The main area of this code block is getting the words from recognized event arguments as follows:

```
System.Collections.ObjectModel.ReadOnlyCollection<RecognizedWordUnit>
words = e.Result.Words;
```

As we have three grammars defined, the collection of the words will have maximum three items, where the first value "draw", and the second and third values hold the values for color and drawing object. Based on the values of color and object type, we have drawn on the canvas.

We have also handled the SpeechHypothesized event handler to enable a quick view to see what you are saying and how the speech recognition engine is trying to identify your commands:

```
private void SreSpeechHypothesized(object sender,
SpeechHypothesizedEventArgs e)
{
    ViewModel.HypothesizedText = e.Result.Text;
}
```

Testing your application

You are all set to run you application. Press *F5* or from the debug menu run the application. By default, you will get an output like the following screenshot:

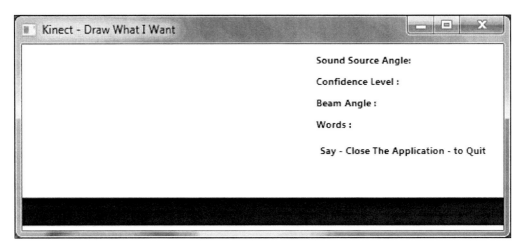

Now say "draw red circle" or "draw green square". You will be able to see the drawn objects on the screen as shown in the next screenshot:

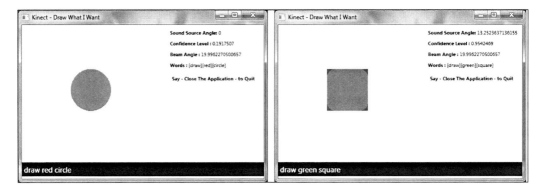

To close the application, just say "close the application"; the application will terminate automatically. While speaking, you can also view the *hypothetical word* in the footer area of the application.

You must have noticed more interesting stuff over here. Check out the **Words** section in the right column shown in the next screenshot. We are able to recognize each and every individual word from the set of recognized sentences.

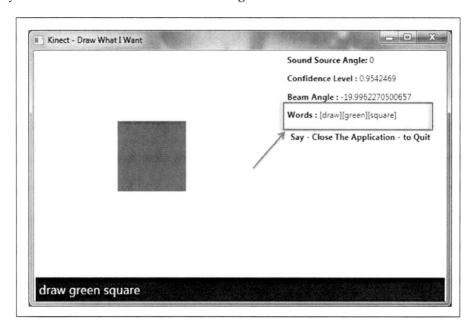

You can simply achieve this by reading the values from the `e.Result.Words` property and iterating through the words as shown in the next code:

```
private void DisplayWords(RecognitionResult result)
{
    StringBuilder sb = new StringBuilder();
    foreach (var word in result.Words)
    {
        sb.Append(string.Format("[{0}]", word.Text));
    }
    ViewModel.Words = sb.ToString();
}
```

Summary

This chapter attempts to highlight certain uses of Kinect SDK Audio APIs and leverage the Microsoft SAPI to build the speech-enabled application. Before delving into any code, we have purposefully harped on about the basics of the speech recognition system and how it works, so that you feel at ease while running the codes. To aid the understanding process we have also provided a well sketched schematic diagram. You have learned how to create your own grammar either by using code or loading from an XML file and finally learned how to load the grammar into the speech recognizer. We have also shown how to create different grammar builders and load them into the speech recognizer one by one. This helps in increasing the versatility of the command set. Finally the chapter ends with a really cool demo to make the contents of the chapter crystal clear to you.

In the next chapter, we will learn about gesture recognition using a Kinect device.

Building Gesture-controlled Applications

9

You've learned about the different features of the Kinect for Windows SDK; also you've seen how things work in the Kinect for Windows sensor and how you can interact with the sensor using the *Kinect for Windows SDK* APIs. We have also explored the Kinect color stream, depth stream, and also skeleton tracking, along with the underlying techniques. However, there is one area that is conspicuous by its absence. Can you guess what it is? It's *gestures*. Gesture recognition is one of the hallmarks of the Kinect. The amount of innovation and research that has gone into the development of gesture technology is unparalleled. *Gestures,* in layman's terms, can be described as bodily actions that convey a message. This simple action could be a waving of the hands, moving of wrists, or a complicated action involving multiple body parts. The technology used for identifying gestures and converting them to a form that can be recognized by gesture-based devices is called **gesture recognition**. Gesture recognition relies on a cocktail of mathematical algorithms and skeleton tracking to recognize and classify the gestures. When we talk about a natural user interface, gesture recognition is the primary thing that comes to minds. Gesture recognition provides a seamless integration of the natural environment and the device.

In this chapter, we will explore different concepts of gesture recognition with the Kinect for Windows SDK. We will look at the different approaches to gesture recognition and apply them in a number of applications.

In this chapter we will walk through the following topics:

- Fundamentals of gesture recognition
- Different approaches to recognizing gestures
- Understanding basic and algorithmic gesture recognition
- Quick introduction to the weighted-network and template-based recognition approaches
- Implementing gesture-enabled applications and controls

What is a gesture

A **gesture** is a human body motion or action that is intended to communicate a message, and these gestures let our application know what we want to do. In the context of the Kinect for Windows SDK, a gesture can be interpreted as a bodily action by which the player conveys some messages or information to the application. It is similar to the concept of typing on a keyboard, or drawing with the help of paper and a pad, or using touch on a touch-based device. In all these cases the input was meant for a particular purpose, which the device needs to understand and then provide the desired output by interacting with the application.

Similarly, a gesture acts as an input for a Kinect device. Based on this input, the application needs to perform certain functions. There is actually no physical connection between users and the device in case of gesture technology. Thus, this technology forms the backbone of the NUI for Kinect.

Approaches for gesture recognition

Recognizing gestures is one of the most interesting processes, and it involves different *calculations*, *algorithms*, *approaches*, and *methodologies*.

 The Kinect for Windows SDK does not provide any built-in APIs for gesture recognition. Therefore, it totally depends on the developers to define their own approaches and write their own logic to recognize and play around with gestures.

The approaches can be varied depending upon the gestures you choose and how you are applying them to your application, thus turning the gestures from simple to complex. We can classify the approaches for gesture recognition in the following ways:

- Basic gesture recognition
- An algorithmic approach
- Weighted-network approach
- Template-based approach

Choosing among the gesture recognition approaches totally depends on the developers and the requirements of the application. Sometimes, a gesture for an application could be simple, for example, just raising both hands, measuring distances between joints; or maybe some advanced gestures such as a swiping motion with both hands. On the other hand, it can be as complex as doing some jumping exercises or swinging a racket.

 Before proceeding with the development of any kind of gesture-related application, make sure that you are clear about the requirements, implications of the gesture, required accuracy, acceptance of processing delay, and the time frame given for development.

Refer to the following diagram to understand the overall high-level interaction happening between the users and the application.

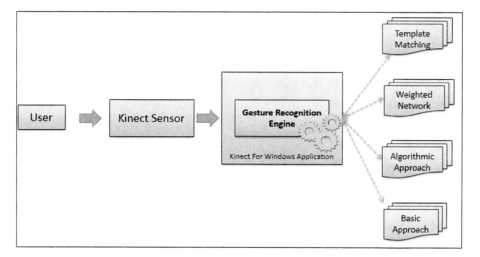

The user interacts with the Kinect sensor, which captures the user's actions and passes them to the application as a skeleton data stream. Gesture-based applications will have a component called the **gesture recognition engine**, which will recognize the gestures based on the user's actions and the approach defined in the application. On recognizing the gestures, the application can then perform the necessary action and notify the user. The recognition engine typically performs the following tasks:

- It accepts user actions in a form of skeleton data
- It matches the data points with predefined logic for a specific gesture
- It executes actions if the gesture is recognized
- It responds to the users

 It's essential to have a good understanding of *skeleton tracking with the Kinect for Windows SDK* to work with gestures. We have covered a detailed discussion on skeleton tracking in *Chapter 6, Human Skeleton Tracking*.

Basic gesture recognition

The fundamental approach of gesture recognition is to play around with the skeleton's joint points and apply basic logic to perform some action. Basic gesture detection depends on some pre-defined set of conditions, known as the **result set**. If the performed action is matched with the result set, we can say that the user has performed a certain gesture, otherwise not.

 Implementing the basic gestures is relatively easy and straightforward, however, this approach is the fundamental base of building any kind of gesture-controlled application.

In this section, we will learn a few approaches to recognize the basic gestures and will build an application that leverages the basic gesture recognition approach.

Gesture-detection technique

Gesture detection depends on the tracked joints of the human skeleton because we define the condition of gestures based on the joints. Before jumping into further details, let's have a quick look at the representation of skeleton joints.

Representing skeleton joints

Each skeleton joint is measured in a three-dimensional (X,Y,Z) plane. The X and Y coordinates specify the location of the joint in the plane, and the player facing the Kinect sensor is in the Z direction.

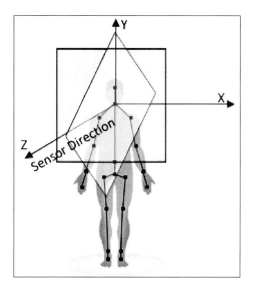

When a joint is represented with X, Y, and Z coordinates in a three-dimensional plane, the X and Y coordinates actually indicate the joint location in the plane, and Z indicates how far the joint is from the sensor. If the joints move from the right-hand side to the left-hand side or vice versa, the X axis of the joint will change. Similarly, for moving joints in the upwards or downwards direction, the value of the Y axis will change. Changes in the Z axis will reflect if the joints move forward or backwards from the sensor.

Calculations for the basic gestures can be done by either of the following:

- Calculating the distance between different joints
- Comparing the joints' positions and the deviation between the joints' positions

Calculating the distance between two joints

Skeleton data representation is three dimensional; however, before looking into the 3D coordinate plane, let's first consider the points in a 2D coordinate plane with only X and Y axis and see how to calculate the distance between two points.

In general mathematics, to calculate the distance between two points, we need to make use of the *Pythagorean Theorem*. The theorem states that:

> *For a right-angled triangle, the square of the hypotenuse is equal to the sum of the squares of the other two sides.*

Refer to the following diagram, which shows how the Pythagorean theorem can be applied to calculate the distance between two joints:

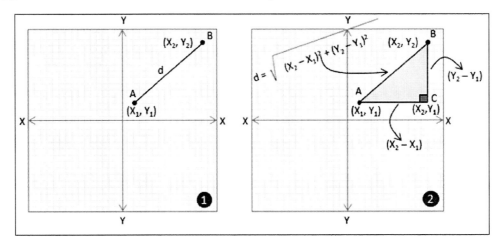

Consider that you have a point A (X1,Y1) and a point B (X2,Y2) in a two-dimensional coordinate plane. You want to calculate the distance (let's call it "d") between point A and point B (refer to the image marked as 1). To calculate the distance using the *Pythagorean theorem,* we have to first draw a parallel line to the X axis from point A and another line from point B, which is parallel to the Y axis. Consider both the lines meeting at point C (X2,Y1). As we know, the X and Y axes are perpendicular to each other; the triangle formed by the points A, B, and C is a *right-angled one* (refer to the image marked as 2).

Now, the value of "d", the distance between points A and B, will be the hypotenuse of the right-angled triangle that was formed by the points A, B, and C. The distance between A and B, now can be calculated using following formula:

$$d = \sqrt{(\text{distance of A,C})^2 + (\text{Distance of B,C})^2}$$

$$d = \sqrt{(X_2 - X_1)^2 + (Y_2 - Y_1)^2}$$

The *Pythagorean theorem* works well for three dimensional planes as well, and the distance between points (X1,Y1,Z1) and (X2,Y2,Z2) can be calculated by the following formula:

$$d = \sqrt{(X_2 - X_1)^2 + (Y_2 - Y_1)^2 + (Z_2 - Z_1)^2}$$

To articulate the discussion on joint distance calculation and put it in the form of code, you can write a method like the following:

```
private float GetJointDistance(Joint firstJoint, Joint secondJoint)
    {
        float distanceX = firstJoint.Position.X - secondJoint.
        Position.X;
        float distanceY = firstJoint.Position.Y - secondJoint.
        Position.Y;
        float distanceZ = firstJoint.Position.Z - secondJoint.
        Position.Z;
        return (float)Math.Sqrt(Math.Pow(distanceX, 2) + Math.
        Pow(distanceY, 2) + Math.Pow(distanceZ, 2));
    }
```

The `GetJointDistance()` method accepts two joints as arguments; it measures the distance from the joints for every axis in the coordinate system and finally returns the distance between the joints.

 `Math.Sqrt` returns the square root value of a specified number, and `Math.Pow` returns the specified power value of a given number.

For example, if you want to calculate the distance between the `HandLeft` and `HandRight` joints, the `GetJointDistance()` method can be invoked as follows:

```
Joint handRight = skeleton.Joints[JointType.HandRight];
Joint handLeft = skeleton.Joints[JointType.HandLeft];
if (handRight.TrackingState == JointTrackingState.Tracked &&
handLeft.TrackingState == JointTrackingState.Tracked)
{
this.GetJointDistance(handRight, handLeft);
}
```

The reason behind checking the `TrackingState` property of joints before calling the `GetJointDistance()` method is to just make sure the joints are tracked and have valid positions for calculating the distance.

It may be possible that Kinect is unable to see the joints and thus TrackingState will not be tracked. However it may also be possible that Kinect can infer the position. Thus you can also use the code based on `TrackingState == JointTrackingState.Inferred` and calculate the distance with one of the joints as tracked and the other as inferred.

Let's try to build a simple gesture application by calculating the distance between joints and see how it works.

Building a clapping-hands application

In this section we will build a clapping-hands application. The application will play a clapping sound whenever the joints of the right and the left hand are very close to each other.

Setting up the project

You can start building this application by creating a new WPF project in Visual Studio. Name the project **Clapping Hands**.

This application needs both the depth and skeleton streams to be enabled and captured. Once you are done with creating the project, you have to perform the following tasks:

- Identify and initialize the Kinect sensor
- Capture the depth stream data from the sensor and display the depth data to the application screen. (You can use color stream or IR data to display on the screen as well; for this application we will be using the depth data)
- Capture the skeleton stream data and detect the first tracked skeleton

By now, you are very familiar with all of the previously mentioned tasks, and can implement it very quickly. Once you are finished with the implementation of these tasks and run the **Clapping Hands** application, if you stand in front of the Kinect sensor, you should be able to view the depth stream data in your application as shown in next image:

Once a skeleton is tracked we can start measuring the distance between the joints. For the time being, leave this application in this state, and let's focus on how to implement the gesture recognizer engine for our application.

Implementing the gesture recognizer

The core of a gesture-enabled application is the gesture recognizer. The gesture recognizer will have a **Gesture Recognition Engine** that will accept the user data, validate the data against predefined conditions, and execute the action depending on the gesture.

First we will create a new `Class Library` project in Visual Studio and give the library a name, **GestureRecognizer**. The default template of the `Class Library` project gives us an empty `Class1.cs` class to start with. Right-click on `Class1.cs` and select **Delete** so that we can start everything from scratch. We can now right-click on the project file in the **Solution Explorer** window and select **Add New Item**. We will be adding four class files into our project as shown in the following screenshot:

Once done, add the `Microsoft.Kinect.dll` assembly as a reference from the **Add Project Reference** option of the project context menu. All the added classes have their own responsibilities, and together all of them will build the gesture recognizer. We will start with the `GestureType.cs` file.

Defining the types of gestures

For any gesture, we need a type to specify what kind of gesture it is. We used the `GestureType.cs` files to define an enumeration for the type of the gesture that is indicated by the `GestureType` enumeration. The definition looks like the following:

```
public enum GestureType
    {
        HandsClapping
    }
```

 You can extend the types of enumerations according to the types of gestures you want. For this demo, we will be using the `GestureType.HandsClapping` enumeration.

Defining the types of recognition results

Along with the type of gestures, every gesture action needs a result, which we can use to notify the user or help us to take further actions. The `RecognitionResult` enumeration defines the following result status for a basic gesture recognition:

```
public enum RecognitionResult
    {
        Unknown,
        Failed,
        Success
    }
```

Creating the event argument for the gesture

Using an event, a class can notify its client when something happens. We have defined `RecognitionResult` for gestures that could be either `Success`, `Failed`, or `Unknown`. Whenever a particular status of the gesture is identified, it's the responsibility of recognition engine to notify back to the application and the end user. The `EventArgs` class is a base for encapsulating any data that can be passed with the event. We have defined the `GestureEventArgs` class, which will hold the `RecognitionResult` event as an argument. This is shown in the following code block:

```
public class GestureEventArgs : EventArgs
    {
      public RecognitionResult Result { get ; internal set; }
        public GestureEventArgs(RecognitionResult result)
        {
            this.Result = result;
        }
    }
```

When a gesture is recognized or failed, the recognition engine will raise an event with GestureEventArgs, which will hold the result in it. You can surely customize it if you want to pass any additional information, message, and so on.

Wrapping up everything with the gesture recognition engine

So far, we have defined the following entities:

* Types of gestures in the GestureType enumeration
* Result of the recognition in the RecognitionResult enumeration
* GestureEventArgs; it holds the arguments for gesture related events

The final and most important part of building the Gesture Recognizer is to wrap up the above components into the GestureRecognitionEngine class and let the recognition engine know the source of the data and what to recognize.

In the GestureRecognitionEngine class we will be handling skeleton joints information, you have to refer to the Kinect assembly namespace in this class file. GestureRecognitionEngine will have a default constructor with two public properties for defining GestureType and assigning skeleton data from the application. This class will also have an event handler for handling the action when the gesture is recognized with GestureEventArgs. The class will look as follows:

```
public class GestureRecognitionEngine
{
    public GestureRecognitionEngine()
    {
    }
    public event EventHandler<GestureEventArgs> GestureRecognized;
    public event EventHandler<GestureEventArgs>
    GestureNotRecognized;

    public GestureType GestureType { get; set; }
    public Skeleton Skeleton { get; set; }
}
```

Add a new method called StartRecognize(), which will be invoked by the recognizer to start recognizing the gesture. The method checks for the GestureType property and calls the corresponding method to match the gesture. As shown in the following code block, the MatchHandClappingGesture() method is called to match the clapping gesture.

```
public void StartRecognize()
{
    switch (this.GestureType)
    {
        case GestureType.HandsClapping:
```

```
                          this.MatchHandClappingGesture(this.Skeleton);
                          break;
                    default:
                          break;
              }
        }
```

The `MatchHandClappingGesture()` method implements the logic or conditions for the clapping gesture. It accepts the skeleton and then calculates the distance between two hand joints as follows:

```
float previousDistance = 0.0f;

private void MatchHandClappingGesture(Skeleton skeleton)
        {
        if (skeleton == null)
        {
              return;
        }

        if (skeleton.Joints[JointType.HandRight].TrackingState ==
        JointTrackingState.Tracked && skeleton.Joints[JointType.
        HandLeft].TrackingState == JointTrackingState.Tracked)
            {
              float currentDistance = GetJointDistance(skeleton.
              Joints[JointType.HandRight], skeleton.
              Joints[JointType.HandLeft]);
              if (currentDistance < 0.1f && previousDistance > 0.1f)
              {
                  if (this.GestureRecognized != null)
                  {
                      this.GestureRecognized(this, new GestureEventA
                      rgs(RecognitionResult.Success));
                  }
              }

              previousDistance = currentDistance;
        }
        }
```

The method first validates the skeleton data for the `null` reference and then returns the control to the application if the skeleton data is `null`. Then it will check if both the `HandRight` and `HandLeft` joints are being tracked. If they are being tracked, it will calculate the distance by calling the `GetJointDistance` method. We have already walked through the piece of code for the `GetJointDistance()` method, and we will use the same code block in this class as well. The `currentDistance` variable holds the distance between the joints. Once the distance is calculated, we are checking the value with a predefined value (`0.1`, which means the joints are very close to each other).

We have used another variable called `previousDistance`, which keeps track of previously calculated distance between joints. This allows the program to only play the sound when the hands are very close to each other and not all the time. Also, the starting value given to `previousDistance` will ensure that even if your hands are together at the starting position, it won't be recognized.

Once the overall condition is satisfied, the `RecognitionEngine` class raises the `GestureRecognized` event handler with `RecognitionResult.Success`. As we did for `GestureRecognized`, you can put some condition where the gesture recognition can fail, and raise the `GestureNotRecognized` event handler.

If we put everything in the form of a class diagram, the overall `GestureRecognitionEngine` class will look like the following:

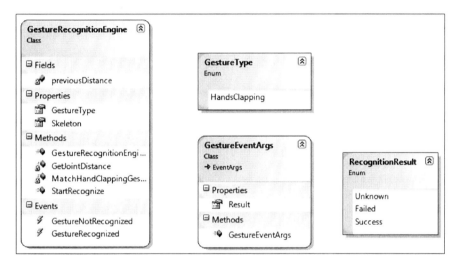

Now you should be able to build the class library. This will produce the `GestureRecognizer.dll` assembly. Our next job will be using the `GestureRecognizer.dll` assembly in our previously built `ClappingHands` application.

Plugging gestures into the application

Resume work with the `ClappingHands` application from the position we left it at. The `GestureRecognizer` library project generates an assembly `GestureRecognizer.dll` that can be used with any Kinect-based application for gesture recognition. Let's integrate this with our `ClappingHands` application and see how it works.

This can be done simply by performing the following steps:

1. Add the `GestureRecognizer.dll` assembly as a reference assembly to the `ClappingHands` application, from the **Add References** window.

2. Add the following namespace in the application:

   ```
   using GestureRecognizer;
   ```

3. Define a new class level variable for the `GestureRecognitionEngine` class, as follows:

   ```
   GestureRecognitionEngine recognitionEngine;
   ```

4. In the `MainWindow_Load` event handler, add the following line just after where you have enabled the skeleton and depth streams:

   ```
   recognitionEngine = new GestureRecognitionEngine();
   recognitionEngine.GestureType = GestureType.HandsClapping;
   recognitionEngine.GestureRecognized += new EventHandler<GestureEve
   ntArgs>(recognitionEngine_GestureRecognized);
   ```

   These lines of code are clear enough; we created an instance of the `GestureRecognitionEngine` class and then set the `GestureType` property and registered the `GestureRecognized` event handler. The definition for the `recognitionEngine_GestureRecognized` method looks like the following:

   ```
   void recognitionEngine_GestureRecognized(object sender,
   GestureEventArgs e)
           {
           kinectSoundPlayer.Play();
           }
   ```

   `kinectSoundPlayer` is an object of the `SoundPlayer` class with a specified sound location for the clapping sound.

   You can download the `Clap.wav` sound files from the book resource location.

5. As a final step, add the following highlighted lines at the end of `SkeletonFrameReady` event handler. This will pass the skeleton data for every frame to `recognitionEngine` and then call the `StartRecognize()` method to verify if the gesture condition is satisfied or not.

   ```
   void sensor_SkeletonFrameReady(object sender,
   SkeletonFrameReadyEventArgs e)
   ```

```
        {
            using (SkeletonFrame skeletonFrame =
            e.OpenSkeletonFrame())
            {
                . . .
                if (firstSkeleton == null)
                {
                    return;
                }

            recognitionEngine.Skeleton = firstSkeleton;
            recognitionEngine.StartRecognize();

            }
        }
```

Testing your application

That's all. Run your ClappingHands application in Visual Studio and then stand in front of the Kinect sensor and perform the gesture we generally make for clapping! You will be able to hear a clapping sound from the application. The following image shows the three different poses for the clapping gesture; when the user's action is similar to pose three, where both the hand joints are very close, the application will play the sound.

The working solution of the ClappingHands application is a sample project available in the ClapingHands directory of the resource location of this book.

In this exercise we have just measured the distance between joint points. We haven't consider the points where the joints are positioned. So, if you clap by putting your hands above your head or below your hips, the application will still play the clapping sound. When we think about making it more precise by identifying a clapping gesture only when the hands are in between the shoulder and hip joint, or not beyond the left or right shoulders, the algorithmic gestures come into play as we need to handle more complex logic than the current one.

A virtual rope workout application

Another simple but interesting solution you can build based on basic gesture recognition is a virtual rope workout application. Choose the joints for your exercise and see how much you can stretch them or how close you can bring them. You can also set a threshold value between two joints and try to reach your targeted distance.

The working solution of a *virtual rope workout* is available in the VirtualRopeWorkout directory of the resource location of this book as a sample project. Sample measurements of the exercises are shown in the following screenshot. You can choose from the options for your exercise type and try to reach the target you have specified, as shown:

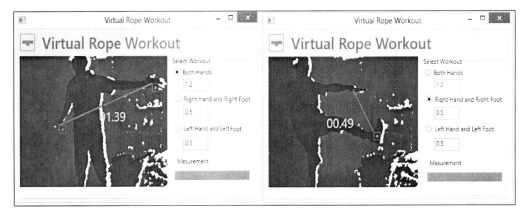

Calculating the distance between joints and performing the actions based on the value of the distance are examples of basic gestures to start with developing and understand how gestures work.

Understanding the positions of joints and calculating the distance are very important for gesture-enabled application development. This is true not only for the basic approaches, but also for algorithmic or other approaches. Overall, the understanding of basic gesture recognition will give you a base for further understanding and implementation of gesture-enabled applications.

Distance calculation will help you measure the distance between joints, but it does not say in which direction the joints are moving or where they are positioned. For example, the distance between the head and the right hand joint can be calculated in different directions, but it does not mean the hand is above the head or below it.

For this kind of calculation, we need to compare with the point-to-point data in the three-dimensional plan. We can come to some conclusions about joint movement and positions based on the change in the direction and values of coordinates. Let's have a look at how we can recognize the gesture of the hands raised up.

Hands-raised-above-head gesture recognition

There are several different types of gesture that can be identified for this scenario. They are as follows:

- Both hands are raised above the head
- Only the right hand is raised above the head
- Only the left hand is raised above the head
- Neither hand is raised above the head

The poses mentioned are shown in the following picture, where the user is facing the Kinect sensor:

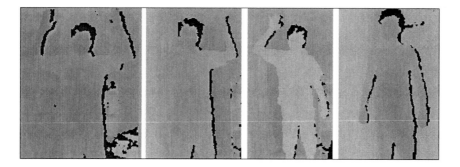

Overall, this gesture recognition involves three different joints; namely, the head, right hand, and left hand. We cannot recognize these gestures by just calculating distances between these three joints; rather, we need to measure the joint positions with respect to the coordinate plane.

So, let's consider that you want to detect if both the hands are raised above the head. Movement of the hands in either the upwards or the downwards direction will be based on the y axis of the coordinate plane. First of all, consider the y axis of the head joint position as the reference point for the other two hand joint positions, let's call them *target points*. Then you need to compare the values of both the targeted joints' y axis movement with respect to the *reference points*. Once the targeted value crosses the reference point, you can say that the gesture is identified. Additionally, you can use a threshold value with reference points to make sure that the targeted joints are crossing as expected.

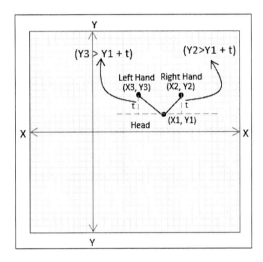

The following code block shows how we can check the gesture of both hands raised above the head:

```
float threshold = 0.3f;
if (skeleton.Joints[JointType.HandRight].Position.Y > skeleton.
Joints[JointType.Head].Position.Y + threshold
            && skeleton.Joints[JointType.HandLeft].Position.Y >
skeleton.Joints[JointType.Head].Position.Y + threshold)
        {
            if (this.GestureRecognized != null)
            {
                this.GestureRecognized(this, new GestureEventArgs
                (RecognitionResult.Success));
            }
        }
```

In the code block we just saw, the first part of the condition checks if the right hand is above the head joint and the second part of the head joint checks if the left hand is above the head. When both are true at the same time, the gesture recognition engine raises a `GestureRecognzied` event.

 Recognizing gestures by comparing different joint positions is really useful and is at the core of algorithmic gesture recognition.

Steps to recognize basic gestures

Gesture recognition based on a calculation between or among joints is a pattern that is implemented using calculation. Yes, overall implementation of gestures is based on similar patterns where you have to use your own logic based on the gesture definitions. Finally, match those patterns based on the joints' information. The following diagram illustrates the overall steps for identifying basic gestures:

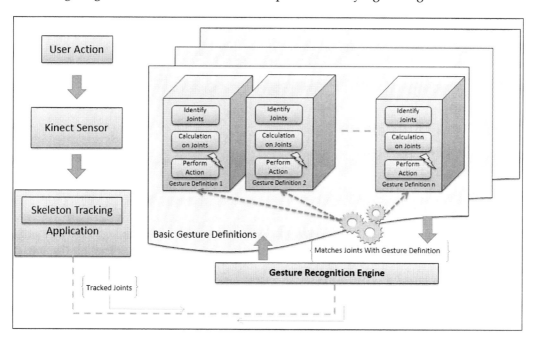

Algorithmic gesture recognition

Algorithmic gesture recognition is built on top of basic gesture recognition, hence the understanding of basic gesture recognition is essential for going ahead with the algorithmic approach. The algorithmic approach uses a set of predefined conditions and parameters to detect and validate a gesture against each of them. With the algorithmic approach, we basically validate a gesture as it is being performed, by ensuring the start points, constraints, parameters, and the end points are always valid.

Which gestures can be considered as algorithmic

You can consider the gestures to be measured by an algorithmic approach when gestures need to be validated against multiple conditions, multiple joints are involved, and where you need to measure the multiple states of gesture. If your application needs all the conditions to be validated and measured based on time or frames, you should go ahead with the algorithmic approach. So, before you go ahead and start implementing, first consider the different boundary conditions, entry and exit criteria for the gestures, and validation states. In general, most of the applications follow the algorithm for regular gesture implementation. Following are a few example gestures which can be considered as algorithmic:

- Hand moving in the same direction
- A swipe to the right or the left
- Zooming in and out
- Waving hands

From the gesture types mentioned, you can understand how the approach could be different from basic gesture detection. The algorithmic approach not only recognizes the gestures, but it also tracks if the gesture is performed correctly or not. Though they are very closely related to each other, we can even say that all the basic approaches are nothing but a smaller set of algorithmic approaches, whereas the algorithmic gestures are more advanced and are calculated with various conditions and parameters.

To summarize, choose the algorithmic approach when the application needs to play around a series of joints. This involves a number of calculations for each and every frame with start criteria, validation of different states, and end criteria.

Understanding the algorithmic gesture detection approach

To help you understand, lets articulate the components that are required for algorithmic gesture recognition in a list:

- Start
- Condition
- Validation
- Finish

To start with any gesture, there will always be an initial position — we call it the "start" position. This is the *entry point* for any gesture and has to be validated before validating other positions. Once the start position is validated and the gesture is being performed by the end user, every single frame has to be validated under the predefined "condition" for the particular gesture types. If any of these conditions fail to satisfy during the complete execution cycle, we can stop the gesture tracking and wait for it to start again. Finally, there should be a condition that triggers the end of the gesture and "validates" the final position, which indicates that gesture recognition is "finished".

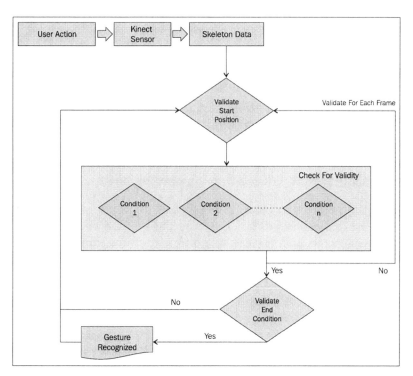

For example, consider you need to perform a `SwipeToLeft` gesture using your right hand. The following images show us the steps for the same, where the user is facing the Kinect sensor:

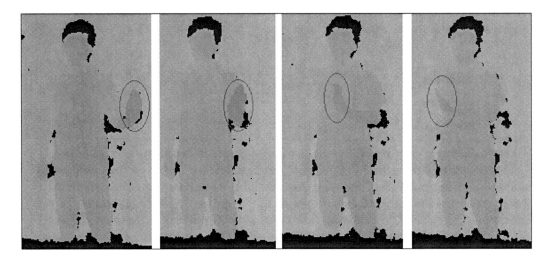

To validate this gesture, you need to perform the following steps very closely:

1. Before starting, *the left hand* joint should be below the left *elbow* and the *spine* joint. Also, the right hand joint should be below the right *shoulder* joint and above the right elbow joint.

2. The user should move the hand from right to left while maintaining the right hand and left hand joint positions.

3. This condition needs to be validated for a couple of predefined frames, and should result in success every time it checks if the hand is moving to the left.

4. After a specific number of frames when the gesture reaches to validate the last condition, it will check if the distance between the right hand joint and the left shoulder has reduced from the starting point.

By considering the preceding points for every skeleton frame, we can determine if a `SwipeToLeft` gesture has been detected or not. The validation should be performed for each and every frame, and you can add a time or frame number to validate.

Implementing an algorithmic gesture

In this section we will learn how to implement the gesture recognition engine by following the earlier approaches. We will be extending the `GestureRecognizer` class library developed earlier. Overall project structures for the new `GestureRecognizer` class library are given in the following screenshot:

In the earlier implementations we passed the `GestureType` enumeration to the gesture recognizer engine to inform it what we need to detect. In this implementation we rather pass the types, the gesture recognizer will return the type of gesture that has been detected. This is because we will have multiple `GestureType` enumerations in these scenarios.

Adding gesture types

Open the `GestureType.cs` file from the **Solution Explorer** and define the following types of gestures.

```
public enum GestureType
    {
        SwipeToRight,
        SwipeToLeft,
        ZoomIn,
        ZoomOut
    }
```

Extending the Event argument

Using Events, the recognition engines can notify the subscriber of events that occur. We have already used the RecognitionResult class for the gesture recognition engine, which would result in either Success, Failed, or Unknown. The EventArgs class is the base class for encapsulating any data that can be passed with an event. The following code block defines the GestureEventArgs class that will hold the RecognitionResult class as well the GestureType property, as an argument:

```
public class GestureEventArgs : EventArgs
    {
      public RecognitionResult Result { get ; internal set; }
      public GestureType GestureType { get; internal set; }

      public GestureEventArgs(RecognitionResult result,
      GestureType type)
        {
            this.Result = result;
            this.GestureType = type;
        }
    }
```

When a gesture is recognized, the recognition engine will raise an event with GestureEventArgs, which will hold the RecognitionResult class as well as the GestureType property.

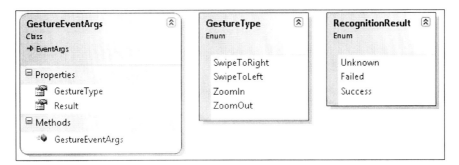

Adding a GestureHelper class

We can add a new class named GestureHelper.cs. The GestureHelper.cs class works as a utility class that contains reusable methods. At this time, we have placed the GetJointDistance() method as a public static method, which has been called to calculate the distance between joints in several places for gesture recognition. Earlier, we had this method inside the GestureRecognitionEngine class; you have to just move the same method inside the GestureHelper.cs class.

Defining the GestureBase class

Now we will create a `GestureBase` class that will contain the basic structure for all the gestures. All the gesture classes will implement the `GestureBase` class to validate the gestures. The GestureBase class is shown in the following code block:

```
public abstract class GestureBase
{
    public GestureBase(GestureType type)
    {
        this.CurrentFrameCount = 0;
        this.GestureType = type;
    }

    public bool IsRecognitionStarted { get; set; }

    private int CurrentFrameCount { get; set; }

    public GestureType GestureType { get; set; }

    protected virtual int MaximumNumberOfFrameToProcess { get {
    return 15; } }

    public long GestureTimeStamp { get; set; }

    protected abstract bool ValidateGestureStartCondition
    (Skeleton skeleton);

    protected abstract bool ValidateGestureEndCondition
    (Skeleton skeleton);


    protected abstract bool ValidateBaseCondition
    (Skeleton skeleton);

    protected abstract bool IsGestureValid(Skeleton skeleton);
    public virtual bool CheckForGesture(Skeleton skeleton)
    {
        if (this.IsRecognitionStarted == false)
        {
            if (this.ValidateGestureStartCondition(skeleton))
            {
                this.IsRecognitionStarted = true;
                this.CurrentFrameCount = 0;
            }
        }
```

```
            }
            else
            {
                if (this.CurrentFrameCount == this.
                MaximumNumberOfFrameToProcess)
                {
                    this.IsRecognitionStarted = false;
                    if (ValidateBaseCondition(skeleton) &&
                    ValidateGestureEndCondition(skeleton))
                    {
                        return true;
                    }
                }

                this.CurrentFrameCount++;
                if (!IsGestureValid(skeleton) && !
                ValidateBaseCondition(skeleton))
                {
                    this.IsRecognitionStarted = false;
                }
            }

            return false;
        }

    }
```

The constructor of the GestureBase class accepts the GestureType property as the parameter and sets it into the class-level public property named GestureType. The abstract base class we just saw has a CheckForGesture() method that accepts the skeleton data and returns a Boolean value to indicate if the gesture was recognized or not.

First, the ValidateGestureStartCondition() method is called to check if the gesture satisfies the start condition. Once the start condition is validated, it will set IsRecognitionStarted to true and set the CurrentFrameCount count to 0. By setting IsRecognitionStarted to true, it indicates that the start position is validated and gesture recognition is in progress. If any further condition fails to recognize the gesture, IsRecognitionStarted will be set to false so that recognition will again start validating the start position.

Once the start position is validated, for all other congestive frames it will call the `ValidateBaseCondition()` and `IsGestureValid()` methods until the frame count reaches the number specified as `MaximumNumberOfFrameToProcess`. The default value of `MaximumNumberOfFrameToProcess` is set to `15`, which means the recognition will validate the stability of the gesture for 15 frames. The `IsGestureValid()` method will validate if the user is still performing the action and moving to the right.

The `ValidateBaseCondition()` method will verify if the user is performing the action in the right way. For example, for the `SwipeToLeftGesture` class, the `IsGestureValid()` method will verify if the hand is moving from the right-to-left direction and the distance between the right hand joint and the left shoulder is decreasing. Whereas, the `ValidateBaseCondition()` method will check if the right hand position is between the shoulder and the spine joint.

Finally, it will validate the final condition by calling the `ValidateGestureEndCondition()` method; also, it will validate the base condition by calling the `ValidateBaseCondition()` method. If the `ValidateGestureEndCondition()` method returns a `true` value, this means the current gesture satisfies all the predefined conditions and the `CheckForGesture()` method will return `true`. At any time, if the condition fails, the `CheckForGesture()` method will return `false` and will reset the gesture by initializing the values.

Once the base gesture class is ready, we can implement any types of gesture that are valid under the given circumstance and can be implemented. For example, here we will follow the example of implementing `SwipeToLeftGesture` using the right hand.

Implementing the SwipeToLeftGesture class

The following code block is a concrete implementation of the `GestureBase` class for a `SwipeToLeftGesture` class:

```
public class SwipeToLeftGesture : GestureBase
{
    public SwipeToLeftGesture() :
    base(GestureType.SwipeToLeft) { }
    private SkeletonPoint validatePosition;
    private SkeletonPoint startingPostion;
    private float shoulderDiff;
    protected override bool
    ValidateGestureStartCondition(Skeleton skeleton)
    {
    // return true if start condition is valid else return false

    }
    protected override bool IsGestureValid(Skeleton
```

```
skeletonData)
{
// return true if current position of gesture is still valid
else return false
}

protected override bool
ValidateGestureEndCondition(Skeleton skeleton)
{
// return true if end condition is valid else return false
}

protected override bool ValidateBaseCondition(Skeleton
skeleton)
{
// return true if base condition is valid else return false
{
}
```

The `SwipeToLeftGesture` class we just saw inherits from the `GestureBase` class and implements all the abstract methods defined in the base class for gesture recognition. The very first thing you notice is the constructor of the `SwipeToLeftGesture` class, where we have set the `GestureType` property to `SwipeToLeft`. This will let our base class know that the current recognition is set for `SwipeToLeft`.

 We haven't given the code block for each and every condition for the validating methods. The conditions for every method will be very logical, as we discussed in the *Understanding algorithmic approach section*. You can get the complete workable solution downloaded from the book's resource location.

Adding the ZoomIn, ZoomOut, and SwipeToRight gesture classes

Similar to the `SwipeToLeftGesture` class, we will have three other classes, namely `SwipeToRight`, `ZoomIn`, and `ZoomOut`, and all of them are inherited from the `GestureBase` base class and implement all the methods, as shown in the following diagram:

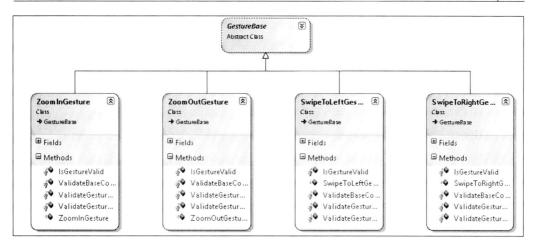

If you want to add any other type of gesture, you just have to define the type of gesture in the `GestureType` enumeration, and implement a new class that derives from `GestureBase`. Finally, write the conditional logic for validating the gesture's start, end, and other conditions.

So far we have defined the `GestureType`, `RecognitionResult`, `GestureEventArgs`, and `GestureHelper` classes, and finally we have implemented different gesture classes derived from the `GestureBase` base class.

Now we need to inject the created gesture class's information to `GestureRecognitionEngine` so that `GestureRecognitionEngine` takes input from the application and instantiates the process of recognition.

Implementing the GestureRecognitionEngine class

Within the `RecognitionEngine` class (`RecognitionEngine.cs`), first remove all the existing code that we have written during the basic gesture recognition and just keep the namespaces.

Add the following class-level member in the class:

```
int SkipFramesAfterGestureIsDetected = 0;
public event EventHandler<GestureEventArgs> GestureRecognized;
public GestureType GestureType { get; set; }

public Skeleton Skeleton { get; set; }
```

Then, create a `List` class of the `GestureBase` class and name it `gestureCollection` to hold lists of different gesture classes:

```
private List< GestureBase > gestureCollection = null;
```

Add a new method, `InitilizeGesture()`, to add all the gestures into `gestureCollection` one by one as shown in the following code block:

```
private void InitilizeGesture()
    {
        this.gestureCollection = new List<GestureBase>();
        this.gestureCollection.Add(new ZoomInGesture());
        this.gestureCollection.Add(new ZoomOutGesture());
        this.gestureCollection.Add(new SwipeToRightGesture());
        this.gestureCollection.Add(new SwipeToLeftGesture());
    }
```

The initialization of all the gestures needs to be done when the application instantiates the `GestureRecognitionEngine` class. This can be done by calling the `InitilizeGesture()` method from the constructor of the `GestureRecognitionEngine` class, as shown in following code block:

```
public GestureRecognitionEngine()
    {
        this.InitilizeGesture();
    }
```

So, when the `GestureRecognitionEngine` class instantiates, the recognition engine will create a list of specified gestures and store them into `gestureCollection`.

The `StartRecognize()` method serves the following two purposes:

- Skips some specified frames after gesture detection
- Invokes the `CheckForGesture()` method for individual gestures

The `StartRecognize()` method is defined as follows:

```
public void StartRecognize()
    {
        if (this.IsGestureDetected)
        {
        while (this.SkipFramesAfterGestureIsDetected <= 30)
            {
                this.SkipFramesAfterGestureIsDetected++;
            }
            this.RestGesture();
            return;
```

```
        }

        foreach (var item in this.gestureCollection)
        {
            if (item.CheckForGesture(this.Skeleton))
            {
                if (this.GestureRecognized != null)
                {
                    this.GestureRecognized(this, new GestureEventA
                    rgs(RecognitionResult.Success, item.
                    GestureType));
                    this.IsGestureDetected = true;
                }

            }
        }
    }
```

This method first checks if any gesture is recognized using the IsGestureDetected property. If the value of IsGestureDetected is true, the method will wait for 30 frames to skip and then will reset the initialization of gestureCollection. This is done to avoid the overlapping of gestures. The next part of the method, which is highlighted, iterates through gestureCollection and calls the CheckForGesture() method by passing the Skeleton data as the argument. Once the gesture is recognized, the CheckForGesture() method returns a true, and in the next statement the GestureRecognized event will be raised with RecognitionResult set as successful and the GestureType property as a GestureType of the current element of gestureCollection.

The following is the code block for resetting the gestures:

```
private void RestGesture()
    {
        this.gestureCollection = null;
        this.InitilizeGesture();
        this.SkipFramesAfterGestureIsDetected = 0;
        this.IsGestureDetected = false;
    }
```

This block of code just reinitializes gestureCollection and resets the class member to the initial state.

Using the GestureRecognitionEngine class

We are done with the implementation of GestureRecognitionEngine, and now it's time to plug it into our applications. The use of GestureRecognitionEngine is similar to that which we used for basic gesture recognition. The only different here is that we have a collection of gestures and instead of passing GestureType to the GestureRecognitionEngine when a gesture is recognized, the recognition engine returns back the recognized gesture type with the GestureEventArgs argument. The following steps show how to use the recognizer in any Kinect application where you want to use this gesture recognizer:

1. Add GestureRecognizer.dll as a reference assembly application from the **Add References** dialog window.

2. Add the following namespace in the application:

   ```
   using GestureRecognizer;
   ```

3. Define a new class-level variable for the GestureRecognitionEngine class, as shown:

   ```
   GestureRecognitionEngine recognitionEngine;
   ```

4. Add the following code snippet to instantiate the GestureRecognitionEngine class and register the event:

   ```
   recognitionEngine = new GestureRecognitionEngine();
   recognitionEngine.GestureRecognized += new EventHandler<GestureEventArgs>(recognitionEngine_GestureRecognized);
   ```

   The lines of code we just saw are clear enough; we created an instance of the GestureRecognitionEngine class and registered the GestureRecognized event handler. The definition for the recognitionEngine_GestureRecognized() event handler is as follows:

   ```
   void recognitionEngine_GestureRecognized(object sender,
   GestureEventArgs e)
       {
           MessageBox.Show(e.GestureType.ToString());
       }
   ```

   Here we are just showing the types of the recognized gestures using a message box. For the actual implementation, you can call for specific actions depending on the types of gestures it recognizes.

5. As the final step, add the following highlighted lines of code at the end of the SkeletonFrameReady event handler. This will pass the skeleton data for every frame to recognitionEngine and then call the StartRecognize() method to verify if the gesture condition is satisfied or not. The code block is as follows:

```
void sensor_SkeletonFrameReady(object sender,
SkeletonFrameReadyEventArgs e)
        {
            using (SkeletonFrame skeletonFrame =
            e.OpenSkeletonFrame())
            {
                . . .
                // getting  skeleton code goes here
                if (firstSkeleton == null)
                {
                    return;
                }

                recognitionEngine.Skeleton = firstSkeleton;
                recognitionEngine.StartRecognize();

            }
        }
```

If you run the application, and perform the necessary actions that recognize these gestures, your application will show a message box with the type of the recognized gesture.

A demo application

The following screenshot shows a **Gesture Detector** application. One side of the application will show us the skeleton with all the tracked joints, and on the other side, it will show us the recognized gestures from the user's actions:

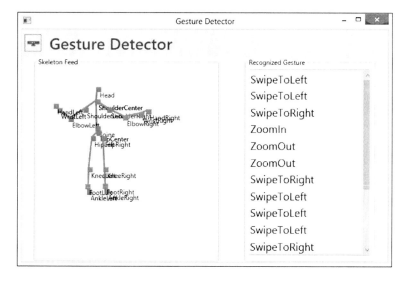

The working solution of the *gesture detector* is a sample project available in the `GestureDetector` folder of the resource location for this book. This application leverages the algorithmic gesture recognition engine we just built, and can detect four types of specified gestures. You will also be able to view the skeleton joints within this application.

Making it more flexible

To take another granular look into the algorithmic gesture recognition approach, and to simplify the implementation, we can further break down the complete *condition block* into multiple smaller modules, and call it them "*phases*". Each phase of a gesture will have its own *result set* or *conditions* that measure the success or failure of the phase. The result of the phases will be dependent on each other, which means recognition will move to the next phase if the previous phase result was passed. It could also happen that all the conditions in a phase are not satisfied. This does not always mean that the phase has failed, it could be that the user is "*on hold*" or "*in progress*" on that particular position for sometime. We can mark the state of the phase as pause and wait for the next action for a few frames. These phases can communicate with one another using *Inter Phase Communication*, to share the information, result, and data with each other. The next screenshot shows how we can divide the complete Gesture Recognition Phase into multiple phases and validate the gestures against each phase:

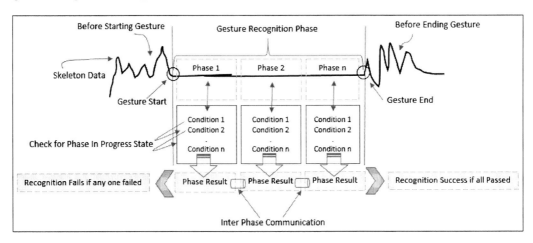

Weighted network gesture recognition

Gesture detection using weighted networks is one of the advanced approaches in gesture detection. In this section we will have a quick walkthrough about this approach and we will see how this works, rather than doing an actual implementation. We have seen most of the measurements of gestures are done on the basis of skeleton joint movements, and for all the earlier cases, joints were clearly visible to the sensors (which we have checked with the joints-tracking state). On the other hand, can we just say that gesture detection of joints can be done only for the tracked joints?

Think about some body movements that are very dynamic in nature. For example, bending exercises (*forward, sideways*) where we initially start with a straight position, then slowly raise our hands forward, and try to touch our toes (*forward bending*) or standing upright with legs apart, keeping one hand on the waist and raising the other hand while trying to bend sideways (*sideways bending*). In both these cases, body movements are dynamic where every time a user cannot reach to same position; moreover, every user can't do it perfectly if we measure with the actual hands and legs joint positions. There is also a good chance of joints overlapping or it could also happen that some of the joints are *going out of Kinect's viewable range*.

Let's consider one more example, the jump exercise. At first look, it appears to be one of the simplest gesture recognition approaches, but that isn't the case. Similar to bending exercises, a jumping exercise can be varied based on the way a user jumps (normal jump, rope workout, high jump, and so on), and based on the movement it could again cause a visibility issue of joints as every user can do it in different ways.

If you want to implement the mentioned exercises with gestures, you really need to think hard on it. This is because they are not straightforward approaches and we can only provide some calculations on joints. Thus, we need some alternative approach that can say to what degree the users are performing the exercise correctly, rather than just saying yes or no. In technical terms, we need a flexible data structure representation that can calculate the probabilities and can reach a decision based on the user's inputs. One of the best approaches to solve this kind of problem with computer engineering is a **Neural network**.

What is a neural network

Neural networks are a set of nodes (called *neurons*) connected with each other as a group. This is similar to the human brain and the synopsis they form. The concept of the neural network came from *human neurons,* and is mostly used for biological neural networks. In Computer Science, we use it as a machine-learning construct that has an input layer (set of input nodes / neurons) and an output layer (set of output nodes / neurons). The input and output layers are connected somewhere in between. This layer is called the *hidden* or *abstract* layer, which has another set of decision-making nodes. The abstract layer consists of another set of nodes (*decision maker*) that are connected with each other, and on combining their decisions a result can be given.

The following diagram shows a very basic neural network with two input nodes (I1 and I2) and one output node (O1). The intermediate layer is an abstract layer with a set of smaller nodes that are connected together. These smaller nodes work as the decision makers; based on the input provided by I1 and I2, the output O1 will be received. This is similar to the nature of neurons in the human brain.

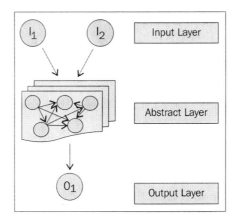

> For more about neural networks, visit
> http://en.wikipedia.org/wiki/Neural_network.

Gesture recognition with neural networks

Gesture detection on a neural network is always based on the probability ratio rather than the exact values. The output would say that the user performed x percent of the exercise correctly and did not perform y percent correctly. Based on this ratio, we can make a decision.

Each node within the network is an algorithm to evaluate small elements of a gesture or movement. Output of one node (action result) will decide which nodes to move next; thus, the sequence flow in this approach will never be the same. Nodes are connected via a link, and each link has an associated value called *weight* (In the following diagram, the weight of the lines denotes the weight of the link). This weight value defines that some links are more important than the others. The purpose of having weights with each of the nodes is to make decisions more accurate. Based on the weight value measured, gestures move on to next step. Higher weight always gets higher preference. At the end of the complete network, we have a resultant calculation called calculated output for the user input action. This is matched with the predefined expected output or the *best-values output* for the detected gesture. As these results are calculated based on probability, it's very common that the result can never be exactly the same and they will have at least some difference or error. If the difference is within a predefined boundary (threshold), the result will be accepted, otherwise the network will perform the operation repeatedly to produce correct or very close gesture-action results.

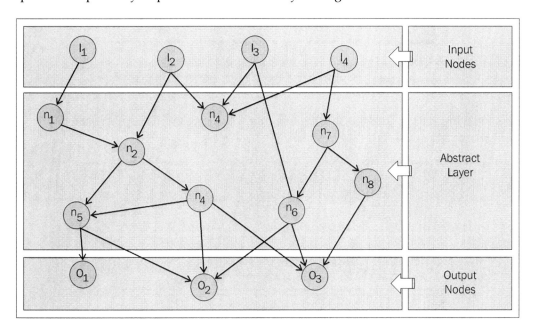

Jump tracking with a neural network – an example

Let's quickly discuss the example of *jump tracking* and see how the weighted network can help to design such kinds of gestures. The following diagram shows us the basic illustration of a jump exercise, which shows two postures of a jump:

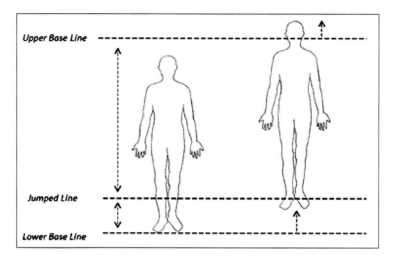

To start with, we can just check if the head joint has crossed the upper base line, and we can draw a weighted graph like the following:

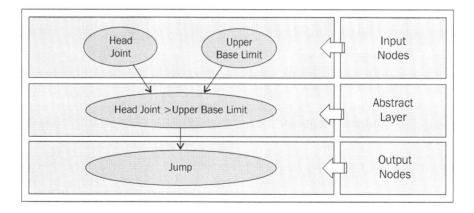

We discussed the different positions of the jump that can cause problems during tracking and measurement. Refer to the following screenshot, which shows the different postures during the jump and some of the cases when the human body parts are not within Kinect's view area:

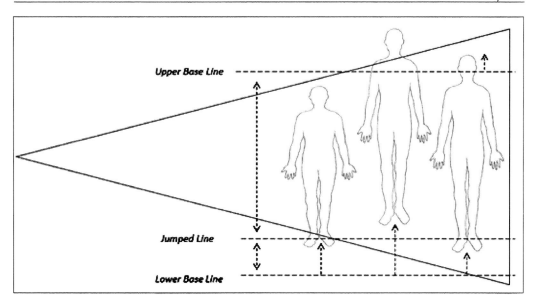

To overcome these kinds of problems, our data graph has to be intelligent enough based on what decisions we take, and whether the user performs the jump operation or not. Typically, the neural network for the jump exercise would look like the following diagram. The weight between the nodes represents the weighted value of that connection. Each node represents a small set of algorithms within the abstract layer.

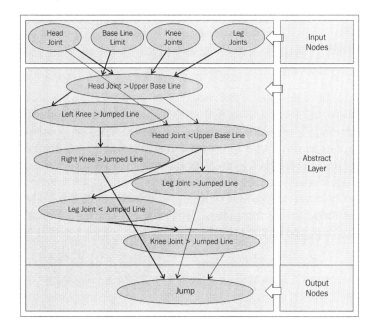

This is just an example of gesture detection using the weighted network approach. While the neural network approach looks very interesting and accurate, building them is not a normal task for the majority of application developers. The implementation of the neural network needs good understanding of fuzzy logic and artificial intelligence, and it is very hard to debug.

Overall, this approach is complex, and it needs more study for implementation. This involves a number of inputs and parameters and they can grow with each and every outcome from every single node. Use it only when gestures are really complex and can change based on user movements or there is a chance that all users cannot perform similar steps.

Template-based gesture recognition

Template-based gesture recognition is also known as pattern-based gestures. This gesture can potentially be used when we are not sure about how robust the recognition is. With this recognition system, the gesture-recognition engine matches the user movements with predefined gestures, and measures how correctly it was being performed. In this approach, gestures are first recorded and stored into a location in the normal way. While matching the gestures, the same set of user actions are taken as input parameters and validated against the stored data. The final result is driven from a probability ratio by matching the data between the existing data set and the data set that is currently being performed. Overall, the template-based recognition system involves the following phases:

- Template creation
- Gesture tracking
- Template matching

The first phase of the template-based recognition system is *template creation*. In this phase, gestures are recorded and stored with joints information along with the metadata. The metadata contains the gesture's name, types of gestures, time interval for the gestures, minimum and maximum duration, and so on. The second phase is all about *gesture tracking* when the user actually performs the actions in front of the sensor and the application passes the information to the gesture recognizer. When the gesture ends, we can compare it with a predefined set of templates to find if the gesture is one of those stored templates. This phase is known as *template matching*. These phases are depicted in the following diagram:

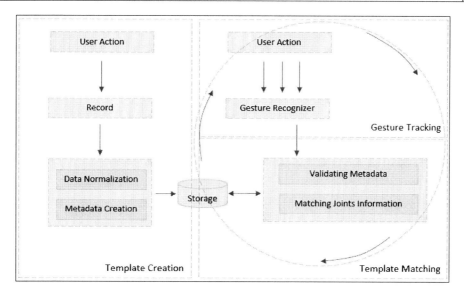

As shown in the preceding diagram, gesture tracking and template matching work side-by-side. While the user is actually performing the action, data can be matched multiple times to see if it is matching correctly. As a data storage, we can use any database, XML, or flat files. You can also choose your own algorithm to match the data from the store location; because most of the times we will get the exact result on match for all the points; rather if we do not get matching results we prefer the nearest values for matching.

Building gesture-enabled controls

Gesture-enabled control is one of the common components of gesture-enabled applications. The controls that we generally use for any applications such as button control and checkbox control do not have built-in support for gestures. The interaction medium for gestures is different than a regular mouse or keyboard. So, to build an application that needs user interaction and needs to execute some events such as *clicking on a button* or *selecting a checkbox* using gestures, we either need to create custom controls or need to hook up the gesture information within existing controls. Following are the tasks involved in building gesture-enabled controls:

- Making a hand cursor
- Identifying the objects
- Enabling actions for objects

Making a hand cursor

The very first task for any gesture-enabled application is to build the *hand cursor*, which will control the application just as a mouse does for any other application. Building the hand cursor is relatively easy, where we just need to map the hand movements with the application elements such as image control.

> In *Chapter 6, Human Skeleton Tracking*, in the *Tracking your hand* section, we have already seen how to track a hand and map it using image control.

In addition to getting the hand movement on the application screen, we need the position of the cursor.

Getting the hand-cursor point

In the application, we need the cursor point on every move so that we can find out the exact position of the screen where the cursor currently is. You can use the following block of code to find out the center position of the cursor on the screen:

```
public  CursorPoint GetCursorPoint()
        {
        Point elementTopLeft = this.PointToScreen(new Point());
        double centerX = elementTopLeft.X + (this.ActualWidth / 2);
        double centerY = elementTopLeft.Y + (this.ActualHeight / 2);
        return new CursorPoint { X = centerX, Y = centerY };
        }
```

The `GetCursorPoint()` method returns the cursor position by calculating the center point of the hand cursor object as the variables of the `CursorPoint` class.

The `CursorPoint` class is defined as below:

```
public class CursorPoint
    {
        public double X { get; set; }
        public double Y { get; set; }
    }
```

> `PointToScreen()` is the method that returns the screen coordinates of the controls, which will be nothing but the top-left positions of the control.

Identifying the objects

The next task, immediately after making the hand cursor, will be the interaction of other objects of your application using that hand cursor. For example, you have a button in your application and you want to click on it using the hand cursor. The hand cursor is a free floating object that is moving based on the hand joints. It does not have any clue about the other controls present in your application, where they are, and how to interact with them. So, the very first thing you have to understand is how the hand cursor knows where the objects are placed and with whom it should interact:

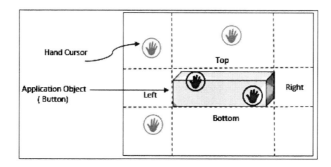

The preceding image illustrates how the hand cursor can identify the object. The complete backend logic is based on the coordinate system. The hand cursor will have a position that will keep changing with every skeleton frame. You will get the position of the hand cursor as `CusrsorPoint` by calling the `GetCursorPoint()` method of the `HandCusror` class.

In a similar way, we can also get the position of the other objects that are used in the application. If we consider that we have a button control, we can simply write an `Extension` method for the `Button` class that will return the `ButtonPostion` class, a custom class that returns the button's `Left`, `Right`, `Top`, and `Bottom` positions. We can do this using the following code block:

```
public static class ButtonExtension
    {
        public static ButtonPosition GetPosition(this Button button)
        {
        Point buttonPosition = button.PointToScreen(new Point());
        return new ButtonPosition { Left = buttonPosition.X,
        Right = buttonPosition.X + button.ActualWidth,
        Top = buttonPosition.Y,
        Bottom = buttonPosition.Y + button.Height };
        }
    }
```

So, for any `Button` object, if you call the `button.GetPosition()` method, it will return the `ButtonPosition` class, which is defined as follows:

```
public class ButtonPosition
    {
        public double Left { get; set; }
        public double Right { get; set; }
        public double Top { get; set; }
        public double Bottom { get; set; }
    }
```

By now you have the center coordinates for the cursor and the boundary range for the button control. From these two set of values you can easily find out if the cursor position falls within the button control, by using the following conditional block:

```
if ((centerX < buttonRange.Left || centerX > buttonRange.Right)
            || (centerY < buttonRange.Top || centerY >
            buttonRange.Bottom))
        {
         // Hand cursor not in button position
        }
        else
        {
            //Hand cursor with in button position
        }
```

You have to calculate the positions for the cursor and the buttons for each and every skeleton frame, and correspondingly validate the earlier conditions to see if the hand cursor is within the range of the objects or not.

Another alternative approach that you can use to find out if the coordinate values fall within the rendered contents is *Hit Testing in the Visual Layer*. Refer to this URL for more information on Hit Testing:

`http://msdn.microsoft.com/en-us/library/ms752097.aspx`

Enabling action for the objects

Until now we have identified the object on the screen using the hand cursor. The next task for us will be executing some actions from the object. We could have easily raised an event when the cursor was within the button position range, but that will not provide a good end user experience. This is because users can move the cursor over multiple objects and finally any of them can be chosen for an action. Now the question is how or when you will fire an event such as a click event. We need to provide something to the user so that they can hold on for some time and wait till the action is complete. This will make sure the user selects what they really want and that the touch was intended. While waiting, we can show a visual indicator to the end user depicting what action they are currently performing, and after a specific time, if the cursor position is still in the valid range, execute the respective action. The complete process of action execution can be classified into the following entities:

- Action Entry
- Action Exit
- Action Completed
- Action Not Started
- Action Status

The following diagram shows the process flow that we need to follow to execute an action:

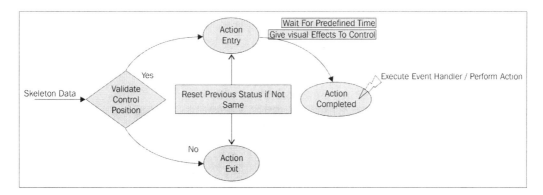

By default, the state will be **Action Not Started**; once the cursor position is identified within the range of objects, the **Action Entry** phase will start. This will validate for a predefined time to check if the cursor is still within range of the object. During this time the application can provide a visual feedback to the end user, and once the time period is over the application fires the intended event by declaring the state as **Action Completed**. If the cursor loses its focus from the object after **Action Entry** or **Validate Control Position**, the state will be called as **Action Exit**. This will reset the timer as well.

So, if we put this in the form of code and consider `ActionEntry` and `ActionExit` as methods, they can be called in the following way:

```
if ((centerX < buttonRange.Left || centerX > buttonRange.Right)
            || centerY < buttonRange.Top || centerY >
            buttonRange.Bottom)
        {
         ActionExit();
        }
        else
        {
         ActionEntry()
        }
```

You can use any approach to display visual feedback to the user. One of the common is using WPF's `DoubleAnimation` class, because using this animation you can specify the start and end values of the animation; when the animation is complete, it fires a `Completed` event. The image below shows a running screenshot of the **Gesture Enabled KinectCam** application. Which changes the Kinect color stream using gesture-enabled button control:

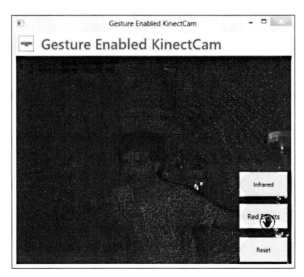

The working solution for **Gestured Enabled Kinect Cam** can be found in the `GesturedEnabledKinectCam` directory of the resource location for this book.

The Basic Interaction – a WPF application

Basic interaction – WPF is a WPF project written in C# that is available for download with the *Kinect for Windows Developer Toolkit*. It demonstrates the basic user interaction model using skeleton tracking and gestures. The following screenshot shows the UI of the reference application. You can explore and play around with the source code of this application, which will give you more context on how you can build and use gesture-enabled controls in an application:

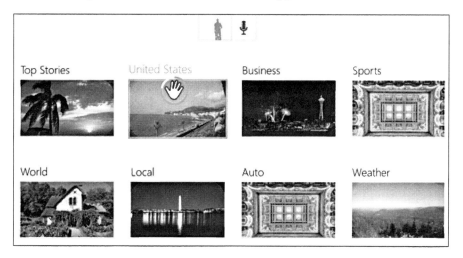

Key things to remember

While gesture detection sounds very inspiring and motivating, and can encourage developers to use their imagination, there are a few options we need to consider while implementing a gesture-enabled application. They are as follows:

- User actions
- Development
- Data matching
- Testing

User actions or inputs are the key elements for any gesture-enabled application. Wrong inputs can mislead the application if they are not handled properly. So, make sure the user knows what needs to be done for what action. This can be done by training them or by providing live feedback in the application's UI.

While developing, make sure you capture all the conditions that come from user input. Also, you must validate the boundary conditions for the entry and exit criteria of the gestures. If the user input matches with the data set, invoke the desire action, otherwise send the message back to the user. This makes your development a bit complex as you need to check for both positive and negative inputs. Before starting development, be aware of the timeline available for implementation, because even an easy gesture can take a good deal of time depending on the criteria and validation scenarios.

 Debugging plays a major role during gesture application development. It's always better to record the gestures once using *Kinect Studio* and play it into the application as long as you need them. Also, use of conditional *breakpoints* can make life even easier. We have discussed this in *Chapter 6, Human Skeleton Tracking*, in the *Debugging the application* section.

If the application is all about matching the data and pattern matching with gestures, data collection plays a crucial role. So, you have to make sure that the data you are collecting for the judgment is normalized with all the factors on which the user can perform the actions. Also, matching stored data with live user action data can affect performance. So make sure you are using the best possible algorithm for matching the data.

And finally, test, test, and test. This is how you can make your application perfect. Testing gesture-enabled applications requires a good amount of time and effort.

Summary

This chapter addressed quick concepts of different gesture-detection approaches, and took them forward into the programming concepts for Kinect. This chapter also guided us through some sample applications related to different gestures. This chapter also gave you a quick overview on building a gesture-enabled control, which is a very common need for any gesture-enabled application. The knowledge, concepts, and sample applications provided in this chapter will encourage and motivate you to use your practical skills for building more complex gestural applications.

10
Developing Applications Using Multiple Kinects

Over the course of the last few chapters, you have gained enough knowledge in developing applications using Kinect for Windows SDK, and now the time is ripe to take the development process one step further by including multiple Kinects in our development domain. Applications can be developed for multiple Kinects using Kinect for Windows SDK. Kinect for Windows SDK supports as many as four Kinect sensors to plug into a single system. With the aid of multiple Kinects, we can make even more feature-rich and interactive applications, such as capturing data from a specific sensor, a failover application where one Kinect acts as a backup and starts automatically when the other one is down, building a security system that detects intrusion in different locations, 3D modeling of data and so on. This takes the app experience to a completely different level.

We need to keep a few things in mind before proceeding to developing applications using multiple Kinects. The area that we need to be careful about is the setting up of the environment for using multiple Kinects. This chapter deals with multiple Kinects, covering fundamentals of development with multiple Kinects, where you will learn how to configure an environment for multiple Kinects, identify and capture data from multiple devices, control individual sensors, and so on. The following areas will be primarily covered in this chapter:

- Setting up the environment for multiple Kinects
- Multiple Kinects – how to reduce interference
- Detecting multiple Kinects
- Developing an application using multiple Kinects
- Controlling multiple sensor status change
- Handling a failover scenario using Kinects
- Challenges faced in developing applications using multiple Kinects
- Applications where multiple Kinects can be used

Setting up the environment for multiple Kinects

In *Chapter 2*, *Getting Started*, we have discussed details about the installation and verification of Kinect device drivers and setting up the development environment. There is not much difference with respect to the setup or the driver installation when we deal with more than one Kinect. The problem will start once you have plugged in multiple devices in a single system. Let's have a look at what will happen if you start plugging in the sensors one by one; we will consider having two Kinect sensors at this time.

Plugging the first Kinect sensor

Once you have plugged in the first Kinect, navigate to **Control Panel | Device Manager**, look for the **Kinect for Windows** node and you will find the list of components detected as shown in the following screenshot:

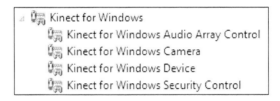

Plugging the second Kinect sensor

Now, plug in another sensor into the system and again navigate to **Control Panel | Device Manager**; look for the **Kinect for Windows** node (if you are already there, you will find the device manager refreshing automatically) and you will find the list of components as shown in the following screenshot:

From the detected component list, it looks like every component is detected twice as there are two Kinects plugged in. If you take a closer look into the list of detected components, you will find that one of the **Kinect for Windows Camera** devices shows the *exclamation mark*.

Double-click on the particular node that shows the warning and check for the device's status. If it shows **This device cannot start. (Code 10)**, it clearly indicates that one of the Kinect cameras could not be loaded due to some reason. This is shown in the following screenshot:

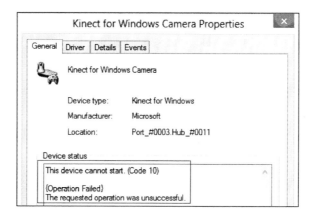

 Most of the time, developers do not notice this warning and start with the development, which causes an exception during the initialization of that particular Kinect sensor.

We will encounter a similar problem with other sensors as well if you try to add more devices. Before going ahead with further development, you should know the reason behind it and how to troubleshoot the issue.

Kinect sensors require an individual USB Controller

Kinect sensors consume a good amount of bandwidth of the USB port; hence, more than one Kinect can't be operated by a single USB Controller. While you are working with multiple Kinects, the only thing you need to take care of is that each of the Kinects has to be connected to a different USB Controller.

A USB Controller is different from a USB port, and multiple USB ports can be controlled by the same controller. The number of controllers your machine has can be seen in the device manager.

At this point, if you change the view of the device manager from **Device by type** to, **Device by connection**, you will find something similar to the following screenshot where you can see that both the Kinect sensors are plugged under a single USB Controller (**293C**):

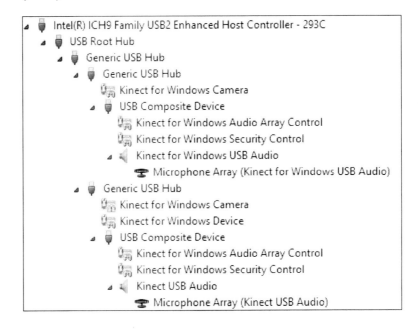

As the USB bandwidth is important, Kinect reserves the bandwidth for the camera for the first time when the drivers load. So, the first Kinect that is loaded will hold the bandwidth it needs. Then, any further connected Kinects will fail to load their camera drivers. Even if you aren't using the first loaded device, it will still hold the bandwidth for its own use. During unload, Kinect releases the bandwidth.

Once you have devices plugged into different USB Controllers, and external power has been supplied for both the devices, you will be able to locate both the devices with camera and audio control within the device manager section as shown in the following screenshot:

To be sure that your devices are plugged into multiple USB Controllers, again change the view to **Device by connection** and you will find that both the devices are connected to different USB Controllers (**293A** and **293C**) as shown in the following screenshot:

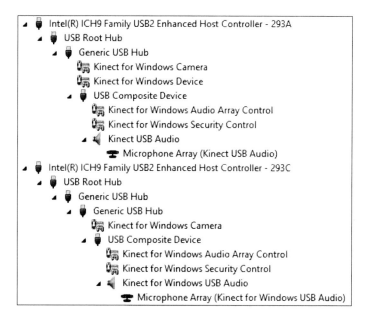

Typically, laptops come with a single USB Controller whereas PCs come with one USB Controller in the front and one at the back. Many of the laptops have the docking station, which has different USB Controllers, while with PCs generally you can change the USB port to try it out or check it from the device manager for the number of USB Controllers. There are a number of external USB Controllers available that you can use in such scenarios.

Multiple Kinects – how to reduce interference

When we talk about multiple Kinects, the first question that comes to our mind is interference. We know that Kinect measures the depth data by reading the IR patterns projected by an IR emitter. When there are multiple sensors placed in the same area the projected IR from the multiple sensors can interfere with one another. In such scenarios, Kinect sensors will return incorrect data, that is, X, Y, and Z values for interference affect the IR dots.

 Why can't Kinect distinguish its own projected IR from the IR projected by other sensors? This could have fixed the interference issue. The answer to this is that the IR laser is not modulated.

You can think of some examples of technology that can modulate the individual patterns coming from each Kinect. Based on the pattern sensor, you can identify its corresponding "dot". However, no support for this exists in Kinect SDK.

When there are multiple Kinects, the IR from each of them can interfere with one another, and as Kinect IR is not modulated, the sensor does not have any clue which IR dots to read. Using Shake 'n' Sense, we can just shake the sensors a little so that the position of the IR dots is moved. So, by shaking the position the IR points are moved a bit and the sensor can read the data on every move. This shake is done generally by an external motor.

The Microsoft Research division at `http://research.microsoft.com/` explains the Shake 'n' Sense technology as follows:

> *Shake 'n' Sense is a novel yet simple mechanical technique for mitigating the interference when two or more Kinect cameras point at the same part of a physical scene. The technique is particularly useful for Kinect, where the structured light source is not modulated. It requires only mechanical augmentation of the Kinect, without any need to modify the internal electronics, firmware or associated host software.*

You can also watch the video of this technology for more understanding of how this technology works, at `http://research.microsoft.com/apps/video/dl.aspx?id=160616`.

With this, you are absolutely ready to start developing and playing around with multiple Kinects. Basic development with multiple Kinects are straightforward and it is similar to what you have done for a single Kinect. The only thing is to take control over individual Kinect sensors. So let's begin with the development and start with detecting multiple Kinects.

Detecting multiple Kinects

The `KinectSensor` class has a static property of type `KinectSensorCollection`, named `KinectSensors`, which consists of the collection of sensors that are connected with the system. The `KinectSensor` class returns the collection of connected Kinect devices with your system. `KinectSensorCollection` is a read-only collection of type `Kinect sensor`. Each `KinectSensorCollection` contains an indexer of the `KinectSensor` object and an event named `StatusChanged`.

The following code block shows the definition of the `KinectSensorCollection` class:

```
public sealed class KinectSensorCollection : ReadOnlyCollection<Kinect
Sensor>, IDisposable
{
        public KinectSensor this[string instanceId] { get; }
        public event EventHandler<StatusChangedEventArgs>
        StatusChanged;
        public void Dispose();
}
```

We need to get hold of the `KinectSensor` property most of the time to get access to the sensor information.

Getting access to the individual sensor

We can get the instance by just defining the position index of the sensor as `KinectSensor.KinectSensors[index];`. The index starts with `0`, which indicates the first device. The following code snippet shows how to get access to an individual sensor when there are two devices connected:

```
// Get the first Sensor
KinectSensor sensor1 = KinectSensor.KinectSensors[0];
// Get the second sensor
KinectSensor sensor2 = KinectSensor.KinectSensors[1];
```

`KinectSensor.KinectSensor.Count` will return the total number of Kinect sensors that are connected.

On the other hand, you can iterate through individual sensors from the `KinectSensorCollection` class as shown in the following code snippet:

```
KinectSensorCollection sensorCollection = KinectSensor.KinectSensors;

        foreach (KinectSensor sensor in sensorCollection)
        {
            if(sensor.Status=KinectStatus.Connected)
                {
                    ...
                }
        }
```

Different ways to get a Kinect sensor's reference

The easiest way to get the instance of the connected sensor using LINQ is shown in the following code snippet:

```
    this.sensor = KinectSensor.KinectSensors.FirstOrDefault(
sensorItem => sensorItem.Status == KinectStatus.Connected);
```

This code returns the first connected sensor from the collection of sensors, or a default one if the collection contains no sensors. You can also use the following code block to get the list of all connected sensors from the list of sensors:

```
var connectedSensors = KinectSensor.KinectSensors.Where(sensoritem =>
sensoritem.Status == KinectStatus.Connected).ToList<KinectSensor>();
```

Developing an application with multiple Kinects

In this demo, we will be developing a small application using two Kinect sensors. To start off with, we will just read some basic information such as device ID, status, and connection ID from the individual Kinect sensors. The fundamentals of this application are very similar to the Kinect Info Box application that we developed in *Chapter 3, Starting to Build Kinect Applications*. The only difference is we will be reading the information for all the connected sensors. Later in the chapter, we will handle the sensor status individually.

Setting up the project

We will start building the application from scratch, so let's first create the solution and set up the project file for the same. Use the following steps to create the project file:

1. Start a new instance of Visual Studio.
2. Create a new project by navigating to **File | New Project**.
3. You will see the **New Project** dialog box. Choose **C#** as our development language and select the **WPF Application** template and type the name as Multiple Kinect Viewer.
4. From the **Solution Explorer** option, right-click on **Reference** folder and select **Add References**.
5. Include a reference of **Microsoft.Kinect** assembly.

Designing the UI

Open the MainWindow.Xaml file from the Solution Explorer. We need a container to display the list of items; the container can be defined using a data template. The basic UI using XAML is shown in the following code block that contains a WPF ListBox control with a template defined. Within the data template, we have placed few Textblock controls (here we have only shown for DeviceID, similarly we can have different Textblock controls for ConnectionID and Status) to display the information for the sensor.

```xml
<ListBox Name="lstsensor" ItemsSource="{Binding}"
  <ListBox.ItemTemplate>
    <DataTemplate>
      <Expander Header="{Binding deviceCount}" >
        <StackPanel>
          <StackPanel VerticalAlignment="Center"
          Orientation="Horizontal">
          <Label FontWeight="Bold" Content="Device ID" />
          <TextBlock Text="{Binding Path=DeviceID}"
          VerticalAlignment="Center" />
          </StackPanel>
        </StackPanel>
      </Expander>
    </DataTemplate>
  </ListBox.ItemTemplate>
</ListBox>
```

You must have noticed that we have used a couple of bindings in the XAML, such as the ItemSource for the ListBox control, and Text for the TextBox control. This is quite understandable as our ultimate goal is to assign the collection of sensor information to the list control.

Creating the KinectInfoCollection

The ListBox property is used to display the basic information of an individual Kinect sensor, which contains the DeviceID, ConnectionID, and Status properties. Create a new class called KinectInfo to hold these basic information as shown in the following code block:

```
public class KinectInfo
   {
      public string deviceCount { get; set; }
      public string DeviceID { get; set; }
      public string Status { get; set; }
      public string ConnectionID { get; set; }
   }
```

The mainwindow.xaml.cs file defines a collection of KinectInfo class, which will contain the list of sensor information:

```
        ObservableCollection<KinectInfo> kinectSensorInfo = new Observabl
   eCollection<KinectInfo>();
```

Getting information from Kinects

Now, it is our time to get information from the Kinect sensor. In the mainwindow.xaml.cs file, include Microsft.Kinect as the namespace.

First, check the number of sensors connected with the system and if it's greater than 0, add the sensor information within the KinectInfo list, and finally assign the list as an item source of the Listbox control. Add the following lines of code in the MainWindow_Loaded event:

```
int count = KinectSensor.KinectSensors.Count;

   this.ViewModel.NumberofDevice = count;
   if (count > 0)
      {
         foreach (KinectSensor sensor in
         KinectSensor.KinectSensors)
           {
             kinectSensorInfo.Add(new KinectInfo
                { deviceCount = string.Format("Device  {0}",
                 numberofDevice++),
                   DeviceID = sensor.UniqueKinectId,
                   ConnectionID = sensor.DeviceConnectionId,
                   Status = sensor.Status.ToString() });
           }
           lstsensor.DataContext = kinectSensorInfo;
      }
```

The preceding code is self-explanatory; we are iterating through the collection of devices and adding the required information into our custom collection. deviceCount is not something that we are getting from the sensor, rather we can calculate manually to get the count index (labeling the devices with a number) for that particular device (for example Device 1, Device 2, and so on.). Finally, we set the DataContext value for 1stsensor as KinectSensorInfo.

Running the application

To run the application, press *F5* or from the **Debug** menu select **Start without debugging**, and you will find the details of both the devices as shown in following output screen. If you have more than two sensors connected before the start of this application, the information of those sensors will be updated automatically:

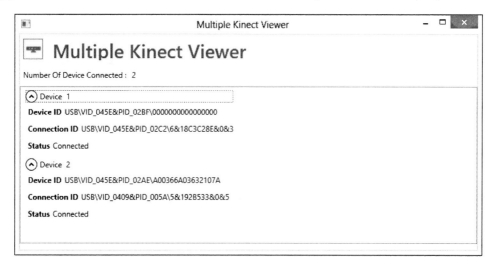

Controlling multiple sensor status changes

Controlling Kinect status changes is one of the key factors and essential for development. Initially in *Chapter 3*, *Starting to Build Kinect Applications*, we have discussed the Status property of the KinectSensor class and how we handle it using the StatusChanged event handler in the *Dealing with Kinect Status* section.

To quickly recall how you can handle the status change, first of all you have to first register for the StatusChanged event as shown below.

```
KinectSensor.KinectSensors.StatusChanged +=
KinectSensors_StatusChanged;
```

The StatusChanged event is attached to the KinectSensor class and raised when the KinectSensor.Status property of a Kinect sensor in the collection changes.

> You really don't need to attach the event handler to each and every instance of the sensor, rather the KinectSensor does a global event registration of the status change event for all the connected sensors.

Finally, whenever there is an event change the event handler is called by sending the StatusChangedEventArgs argument. This event's argument holds the KinectStatus property and the reference of KinectSensor for the Kinect device, by which this event has been raised. Refer to the following code block:

```
void KinectSensors_StatusChanged(object sender,
StatusChangedEventArgs e)
        {
            KinectSensor sensorStatus = e.Sensor;
    //handle the status here
        }
```

As shown in the preceding code block, the sensorStatus property holds the reference of Kinect, which has the changed status. Now we will see how we can extend to the Multiple Kinect Viewer application with status change in the next section.

Extending Multiple Kinect Viewer with status change

In the very first step we will make the KinectInfo class to implement the INotifyPropertyChange interface, as we need to update the status as and when the status changes. These changes are highlighted in the following code block:

```
public class KinectInfo : INotifyPropertyChanged
    {
        public string deviceCount { get; set; }
        public string DeviceID { get; set; }
        private string status;
```

```
public string Status
    {
        get
        {
            return this.status;
        }
        set
        {
            this.status = value;
            this.OnPropertyChange("Status");
        }
    }
    public string ConnectionID { get; set; }

    public event PropertyChangedEventHandler PropertyChanged;

    public void OnPropertyChange(string propertyName)
    {
        if (this.PropertyChanged != null)
        {
            this.PropertyChanged.Invoke(this, new
            PropertyChangedEventArgs(propertyName));
        }
    }
}
```

With this change in the code, the Status property of KinectInfo class should automatically reflect to the UI whenever there is a status change.

Registering and handling the status change

The StatusChanged event will only fire if the event handler is attached with the KinectSensor class. To do so, attach the event handler on the MainWindow() method as shown in the following code block:

```
public MainWindow()
    {
        InitializeComponent();
        Loaded += new RoutedEventHandler(MainWindow_Loaded);
        KinectSensor.KinectSensors.StatusChanged += new
        EventHandler<StatusChangedEventArgs>
        (KinectSensors_StatusChanged);
        this.ViewModel = new MainWindowModelView();
        this.DataContext = this.ViewModel;
    }
```

When there is a change in the sensor status, the `StatusChanged` event will fire with the `StatusChangedEventArgs` argument, which contains the reference of the sensor that causes the status change. In the following code block, we are matching the `ConnectionID` value of the device from the list of sensor elements with the `ConnectionID` value of the sensor that raised the `StatusChanged` event:

```
void KinectSensors_StatusChanged(object sender, StatusChangedEventArgs
e)
    {
        KinectInfo kinfo =
        this.kinectSensorInfo.FirstOrDefault(item =>
        item.ConnectionID.Equals(e.Sensor.
        DeviceConnectionId));
        if (kinfo != null)
        {
            kinfo.Status = e.Status.ToString();
        }
    }
```

If the ID gets matched, we are just updating the `Status` value of the particular element from the list. As we have already implemented the `PropertyChanged` attribute, the data will bind automatically with the UI.

Running the application

Run the Multiple Kinect Viewer application again. First you will find that both the devices have `Connected` status as shown in the left part of the screenshot. Then try to unplug one of the sensors, thereby disconnecting it from the system. You will find the status is getting updated automatically. Refer to the right part of the screenshot, where the **NotPowered** status is shown for the Device 2:

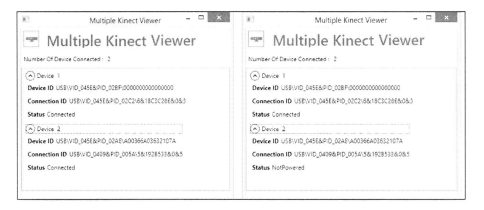

Identifying the devices automatically

With the help of the StatusChanged event, you can also identify the device automatically when they are connected to the system. Just consider the scenario where you have one device connected when you run the Multiple Kinect Viewer application; you will find the list item showing only one device connected.

Now, if you plugged in another device, the list won't reflect the information of a newly-added device as our system knows there is a new device connected, but our application is still not aware about it. In such scenarios we can make use of the StatusChanged event itself to identify when the sensor is getting connected, because the StatusChanged event can recognize the new devices when it's connected. So, if the event is registered, the application invokes the event handler for a status change for a new connected device as well. To recognize and update the collection of devices in our application, we have to add a few extra lines of code in the StatusChanged event handler as shown in the following code block:

```
KinectInfo kinfo = this.kinectSensorInfo.FirstOrDefault(item => item.
ConnectionID.Equals(e.Sensor.DeviceConnectionId));
            if (kinfo != null)
            {
                kinfo.Status = e.Status.ToString();
            }
            else
            {
                kinectSensorInfo.Add(new KinectInfo { deviceCount
                = string.Format("Device  {0}", numberofDevice++),
                DeviceID = e.Sensor.UniqueKinectId, ConnectionID =
                e.Sensor.DeviceConnectionId, Status = e.Sensor.Status.
                ToString() });
            }
```

The changes we made here reflect that if the device ConnectionID value does not match, then the device is not in the list and the item needs to be added to the list. That's all.

Run the application with one sensor plugged in as seen in the left part of the following screenshot. Then plug in the other sensor; you will get the list updated with two sensors as shown in the right part of the following screenshot:

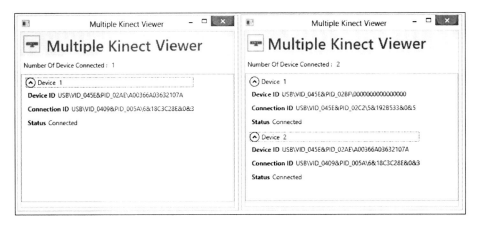

Integrating with KinectStatusNotifier

We have developed one KinectStatusNotifier component as part of the *Building KinectStatusNotifier* exercise in *Chapter 3, Starting to Build Kinect Applications*, which is not self-executable; it generates a `KinectStatusNotifier.dll` assembly, which can be used with a Kinect-based application. We have also integrated the same with the Kinect Info Box application in the *Using KinectStatusNotifier* section. If you follow the same steps with the Multiple Kinect Viewer application, you will be able to see a system tray notification with a status change as shown in the following screenshot:

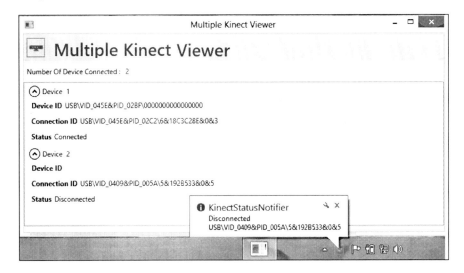

Well, using `KinectStatusNotifier`, you can customize the notification messages and display other information as well on status change. As shown in the following screenshot, you can see that we are able to identify which device status is getting changed and the status as well as the Device ID:

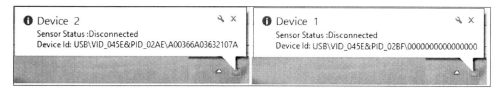

To achieve this, you just need to disable the Auto Notification feature from the Status Notifier by using the following code:

```
this.notifier.AutoNotification = false;
```

By doing this, the `KinectStatusNotifier` will stop showing automatic notifications in our system and the control is transferred to the user. In the next step, in sensor status change, read the information from KinectInfo Collection, and invoke the notification message as shown in the following code block:

```
if (kinfo != null)
    {
       kinfo.Status = e.Status.ToString();
       this.notifier.NotifierTitle = kinfo.deviceCount;
       this.notifier.NotifierMessage = string.Format("Sensor
       Status :{0} \nDevice Id: {1}", kinfo.Status,
       kinfo.DeviceID);
       this.notifier.NotifyStatus();
    }
```

As you can see from the preceding code, we are assigning the `NotifierTitle` property with the `deviceCount` property and assigning the `NotifierMessage` property with `Status` as well as `DeviceId`. Then, we are calling the `NotifyStaus()` message explicitly to notify us in the system tray.

Until now, we have discussed how we can configure, connect, and check the status of multiple Kinects. Now let's have a look at how we can use two Kinect sensors and capture the depth and color stream data.

Capturing data using multiple Kinects

If your sensors are connected properly and you are able to access individual Kinects, capturing data from multiple sensor is fairly easy. You are already familiar with capturing color and depth data stream from a sensor, so rather than going into a step-by-step discussion, just look at the following steps for capturing data:

1. Identify the individual Kinect sensors.
2. Attach the event handler to the individual Kinect sensors.
3. Handle the events for the attached event handler.
4. Check the sensor status and control the start and stop based on your requirement.

Using these steps you can a build an application that can capture different data streams from the Kinect sensor as shown in the following screenshot:

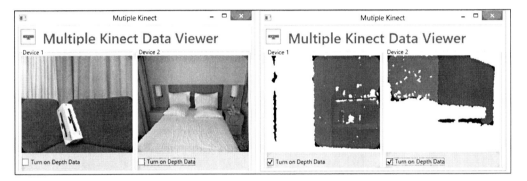

Both these images show that the color and depth data are being captured from multiple Kinects.

 The overall implementation will be the same as we did for individual Kinect sensors, except identifying and attaching an event handler for a particular sensor. You can enable the color, depth, as well as the skeleton stream for multiple Kinects. Skeleton processing requires heavy CPU processing, so make sure your CPU has enough power to process skeleton data for both the sensors.

This application is available for download from the book resource location.

Handling a failover scenario using Kinects

One of the very useful scenarios where you can use multiple Kinects is failover. Failover is used to make the system more fault-tolerant by providing automatic switching to a redundant or standby system. Here, we can consider Kinect as a system, if you are building one Kinect application that needs to be run constantly to capture data. It could happen, that one system fails (gets disconnected, power turns off) and your application fails to capture data. In such a situation, you can start the other connected sensor automatically to capture data and turn it off once the first device starts again.

You can easily build this scenario with the knowledge you have gained in this chapter. The `StatusChanged` event handler is the key here. You can monitor sensor status and once it's getting disconnected or powered off, start the other connected sensor.

The following screenshot shows a failover application built using Kinect sensors, where the primary sensor returns color stream data and the other sensor works as a backupand activity logs showing the device information along with the start time. Once one sensor is down, the other sensor automatically starts capturing the data:

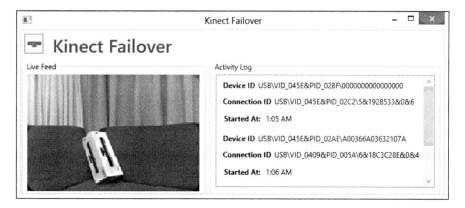

This application is available for download from the book resource location.

Challenges faced in developing applications using multiple Kinects

Building an application using multiple Kinects is complex when it comes under data synchronization or merging. Following is a list of a few challenges that can be faced while using multiple Kinects:

- Interference
- Synchronization of frames
- Data smoothing

Applications where multiple Kinects can be used

One common scenario with multiple Kinect sensors is the failover application, which we have already discussed. Additionally, we can use multiple Kinects in the following places:

- 3D body scanner using multiple Kinects
- Robotics
- 3D-view construction of an environment
- Tracking objects in 3D
- Building security solutions

Summary

This chapter mainly works as an introductory chapter for building applications using multiple Kinects. Dealing with multiple Kinects is very easy, as it is doing nothing but taking care of individual Kinect sensors. But the first major hurdle we usually face is while configuring both the Kinects so that Windows can recognize both the devices correctly, and the devices work properly without interfering into each other's functioning. Some of the most common errors involved in setting up multiple Kinects to work with Windows have been highlighted and the method of troubleshooting has also been dealt with in fair detail. We have also demonstrated how the devices can work together without overlapping individual domains. We have developed a small application using multiple Kinects to track and notify the status change of individual sensors. We have also built a couple of demos that show the uses of multiple Kinects.

11
Putting Things Together

Over the course of the previous chapters, we have explored the various aspects of the *Kinect for Windows SDK* and have seen how the SDK helps us to interact with a Kinect device to build interactive applications. You have seen how Kinect returns depth information of objects, how it tracks a human skeleton, or even how it recognizes human voice, and you have also learned about building gesture-enabled applications.

Finally we have reached the last chapter of this book. In this chapter, we will go beyond the Kinect SDK and will explore how we can take advantage of this motion-sensing device by integrating it with other devices. Additionally, we will also look into a couple of solutions available with the Kinect for Windows Developer Toolkit.

The objective of this chapter is not to discuss step-by-step codes, but rather we will walk through the different possibilities of using Kinect by integrating it with other devices, such as Windows Phone, a Netduino microcontroller. In this chapter we will be discussing about the following:

- Taking Kinect to the Cloud
- Remoting Kinect using Windows Phone
- Connecting Kinect with a Netduino microcontroller
- Using Kinect for augmented reality
- Introduction to face tracking using Kinect
- Working with XNA and a 3D avatar

Taking Kinect to the Cloud

When you take Kinect to the Cloud, the sky is the limit for making applications. In this section we will discuss how to design a very simple application that can upload image frames to the Cloud using *Windows Azure*.

Required components

To build this solution, we will be using the following technologies:

- Windows Azure
- Windows Azure SDK
- Kinect device and the Kinect for Windows SDK

The following diagram shows the overall application design. This diagram describes how the Kinect device is connected with Windows Azure Storage via the Kinect for Windows SDK and Windows Azure SDK:

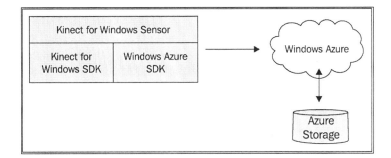

Windows Azure

We will use Windows Azure cloud storage for read/write operations of the image streams. Windows Azure storage has *Blobs*, *Tables* and *Queues*.

Blobs are used for storing larger files, which can be uploaded or downloaded as chunks called a blob. As of today, blobs allow you to store files up to 1 TB.

Tables should not be confused with the SQL Azure tables. The Azure storage table is similar to SQL tables, but are non-relational tables. Tables are created as entities and differentiated by a partition key and a row key. The Azure table can hold up to 100 TB of data and is capable of providing a throughput of 500 entities per second per partition. (The throughput can go up to few thousands per second when multiple partitions are involved.)

Queue storage mimics the behavior of a conventional queue accepting messages in a *First In First Out* (FIFO) format. A message can be up to 64 KB and can hold any number of messages and a queue can store a total of 100 TB.

 For more information on Azure Storage Services please visit `http://msdn.microsoft.com/en-us/library/windowsazure/ee924681.aspx`.

The Windows Azure SDK

The *Windows Azure SDK* allows you to develop Cloud-based applications in your favorite language. As in our example we will use the SDK for .NET.

 The SDK is freely available at `http://windowsazure.com` for download.

The SDK offers two ways of communicating with Azure Storage:

- REST API
- Storage services

The *REST API* allows the programmer to transfer content over a REST protocol without worrying about the platform.

In our case, since we are using .NET we will take the advantage of Storage services to insert the image frames to store an image frame in Azure tables.

The Kinect for Windows SDK

This is something that you are already familiar with. The Kinect SDK has a bigger edge running on the native .NET platforms, and therefore integrating with Azure is as simple as referring the Azure SDK to the application.

In this concept, we will poll the Kinect device at regular intervals and update the storage in Windows Azure with image frames.

Designing the solution

Let's start with the schema for the entity as shown in the following screenshot to which we are going to upload the image frame:

In order to create a table entity, we are inheriting our custom type CamAudit from TableEntity using the following code block:

```
public class CamAudit : TableEntity
    {
    public DateTime ShotTime
    {
        get { return DateTime.Parse(this.RowKey); }
        set { this.RowKey = value.ToString(); }
    }

    public string Location
    {
        get { return this.PartitionKey; }
        set { this.PartitionKey = value; }
    }

    public byte[] Picture { get; set; }
}
```

As we have already discussed that the entity has to be differentiated by the RowKey and PartitionKey properties, in our case we have to decide the unique timestamp when the image is captured to be the row key, and the location (assuming we have Kinect placed in multiple locations) as the partition key. The image shot will be uploaded as a byte array using the picture property.

Following is the code that will insert the picture in to the storage table:

```
// Retrieve the storage account from the connection string.
        CloudStorageAccount storageAccount =
        CloudStorageAccount.Parse(
```

```
CloudConfigurationManager.GetSetting
("StorageConnectionString"));

// Create the table client.
CloudTableClient tableClient =
storageAccount.CreateCloudTableClient();

// Create the CloudTable object that represents the
"people" table.
CloudTable table =
tableClient.GetTableReference("CamAudit");
table.CreateIfNotExists();

// Create a new customer entity.
CamAudit cam = new CamAudit();
cam.ShotTime = DateTime.Now;
cam.Location = cameraLocation;
cam.Picture = this.GetCurrentImageAsByteArray();

// Create the TableOperation that inserts the customer
 entity.
TableOperation insertOperation =
TableOperation.Insert(cam);

// Execute the insert operation.
table.Execute(insertOperation);
```

Now that our code for the Azure part is ready, for the remaining part the Kinect captures the image at regular intervals and uploads it to Azure.

We have already discussed about how we can capture image frames and save them as images in local storage in *Chapter 4, Getting the most out of the Kinect camera* in the *Capturing and saving images* section. We can plug in similar code to get this current solution running. Here we just need to get the image byte's array, as shown in the highlighted code block.

Real-time implementations

Once the data is uploaded to Azure, it is ready to be consumed by any platform and from anywhere. Since the Azure table service also supports REST, you can pretty much access the data from any device or platform with absolutely no code specific to Azure.

For example, let's assume that using the earlier code we uploaded a picture using the following parameters:

- ShotTime: 02/21/2012 6:46:31 PM

- Location: KinectDevice1

- Picture: <<Some Picture>>

This inserted data can be retrieved using the following URL:

```
http:// <<azure storage account>>.table.core.windows.net/
CamAudit (PartitionKey= KinectDevice1, RowKey='02/21/2012
6:46:31 PM')?$select=Picture
```

Refer to the following diagram which shows how the data captured by the Kinect sensor can be consumed by different application from Windows Azure:

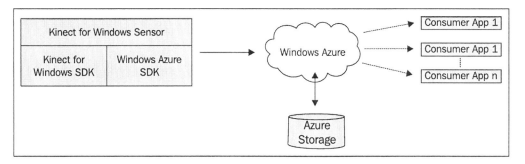

Now you can monitor location where you have placed the Kinect sensor and get the information you need from a URL. Your imagination is the only limit when developing applications based on this concept.

 Using this approach you can try to extend the solution of *Human Intrusion Detector*, which we developed in *Chapter 6, Human Skeleton Tracking*.

Remotely using the Kinect with Windows Phone

We have already learned how to leverage the Kinect sensor using Azure. Now we will take it one step further by integrating it with Windows Phone along with the solution that we have previously built. In this application, we will try to send a command from a Windows Phone that will be passed to a Kinect device through Azure.

The overall solution will look like the following diagram:

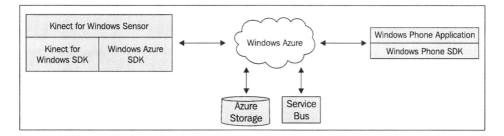

Required components

As this is an extension of the previously designed solution, along with the previously used components we will be using the following:

- Windows Azure Service Bus
- Windows Phone SDK

The Windows Azure Service Bus

Service bus allows us to send or receive messages between two platforms remotely. It also supports different modes of messaging.

 For more information about Windows Azure Service Bus refer to `http://www.windowsazure.com/en-us/home/features/messaging/`.

In our application, we are going to use a WCF service to point to a remote endpoint hosted in Windows Azure Service Bus and communicate between a Windows Phone and a Kinect device.

The Windows Phone SDK

Windows Phone SDK runs on a .NET runtime with Silverlight or XNA as a platform for building applications. In our application we are going to consume a WCF service whose endpoint is in the Cloud and hosted on your local machine or where the Kinect application is running.

 The Windows Phone SDK is freely available at `http://windowsphone.com` for download.

Designing the solution

Let's start with creating a namespace in Azure. For this you will need to create a service as shown in the following screenshot:

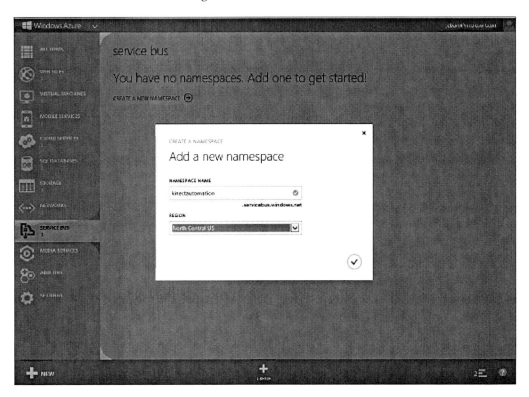

You will be required to create a unique namespace for communication. For our example, we will be using `http://kinectautomation.servicebus.windows.net`. Now that the endpoint is created in Azure, we will write a WCF service that uses this URL as the endpoint.

The service that we are creating here communicates with the Kinect device and instructs it to take a picture and upload it to Azure as discussed in the earlier design. This WCF service will be hosted on the same machine where the Kinect device is connected. The WCF service will not be any different than the classic service.

We can define the WCF attributes as follows:

- ServiceContract: IKinectService

- OperationContract: TakePicture

Assuming that you have defined the ServiceContract and the OperationContract attributes as previously mentioned and implemented them, our next task is to make the service listen to the endpoint we created in Azure.

To do this, we will need to define a custom behavior through which a remote endpoint can be connected. This can be done using the following code snippet:

```
private TransportClientEndpointBehavior serviceEndpointBehaviorValue;
        private TransportClientEndpointBehavior
        ServiceEndpointBehavior
        {
            get
            {
                if (serviceEndpointBehaviorValue == null)
                {
                    serviceEndpointBehaviorValue = new
                    TransportClientEndpointBehavior();
                    serviceEndpointBehaviorValue.TokenProvider =
                    TokenProvider.CreateSharedSecret
                    TokenProvider(
                        "username",
                        "token"
                    );
                }

                return serviceEndpointBehaviorValue;
            }
        }
```

This property defines a custom behavior that uses the token provided for the authentication. The username and the token for the namespace that you have created can be captured from the *Azure Dashboard*.

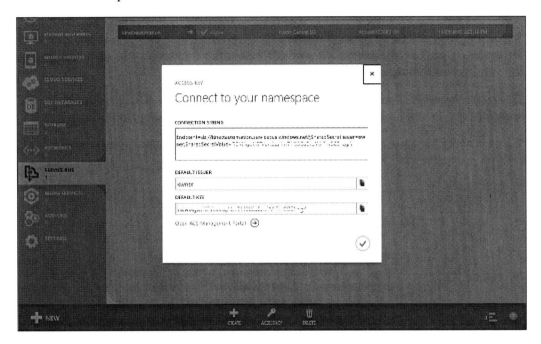

Refer to the following code block:

```
ServiceHost host = new ServiceHost(new KinectService());
        ServiceEndpoint endpoint =
        host.AddServiceEndpoint(typeof(Application
          namespace.IKinectService), new
          BasicHttpRelayBinding(),
          "https://kinectautomation.servicebus.windows.
        net/soap12/");
        endpoint.Behaviors.Add(ServiceEndpointBehavior);
        host.Open();
```

In this code block, `KinectService` is the type that implements `IKinectService`.

As you can see, we are using *SOAP 1.2* as the protocol for listening to the endpoint. When the preceding set of code is executed, there will be a connection opened between the application and Azure. The WCF service will be self-hosted, listening to the remote endpoint we just defined. Now whenever you call the service method `TakePicture` from any device that can access the Internet, the piece of code implemented inside the `OperationContract` implementation will be called. In our case, we will take a new picture and upload it to Azure.

Now that the *Kinect and Azure* part of code is ready, we will build the application for Windows Phone, which can connect to Azure using the following code block:

```
private KinectReceiverClient serviceClientValue;
    public KinectReceiverClient ServiceClient
        {
            get
            {
                if (this.serviceClientValue == null ||
                        this.serviceClientValue.State ==
                        CommunicationState.Closed ||
                        this.serviceClientValue.State ==
                        CommunicationState.Closing ||
                        this.serviceClientValue.State ==
                        CommunicationState.Faulted)
                {
                    this.serviceClientValue = new
                    KinectReceiverClient("BasicHttpBinding_
                    IKinectReceiver");
                }

                return this.serviceClientValue;
            }
        }


    public Action<bool> KinectCommandCallback { get; private set;
    }

    public void SendCommandToKinect(Action<bool> callbackMethod,
    string command)
        {
            Deployment.Current.Dispatcher.BeginInvoke(() =>
                {
                    this.KinectCommandCallback = callbackMethod;
                    this.ServiceClient.SendMessageCompleted += new
                    EventHandler<SendMessageCompletedEventArgs>
                    (ServiceClient_SendMessageCompleted);
                    this.ServiceClient.TakePictureAsync();
                }
                );
        }

    private void ServiceClient_SendMessageCompleted(object
    sender, SendMessageCompletedEventArgs e)
        {
```

```
        this.KinectCommandCallback(e.Error == null &&
        string.Compare(e.Result.Acknowledgement, "ok",
        StringComparison.InvariantCultureIgnoreCase) == 0);
   }
```

The code that we just saw will call the WCF method that is hosted on your machine and is listening to the Azure port.

Real-time implementations

We make an asynchronous call to the WCF endpoint, which is triggered on the machine to which the Kinect is connected, and it works just like any normal WCF service. From here you can choose to upload the picture to Azure, then read the same, and display it in your phone.

You can use the concepts that we just discussed to build a complete home security system using Kinect, Windows Azure, Windows Phone, and Windows 8. Refer the following URL for more information http://abhijitjana.net/2012/04/16/home-security-system-using-kinect-azure-windows-phone-and-windows-8/.

Using Kinect with a Netduino microcontroller

Another fun part of development is when we integrate Kinect with a *microcontroller* and send signals or data from a Kinect-based application to do some activities. With the microcontroller, we can wire up different electronic gadgets, such as a 7-segment board, digital alarm, LED display board, and many more.

Integrating these two technologies can help us to build a robust and real-life application, such as a home automation system, security system, controlling a robot, and so on. In this section we will learn how we can connect a *Netdunio microcontroller* with a Kinect and control the Netdunio on-board LED.

Required components

Other than *Kinect, the Kinect for Windows* SDK, and *Visual Studio,* to build this solution we need the following components:

* Microsoft .NET Micro Framework
* Netduino
* Netdunio SDK (32-bit or 64-bit depending on the Operating System)

Microsoft .Net Micro Framework

The *.Net Micro Framework* is a subset of the *.Net Framework,* which does not require a host operating system to run. The Micro Framework has a hardware abstraction layer, which allows us to deploy the solution on a microcontroller and run it.

 You can download the Micro .NET Framework and find additional information on the Micro Framework website located at http://www.netmf.com/.

Netduino

Netdunio is an *Open Source Microcontroller,* which runs on the Microsoft .NET Micro Framework. Why is this an Open Source Microcontroller? Because the detailed specifications of this board are completely open/public. You can build a device on your own or you can purchase a pre-built one. The Netdunio family consists of three types of electronics boards:

- Netduino
- Netduino Mini
- Netduino Plus

The following screenshot shows a *Netduino Plus* device with a USB cable plugged in, which we will be using for this solution:

The Netduino SDK

The *Netdunio SDK* installs the device driver that talks to the Netduino device. This SDK is available for both 32-bit and 64-bit devices. Make sure you select the one based on your operating system. Install it before connecting the Netduino to the computer.

Once you plug in the Netduino to your computer using the USB cable, you should see the LED on the board lighting up, as shown in the following screenshot:

 For more information on Netduino devices, its platform, its family and Netdunio SDK, refer to the Netduino website http://www.netduino.com/.

To get started, we take a quick look at the Netduino SDK and Netduino microcontroller. Let's try to create an application to build the on-board LED light.

Blinking of the on-board LED

Once you have the .NET Micro Framework and Netdunio SDK installed, you will find a **Micro Framework** template in the **Installed Templates** section in the **New Project** dialog window of Visual Studio. Select **Netdunio Plus Application** from the right panel as shown in the following screenshot and then choose a project name and select **OK**.

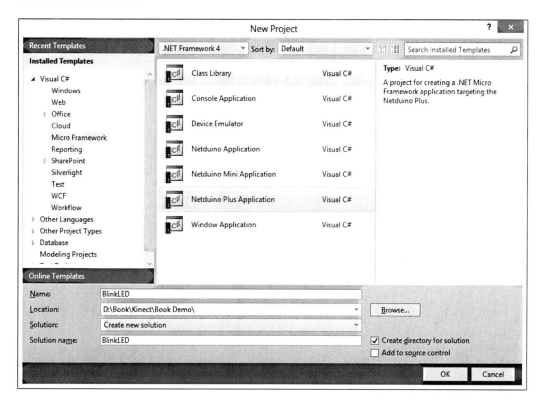

The default template for the Netduino Plus application contains all the assembly files required to start building an application. These references includes the required DLL files for the Microsoft .NET Micro Framework and the Netduino SDK. The following screenshot shows the added assembly (in Solution Explorer) and the used namespaces:

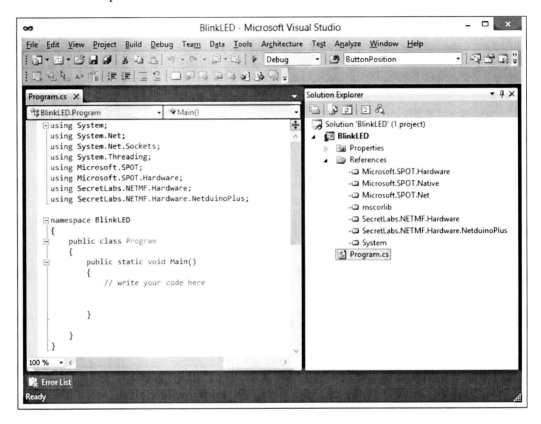

Replace the Program class with the following code block:

```
public class Program
    {
        public static void Main()
        {
            var OnBoardledPort = new OutputPort(Pins.ONBOARD_LED,
            false);
            for (int i = 0; i < 10; i++)
            {
                OnBoardledPort.Write(true);
                Thread.Sleep(200);
                OnBoardledPort.Write(false);
```

```
                    Thread.Sleep(200);
                }
            }
        }
```

In this code block, we have first set up the on-board LED and set it to `false` so it is turned off. Within the loop, we are turning it on and off ten times. The `Thread.Sleep()` method is used to add a pause in between the blink.

Changing the Deployment Transport

When we run the application, code is first deployed to the Netduino board and then it starts its execution. By default, Visual Studio runs the application in an emulator. Change the **Deployment** target from **Emulator** to **USB** and select the **NetduinoPlus_NetduinoPlus** device from the **Device** drop-down as shown in the following screenshot. You will get the following details from the **Project Property** window in the **.Net Micro Framework** tab:

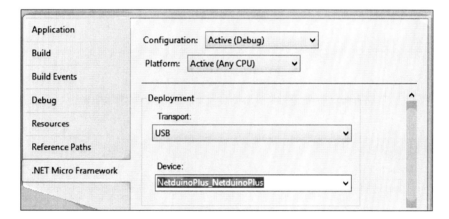

 The device information will be available in the device drop-down only if the Netduino device is plugged in to the computer and the device drivers are installed.

Running the application

If you run the application now from Visual Studio you will find that the blue LED light is blinking (we have restricted our code to blink only 10 times).

You can also find a similar project examples from the Netduino website at http://www.netduino.com/projects/. Play around with them in order to explore what the Netduino can do.

So far we have seen the basics of a Netduino application; let's have a look at how we can integrate it with a Kinect sensor.

Connecting Kinect to a Netduino

At first, it may look very easy to add the Kinect reference with the Netduino application and get it working. But this won't work. The `Microsoft.Kinect.dll` requires *.NET Framework 4.0*; whereas the Netduino works on a subset of the .NET Framework, which is the Microsoft .NET Micro Framework. These two frameworks aren't directly compatible. However, we can connect the devices over the Internet either by using socket programming or sending web requests as shown in the following diagram:

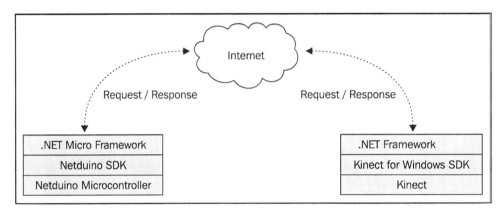

Using an Internet connection

The Netduino Plus device has an *Ethernet port* and an *Ethernet router*. You can plug the Ethernet cable into the device and connect it to the Internet.

The following code block will give you the IP address of your device, which you can use for further communication with the Netduino:

```
Microsoft.SPOT.Net.NetworkInformation.NetworkInterface.
GetAllNetworkInterfaces()[0].IPAddress
```

The typical structure for the development environment for this kind of application will look like the following screenshot:

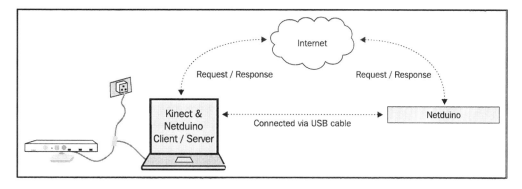

Listening to the request

Once the development environment is set up and both the computer and the Netduino are connected to the Internet, you should able to ping the IP addresses of the Netduino. Further development is straightforward using basic socket programming.

 Get more information about the `Socket` class and its methods from `http://msdn.microsoft.com/en-us/library/attbb8f5.aspx`.

You can use the following code block within your Netduino application, which listens for an incoming request:

```
public class Program
{
    private static Socket socket = null;

    private static OutputPort OnBoardledPort = new
    OutputPort(Pins.ONBOARD_LED, false);

    public static void Main()
    {

        socket = new Socket(AddressFamily.InterNetwork,
        SocketType.Stream, ProtocolType.Tcp);
        socket.Bind(new IPEndPoint(IPAddress.Any, 80));
        socket.Listen(100);
        while (true)
        {
            using (Socket clientSocket = socket.Accept())
```

```
            {
                int available = clientSocket.Available;
                if (available > 0)
                {
                    byte[] buffer = new byte[available];
                    int byteCount =
                    clientSocket.Receive(buffer, available,
                    SocketFlags.None);
                    string request = new
                    string(Encoding.UTF8.GetChars(buffer));
                    if (request.IndexOf("SkeletonTracked") > 0)
                    {
                        for (int i = 0; i < 10; i++)
                        {
                            OnBoardledPort.Write(true);
                            Thread.Sleep(200);
                            OnBoardledPort.Write(false);
                            Thread.Sleep(200);
                        }
                    }
                }
            }
        }
    }
}
```

Once a request reaches the socket, we can just check if the request has specific information on which Netduino intends to execute an action. As in the preceding highlighted code, we are just blinking the LEDs when the request contains the information SkeletonTracked.

Sending a request from a Kinect application

The final part of this solution is to send information from a Kinect application. This information could be anything, such as some depth information, player information, joint information, or even a signal based on the speech command. In the following code block, we have used the skeleton tracking features of the Kinect for Windows SDK

```
void sensor_SkeletonFrameReady(object sender,
SkeletonFrameReadyEventArgs e)
    {
. . .
        Skeleton firstSkeleton = (from trackskeleton in
        totalSkeleton
```

```
where trackskeleton.TrackingState ==
SkeletonTrackingState.Tracked  select
trackskeleton).FirstOrDefault();

    if (firstSkeleton != null &&
    this.CurrentSkeletonID !=
    firstSkeleton.TrackingId)
    {
        this.CurrentSkeletonID = firstSkeleton.TrackingId;
        SendSignalToNetduino();
    }
}
}
```

In this code, we just send a signal to the Netduino application when there is a new skeleton tracked by calling the `SendSignalToNetduino()` method, which can be written as follows:

```
private static void SendSignalToNetduino()
    {
        WebRequest webRequest =
        WebRequest.Create("http://xxx.xxx.xxx.xxx/
        SkeletonTracked");
        Stream objStream;
        objStream =
        webRequest.GetResponse().GetResponseStream();
    }
```

In this code block, we are creating an instance of the `WebRequest` class and sending the requests to the IP address of the Netduino application.

 Instead of sending a web request, you can also send requests using the `Socket.Send()` method with request messages.

If both applications are running, whenever the sensor tracks a skeleton with a new tracking ID you will see that the on-board LED is blinking.

Taking it further

What we have discussed so far demonstrates how these two devices can work together. You could extend this application by connecting an alarm to the Netduino and playing it with a human skeleton track.

To take it to a more advanced stage, you can program a robot using a Netduino microcontroller and control it using the Kinect sensor.

 If you are new to the Microsoft .NET Micro Framework and Netduino microcontroller, you can refer to the books *Getting Started with Netduino*, *O'Reilly Media* by Chris Walker and *Getting Started with Internet Things*, *O'Reilly Media* by Cuno Pfister.

While the cross-device application with Kinect is interesting and gives you other areas of development to explore, there are some additional programming features that you can use with the Kinect sensor to build more real-life applications.

Augmented reality applications

Augmented reality is another great innovation in the computer world. This is a process where we can mix up the real-world data and computer-generated objects. It overlays computer images, video, audio, and other objects from computer screens onto real-time environments. The Kinect sensor will be used to obtain the player data by capturing depth information or skeleton information and positioning it in the application. For example, you could place a virtual hat on a player's head. You can just perform this by tracking the human skeleton and positioning one hat image based on the head joint position.

For a quick example of an augmented reality application, you can take a look at the *Green Screen* sample application available with the Kinect for Windows Developer Toolkit. The *Green Screen* application renders the player body over the background image by removing the live background pixels of the player index using depth data as shown in the following screenshot:

Working with face tracking

The face tracking SDK comes with the *Kinect for Windows Developer ToolKit*. The Face tracking SDK detects and tracks the positions and orientations of faces and it can also animate in real time the eyebrow positions and the mouth shape .The face tracking SDK could be used in several places such as recognizing facial expressions, NUI interaction with the face, and face-related tasks.

Using the face tracking SDK we can perform the following tasks:

- Track one or more faces
- Track 100 points on a face. Following image shows 87 tracked points out of a total of 100 points:

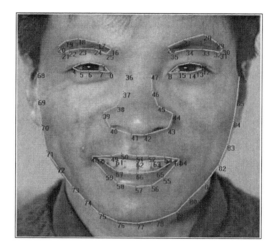

Image courtesy of
`http://msdn.microsoft.com/en-us/library/jj130970.`

- Animate lips, jaw, brows, and so on

The developer toolkit installs two libraries for face tracking (compiled in 32- and 64-bit versions):

- `FaceTrackData.dll`
- `FaceTrackLib.dll`

If you are building an application using C++, you can use the libraries directly. But with a managed application, you should use the wrapper.dll, which is available as follows:

- Microsoft.Kinect.Toolkit
- Microsoft.Kinect.Toolkit.FaceTracking

The `FaceTrackFrame` class is the core of the face tracking system, which represents the face for every frame. You can get the face point and shape information from the instance of this class itself. The following screenshot shows the properties and methods of the `FaceTrackFrame` class:

You can find the details for the face tracking APIs by exploring the documentation available with the developer toolkit. The Kinect SDK developer toolkit also has two sample applications that leverage the features.

 Read more information about Face Tracking using the Kinect SDK at http://msdn.microsoft.com/en-us/library/jj130970.aspx.

Working with XNA and a 3D avatar

You can use the Kinect SDK with an XNA game. For that you must install *XNA Game Studio 4.0* on your computer. Using XNA you can build 3D interactive solutions with Kinect.

One great example of using an XNA application with a Kinect sensor is controlling a 3D avatar using human skeleton joint movements. *Avateering*, which is available with the Kinect for Windows Developer Toolkit, uses skeleton joint orientation and moves a 3D avatar based on that.

The following screenshot shows a sample avatar that uses the XNA *Avateering* application:

 Image courtesy of
http://msdn.microsoft.com/en-us/library/jj131041.asx.

Summary

In this chapter, you have learned how Kinect can be used with a range of other Microsoft technologies along with other devices. You have learned how you can connect Kinect with Windows Azure and control the Kinect sensor using Windows Phone. You were also introduced to the Netduino microcontroller and how Kinect worked with it. Finally, we also had a quick look at the face tracking SDK, an augmented reality application, and the 3D *Avateering* sample application which are available as a part of Kinect for Windows Developer Toolkit. Overall, this chapter gives you a quick view on how Kinect can be used in different areas.

Index

I

image format
  binding 99, 100
  color image format, changing 100, 101
ImageFrame class 99
ImageFrame.Format 97
ImageFrame property 105
image frames 78
images
  capturing 102, 103
  saving 102, 103
  saving, directly 104-106
  saving, periodically 103, 104
Infrared (IR) emitter 12, 13
InitilizeGesture() method 292
INotifyPropertyChanged 63
installation
  Coding4Fun Kinect toolkit 117-119
InstalledRecognizers method 244, 254
intrusion detector camera application
  about 174, 175
  night vision, creating 176
IR depth sensor 11, 121
IR emitter 11, 121
IR stream data
  capturing 114
IsEnabled property 126
IsGestureValid() method 289

J

JitterRadius property 199

K

Kinect
  about 7, 8
  audio signal processing 217
  connecting, with Netduino 348
  removing, Windows Phone used 336
  taking, to Cloud 332
  using, areas 16, 17
  using, with Windows PC speech
    recognition 240-242
  with Netduino microcontroller 342

Kinect audio
  recorded audio, playing 225
  record, starting 224
Kinect audio configuration
  about 212
  Kinect Microphone Array, using 214
  Kinect USB Audio, troubleshooting 213
  verifying 212
KinectAudioSource class 233
KinectCam
  about 82
  color image, capturing 86
  data binding 84, 85
  extending 98
  frame format, calculating 101
  frame number, getting 98, 99
  frame rate, calculating 101
  image format 99
  image format, modifying 99
  images, saving directly 104-106
  project, setting up 83
  running 94
  setting options, actions 83
  working 83
  XAML application, designing 84, 85
Kinect camera 77
Kinect, connecting with Netduino
  about 348
  Internet connection, using 348
  request, listening to 349, 350
  request, sending from Kinect
    application 350, 351
Kinect device
  microphone array 211
Kinect, for Developer Toolkit
  about 42
  Face Tracking SDK 42
  Kinect Studio 43
Kinect, for Windows
  color camera 10
  components 8, 9
  image 9
  internal view 9
  IR depth sensor 11
  IR emitter 11

SpeechRecognized event 244
SRGS 246
SSL 218
STA 225
StartKinectCam 89
StartRecognize() method 292, 294
StartSenosr() method 58
StatusChanged event 67, 324
StatusChangedEventArgs class 68
StatusChanged event handler 329
StatusChanged property 324
StatusNotifer class 74
StausChanged events 68
stereo triangulation 124
Stop() method 60
system requirements, Kinect for Windows
    SDK
  development tools 21
  Kinect sensor 21
  supported operating systems 20
  system configuration 20

T

Tables 332
template-based gesture recognition
  about 302
  gesture tracking 302
  phases 302
  template creation 302
  template matching 302
Tilt motor 13, 14
TrackingID property 185

U

UnloadAllGrammars method 250
User Access Control (UAC) 24
user actions 310
user interface (UI) 238

V

ValidateBaseCondition() method 289
Validate Control Position 308

ValidateGestureEndCondition()
    method 289
ValidateGestureStartCondition()
    method 288
ValueChanged event 149
Visual Studio project
  creating 50
  Kinect libraries, adding 52, 53

W

WCF attributes 339
weighted network gesture recognition
  about 297
  neural network 298
  neural network, using 298, 299
Windows Azure
  about 332
  blobs 332
  queue 333
  tables 332
Windows Azure SDK 333
Windows Azure Service Bus 337
Windows_Loaded event 153
Windows PC speech recognition
  Kinect, using with 240, 242
Windows Phone SDK 337
Windows SDK
  Kinect 19
Words property 257
WPF application 309
WritePixels method 116

X

XNA
  working with 355

Y

YUV image stream 80

Thank you for buying
Kinect for Windows SDK Programming Guide

About Packt Publishing

Packt, pronounced 'packed', published its first book *"Mastering phpMyAdmin for Effective MySQL Management"* in April 2004 and subsequently continued to specialize in publishing highly focused books on specific technologies and solutions.

Our books and publications share the experiences of your fellow IT professionals in adapting and customizing today's systems, applications, and frameworks. Our solution based books give you the knowledge and power to customize the software and technologies you're using to get the job done. Packt books are more specific and less general than the IT books you have seen in the past. Our unique business model allows us to bring you more focused information, giving you more of what you need to know, and less of what you don't.

Packt is a modern, yet unique publishing company, which focuses on producing quality, cutting-edge books for communities of developers, administrators, and newbies alike. For more information, please visit our website: www.packtpub.com.

Writing for Packt

We welcome all inquiries from people who are interested in authoring. Book proposals should be sent to author@packtpub.com. If your book idea is still at an early stage and you would like to discuss it first before writing a formal book proposal, contact us; one of our commissioning editors will get in touch with you.

We're not just looking for published authors; if you have strong technical skills but no writing experience, our experienced editors can help you develop a writing career, or simply get some additional reward for your expertise.

3D Graphics with XNA Game Studio 4.0

ISBN: 978-1-84969-004-1   Paperback: 292 pages

Create attractive 3D graphics and visuals in your XNA games

1. Improve the appearance of your games by implementing the same techniques used by professionals in the game industry

2. Learn the fundamentals of 3D graphics, including common 3D math and the graphics pipeline

3. Create an extensible system to draw 3D models and other effects, and learn the skills to create your own effects and animate them

XNA 4.0 Game Development by Example: Beginner's Guide – Visual Basic Edition

ISBN: 978-1-84969-240-3   Paperback: 424 pages

Create your own exciting games with Visual Basic and Microsoft XNA 4.0

1. Visual Basic edition of Kurt Jaegers' XNA 4.0 Game Development by Example. The first book to target Visual Basic developers who want to develop games with the XNA framework

2. Dive headfirst into game creation with Visual Basic and the XNA Framework

3. Four different styles of games comprising a puzzler, space shooter, multi-axis shoot 'em up, and a jump-and-run platformer

Please check **www.PacktPub.com** for information on our titles

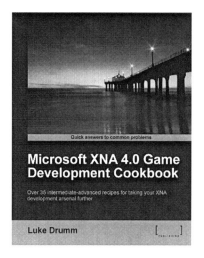

Microsoft XNA 4.0 Game Development Cookbook

ISBN: 978-1-84969-198-7   Paperback: 356 pages

Over 35 intermediate-advanced recipes for taking your XNA development arsenal further

1. Accelerate your XNA learning with a myriad of tips and tricks to solve your everyday problems

2. Get to grips with adding special effects, virtual atmospheres and computer controlled characters with this book and e-book

3. A fast-paced cookbook packed with screenshots to illustrate each advanced step by step task

4. Apply the techniques learned for wiring games for PC, Xbox 360 and Windows Phone

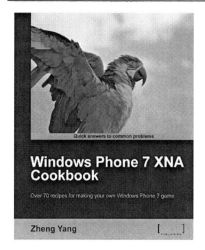

Windows Phone 7 XNA Cookbook

ISBN: 978-1-84969-120-8   Paperback: 450 pages

Over 70 recipes for making your own Windows Phone 7 game

1. Complete focus on the best Windows Phone 7 game development techniques using XNA 4.0

2. Easy to follow cookbook allowing you to dive in wherever you want.

3. Convert ideas into action using practical recipes

Please check **www.PacktPub.com** for information on our titles

CPSIA information can be obtained at www.ICGtesting.com
Printed in the USA
BVOW06s2331250813

329378BV00003B/55/P